THE
GRAND
TACTICIAN

Khrushchev's Rise to Power

THE
GRAND
TACTICIAN

Khrushchev's
Rise to Power

by

LAZAR PISTRAK

FREDERICK A. PRAEGER, *Publisher*
New York

BOOKS THAT MATTER

Published in the United States of America in 1961
by Frederick A. Praeger, Inc., Publisher
64 University Place, New York 3, N. Y.

Second Printing, May 1961

© 1961 by Frederick A. Praeger, Inc.

LIBRARY OF CONGRESS CATALOG CARD NUMBER: 61-9229

This book is Number 87 in the series
of *Praeger Publications in Russian History
and World Communism*

MANUFACTURED IN THE UNITED STATES OF AMERICA

TO NINA

Preface

However Khrushchev's political career may end, his name will appear in the annals of world history as that of a recognized leader of the U.S.S.R. and as a world figure who left a deep imprint on foreign relations in the 'fifties and the 'sixties of this century. In the short period since Stalin's death, Khrushchev, a man hardly heard of outside the borders of the Soviet Union at the time of his accession to power, has become one of the most widely known of world political leaders.

None of the Marxist or Communist leaders of the past has been known to so wide an audience as has Khrushchev. Marx and Engels were known only to limited groups of economists and philosophers and to small revolutionary circles, predominantly in Europe. Lenin emerged from obscurity after the revolution he had staged, but neither he nor his successor, Stalin, had personally contacted so many people within and outside the Soviet Union as has Nikita Khrushchev.

His name is identified with such bold moves as the de-Stalinization speech of February, 1956, the two dramatic purges of 1957, far-reaching changes in Soviet economic life, and spectacular achievements in the exploration of outer space. A spokesman of reform against the abuses of the Stalinist terroristic era, he has succeeded in consolidating his leadership of the Party and control over those other components of the totalitarian dictatorship—the secret police, the military caste, and the managerial class—which sought a more independent role in the structure of the Soviet regime after Stalin's death. On the other hand, he has also succeeded in curbing the intelligentsia who hoped in the early spring of 1953 that the death of the dictator would bring an end to the icy winter of the Stalin era.

Like his predecessors, Khrushchev has played an exclusive role in formulating Soviet foreign policy, but he differs from them in that he introduced the use of personal diplomacy and in that he himself has become an instrument of that policy. In the last five years he has visited no less than eighteen countries, some of them two and three times. The picture of himself which he conveyed to the millions of people who saw him in person and on television screens has been that of a man of tremendous vitality and energy, simplicity and earthiness, wit and likableness, shrewdness and stuffiness, and unrestraint and rage. A popularizer of Communist ideas and an ardent defender of "peaceful coexistence" of worlds with different social systems, he has become the most controversial personality in our time. Yet all that is officially known about Khrushchev's life is crowded in brief sketches published in Soviet encyclopedias and political dictionaries.

Biographies of political personalities are considered incomplete if based only on the dry facts of political activity and not supplemented with an insight into their private lives. Without such an insight, the contours of the subject are blurry, resembling an underexposed or underdeveloped photograph. Biographers spare no effort in collecting data concerning all aspects of the life of their subject. In non-Communist democratic states, public figures can hardly conceal the circumstances of their personal lives. For in the democracies there is a free press, and, in addition, political leaders must make the facts of their lives public in order to gain election to office. In Communist countries, however, where secrecy is the rule, Communist leaders are free from any obligation to present their record to the people. The Party vouches for their fitness, and the Party releases exactly as much information as it deems necessary. The "record" contains dry data about their political activity—but not a word about their personal lives. A distinction, however, should be made between the founders of Communism and those whose political careers began after the Revolution of 1917. Lenin, for instance, lived most of his life in an open society, and thus his political and personal life was watched and known by friends and enemies alike. Khrushchev and most of the present members of the Kremlin's ruling circle grew up politically and became prominent in the Stalin era, during which all the features of an open society crumbled under the blows of the totalitarian dictatorship. This is why excellent biographic material on Lenin is available, and why this attempt to write Khrushchev's biography can be only a partial success.

Even when the political history of a Soviet leader is officially set down, it is not a factual account. It is rather a legend interwoven with the larger legend of the development of Communism and the Soviet state as a whole. If, in the course of events, the status of a leader is changed, his political history is revised; or, if a leader is purged, his biography is completely omitted. The fact is that nothing is eternal in the Soviet encyclopedias and history books. Stalin, during his lifetime, was confident that his name would dominate forever the histories of the Communist Party. And Beria and Molotov—as well as Malenkov, Kaganovich, Bulganin, Zhukov—expected their names to find a well-deserved niche in those histories, too. How wrong all these Communist leaders were is apparent from the new version of the Party's history which was published in 1958-59. Two decades have passed since the first version appeared—a version which was publicized as the fundamental textbook of the Communist movement and was disseminated in tens of millions of copies in almost every language of the world. Now that version of history is no longer valid. In the new version, for example, many of the fables about Stalin's deeds that once adorned the Party's history have been extirpated, and in this latest version some of Stalin's victims have reappeared while at the same time the names of those purged by Khrushchev have vanished.

The official biographies of Khrushchev must therefore be held suspect, and of course they can by no means be regarded as final. Future encyclopedias and dictionaries will undoubtedly revise some of the information to bring it in line with whatever picture of the leader is desired at the time. There have already been attempts made in this direction.

Thus far sixteen official or semiofficial Soviet biographical sketches of Khrushchev have appeared. In addition, Khrushchev has volunteered bits of information about himself and his family in his speeches and his talks with visitors to the Soviet Union. Yet there is still insufficient information to produce a comprehensive biography of Khrushchev. What this book attempts to do, then, is to construct the man from what is known of his political career, from the events in which he participated, from his contributions to the establishment of the Soviet totalitarian dictatorship. It is not a biography in the usual sense of the word; it is, instead, a presentation of the facts and circumstances which made it possible for Khrushchev to emerge from the gray mass of Russia's population and become the strongest man in the Kremlin. It is hoped that the reader will obtain from this account not only a political profile of this Soviet leader but also some insight into the man himself.

Numerous stories about Khrushchev's past circulate outside the Soviet Union, and many of them find their way into print. Since such stories either contradict well-known facts or cannot be verified, this writer has chosen to disregard them and to rely mainly on Soviet official documents and on the record which emerges from Soviet newspapers, magazines, and books.

—L. P.

AUTHOR'S ACKNOWLEDGMENT

The author wishes to express his deep appreciation to Boris I. Nicolaevsky, George Denike, and Seweryn Bialer both for reading the manuscript in part as well as for their valuable suggestions. For editing the final manuscript, the author is greatly indebted to Miss Dorothy Dillon. He also acknowledges the assistance rendered him by Mr. Konrad Kellen in the editing of the first version of the manuscript.

Invaluable service was rendered to the author by his wife, Nina, whose advice and innate understanding and patience helped shape many a chapter.

CONTENTS

I

The Ukrainian Overture

1

The Belated Bolshevik

> It is not difficult to be a revolutionary when the revolution has already flared up and is at its height. . . . —V. I. Lenin, *Sochineniya*, 4th ed.; xxxi, 77.

Khrushchev was born on April 17, 1894, in Kalinovka, a village in the province of Kursk. During the collectivization of Soviet agriculture in the early 'thirties, Kalinovka became the center of a collective farm, which was named after Khrushchev following his rise to prominence as a Party worker. Khrushchev is also identified with his birthplace by the fact that he shows great personal interest in the Kalinovka collective farm. He has visited it several times and urged its management to spare no effort in taking the lead over other farms in the district.[1] In 1956, he told a group of visiting French Socialists to come to Kalinovka five years later and see what the collective farm system could accomplish.

The national origin of the Khrushchevs is shrouded in obscurity, for it is a Soviet policy to refrain from listing the national origin of Communist leaders. Several experts on Ukrainian affairs maintain that he "seems to be definitely Russian."[2] But there are also indications which point to either Polish or Ukrainian extraction. "Khrushch" ("Chruszcz" in Polish transcription) is a family name encountered in Poland. In 1493, a man by this name came from Poland to Moscow, adopted the Orthodox faith,

3

and was christened Ivan Ivanovich Khrushchev. This Polish emigrant was the founder of an old Russian aristocratic family line which was registered in the genealogical books of Kursk and of five other Russian provinces.[3] It is, of course, possible that after several centuries the Kursk branch of the family became impoverished and fell to the status of peasants. The hypothesis of Khrushchev's Ukrainian origin can be supported by the fact that the Kursk province is adjacent in the south and west to three Ukrainian provinces and that, at the time of his birth, approximately one-fifth of its inhabitants were Ukrainians. Khrushchev himself has stated that his native language is Russian, although he knows Ukrainian "rather well." [4] All these facts are not, of course, conclusive evidence of his belonging to one or another nationality.

Recent official accounts of Khrushchev's life report that his family belonged to the "poorest group of rural population" [5] and that his father, Sergei, was a miner "from the village of Kalinovka" [6] who, "like many other poor, landless peasants of Kalinovka," worked in the Doniets Coal Basin (Donbas).[7] According to these sources Khrushchev spent his childhood in Kalinovka.[8] It is, of course, possible that at some point of Khrushchev's early life his family moved from Kursk province to the Doniets Coal Basin. All that is known about Khrushchev's mother is that her full name was Ksenia Ivanovna Khrushcheva and that she died in February, 1945.[9]

"Life did not pamper me; it was stern[10] . . . I began working when I learned to walk. Till the age of fifteen I tended calves, then sheep, and then the landlord's cows. I did all that before I was fifteen." [11] In these terms Khrushchev recently described his childhood. One of the official Soviet biographical sketches of Khrushchev's life relates that he began to work at an early age, "first as a sheepherder, then as farmhand in Kalinovka and in the neighboring villages." [12]

In the winter Khrushchev attended an elementary parochial school. The subjects taught in the parochial schools were: "Law of God, church songs, Church-Slavonic and Russian (civilian) reading and writing, and elementary knowledge of arithmetic." Children attending the two-grade school received, in addition, "elementary information on the history of the Church and of the Fatherland." Attendance at church services was obligatory.[13]

Khrushchev has never stated how long he attended the parochial school, but at the age of fifteen, he joined his father who worked as a miner in the area of Yuzovka, the center of the Doniets Coal Basin.

Yuzovka was founded in 1869, when a British subject, John Hughes, received a concession and a subsidy from the Czarist Government to build iron works. The town was named after its founder and is spelled Hughesovka by the British. At the end of the 'seventies about four thousand people were employed in the mines and shops in and around Yuzovka. At the beginning of this century, Yuzovka had a population of 32,000. The town had an Orthodox parochial school and two elementary schools —one English and one Russian; one hospital, one physician, and an assistant physician; a pharmacy; one printing shop; one book store; five photographers; one notary public; an English Club; and one consumers' cooperative serving the employees of the Hughes iron works.

Old Yuzovka was divided into two parts: the more or less comfortable settlement, called the English Colony, where the mine and factory owners and the technical personnel lived; and the workers' settlement, adjacent to the places of their employment, consisting of barracks and temporary mud huts, with unpaved streets, without central water supply or sewers: these settlements were called *Sobachevka* (from the word *sobaka*— dog) and "Shanghai." Here and in similar settlements of Russia the poorest peasants, forced out from their native villages by misery and hopelessness, were transformed into industrial workmen.

In the 'seventies most of the inhabitants of the "dog" settlements were former serfs. To them the most primitive life in a growing industrial center must have been more acceptable than life in the countryside where, despite the abolition of serfdom promulgated by the Czarist regime in 1861, the liberated serfs economically were still almost completely dependent upon the big landlords. But once enrolled in the labor ranks, the feeling of solidarity, self-respect, and hope began to grow and, with it, the demands for a better life. The month of April, 1874, wit-

nessed the first labor strike and demonstration in Yuzovka. Other
strikes followed in the 'eighties, and in 1898, the workers struck
until their workday was shortened from twelve to ten and a half
hours. At the beginning of this century economic strikes became
more frequent and reached a peak during the Revolution of
1905.[14]

Khrushchev's father belonged to the first generation of the
"proletarized" peasants, and, after he had settled in Yuzovka, he
placed his sheepherding son, Nikita, in the Bosset factory to
learn the trade of a fitter. Here, young Khrushchev for the first
time saw East meeting West—the contrast between Western
technological know-how and civilization and Eastern technical
backwardness and primitive life. Khrushchev's present urge to
"catch up and overtake" the West was perhaps born in this
atmosphere of sharp contrast.

There is no substance at all to Khrushchev's claim that he,
like his father, worked there as a miner,[15] since none of the
Soviet official descriptions of Khrushchev's life supports that
claim. They state that he worked in the Donbas as a fitter in
factories and mines.[16] After he had learned to repair mining
machinery, he worked as a repair mechanic in the pits. Some
Soviet sources report that he also learned to operate the lift
cage.[17] He also worked for a time at a coke and chemicals plant.[18]

"When young Nikita Khrushchev descended into the mine for
the first time, he was spared any feeling of loneliness, in spite of
the fact that work in the prerevolutionary Donbas was like
prison hard labor." These are the terms in which some Soviet
sources describe the work conditions which Khrushchev found
in the Doniets coal fields. In an interview with a correspondent
of Le Figaro, Khrushchev was cautious enough not to compare
prerevolutionary working conditions in the Doniets coal pits with
"prison hard labor." "When I read Emile Zola's book Germinal,"
Khrushchev said, "I got the impression that he was writing not
about France but about the mines in which my father and I were
working. The lot of the workers was the same in France as in
Russia." [19]

None of the Soviet biographical sketches of Khrushchev's life
published in Soviet encyclopedias and political dictionaries mentions his social or political activity in the years preceding the 1917

Revolution. But booklets recently disseminated by Soviet embassies imply that he played an active role in the labor movement at that time.* Young Khrushchev, they say, was "a bright lad with a nimble wit and rapidly became a favorite among the miners." [20] "He was a young man with a keen and inquisitive mind, and soon began to take active part in the workers' cause," one reads in a pamphlet published in the United States on the occasion of Khrushchev's visit to this country. [21] Khrushchev himself, pointing to his past, said in an interview with French trade unionists that he not only participated in strikes but "enjoyed the confidence of the workers in spite of his youth" and was "more than once" a member of their delegations who carried on negotiations with the management. [22] In order to determine to what extent, if at all, these claims can be justified, it is necessary to take into consideration the following facts.

Until the age of fifteen Khrushchev was a sheepherder and farm hand in his native village. This would indicate that he came to the Donbas around 1909-10. A Soviet study on the labor-union movement in the Donbas prior to the Bolshevik Revolution points out that those years were the years of the "greatest decline" of the labor movement in the Doniets basin. [23] It was not until 1912 that the strikes reached appreciable proportions. Various revolutionary parties—Mensheviks, Socialist Revolutionaries, and Bolsheviks—driven underground after the defeat of the revolution of 1905, began to regroup their ranks. Young workers interested in the labor movement devoted their spare time to educating themselves and reading legal and illegal political literature, and to lending a helping hand to the underground and semilegal political groups. In 1912, *Pravda* had begun to appear as a legal publication. Over thirty groups had been organized in the Ukraine alone to obtain new subscriptions and donations, with three of these groups in the very town of Yuzovka, [24] where Khrushchev pursued his trade. At this time, Lazar Kaganovich, only one year older than Khrushchev, had already been active in the Bolshevik Party. In fact, during World

---

* It is noteworthy that Soviet domestic publications lack any information about Khrushchev's prerevolutionary social or political activity. It would seem that the Soviet Ministry of Foreign Affairs has been instructed to project the Soviet leader as an early fighter for worthy causes, particularly in those non-Communist countries which he was to visit.

War I, Kaganovich headed an illegal Bolshevik group in Yuzovka, which was one of eighteen groups in the Doniets basin.[25]
In 1913, over fifteen thousand miners and metal workers struck
in that area, putting forward economic as well as political demands.[26] Three thousand five hundred workers struck in that
year near Khrushchev's adopted town of Yuzovka, protesting
wage cuts and demanding the dismissal of the most hated
representatives of the management.[27] With the outbreak of the
war in September, 1914, 30 to 40 per cent of the miners were
called to the armed forces.[28] The strike movement slowed down
considerably but soon resumed, and reached a new peak in the
spring of 1916, when fifty thousand workers struck in the Doniets
basin, demanding a 50-per-cent wage increase.[29]

When the war broke out, Khrushchev was over twenty years
old. Though no doubt eligible for service in the Czarist army on
grounds of health—his present condition would seem to indicate
that he must have been an able-bodied youth—he did not serve.
Probably he was exempted from military service because of the
nature of his work, since fitters or cage operators were considered specialists and harder to replace. In that or another
capacity, he worked from 1914 to 1918 in Yuzovka.[30]

During the war, the Czarist police arrested scores of strike
leaders, and thousands of workers exempted from service because of their skills were deprived of their privilege and called
to the army.[31] There can be little doubt that had the youthful
Khrushchev been an active participant in any of this political
unrest, his official biographies would have reported this fact in
detail, as do the biographies of other Soviet leaders. In addition
to the Modestov book, there are a number of other Soviet studies
dealing with the prerevolutionary labor movement in the Doniets
basin. In these sources, the leaders of the Doniets strikes, particularly those who belonged to or sympathized with the Bolshevik movement, are mentioned by name, but Khrushchev is
not among them.

If there is substance to Khrushchev's claim that he represented
the workers' cause in negotiations with the capitalists, a logical
explanation for the failure of the accounts to mention him would
be that he did not negotiate with them as a sympathizer with
the Bolshevik cause. Possibly the complicated situation prevail-

ing at the time can shed some light on this.

It is possible, of course, that Khrushchev had been involved to some extent in strikes after the overthrow of the Czarist regime, when trade unions sprang up with feverish speed and strikes became legal. However, in an interview with French trade unionists, Khrushchev said that he "never worked in the trade unions," [32] which would indicate that he could hardly have played a major role in organizing or settling strikes. In general, Soviet biographies of Khrushchev are silent about his political activity during the period between March, 1917, when the Czarist regime was overthrown, and January, 1918, when the Bolsheviks seized power in the Ukraine. The question arises whether Khrushchev belonged to any political party at all, since he did not join the Communists until some time in 1918.

"In Yuzovka," says a study of the Ukrainian Academy of Sciences, "the Mensheviks had a considerable influence on the masses." [33] There were a number of regions in the Doniets basin where anti-Bolshevik democratic parties resisted the Bolsheviks even after the Bolshevik upheaval in November, 1917. Among those places Yuzovka was particularly prominent. There the overwhelming majority of the deputies of the local Soviet belonged to the Mensheviks and Socialist Revolutionaries. "Several times new elections to the Soviet had been held, but every time the . . . Mensheviks and the Socialist Revolutionaries seized the preponderant majority of seats in the Soviet," [34] one reads in the same Ukrainian source. Even on the eve of the Bolshevik Revolution in November, 1917, the election results favored those parties. The biographical sketches of Khrushchev published in Soviet encyclopedias and political dictionaries do not contain any information about his political leanings at the time the Yuzovka Bolsheviks fought against the Mensheviks and Socialist Revolutionaries. Attempts to build up Khrushchev's role in the 1917 Revolution have been made, but the claims are so vague and unspecified that they can be disregarded. In 1948, for instance, in an article devoted to the "City Named After Stalin" (formerly Yuzovka), Khrushchev is said to have had an "active part" in the revolutionary events of 1917.[35] The vagueness of this statement becomes obvious if it is compared with the exactitude with which the same article describes Lazar Kaganovich's merits,

crediting him with having played an important role in the
strengthening of the Yuzovka Bolshevik organization in 1916,
with having been a member of the Yuzovka Bolshevik Party
Committee from the first day of the 1917 Revolution, and having
been the leader in the struggle of the Yuzovka Bolsheviks against
the Mensheviks and Socialist Revolutionaries. Another attempt,
even more indefinite than the first one, has been made in the
press releases and the special booklets published by or under
the auspices of the Soviet embassies abroad. They claim that
Khrushchev's "keen, searching mind and working-class background brought him into the very middle of the struggle for
freedom," [36] or that "the general revolutionary upsurge absorbed
him completely." [37]

Only one Communist source is specific about Khrushchev's
activity after the overthrow of the Czarist regime. The Polish
Communist weekly *Polityka* revealed that "Khrushchev acted
for the first time 'in the name of the Revolution' when he had
become chairman of a peasants' committee in Kalinovka and,
together with others, divided the landowner's estate among the
peasants." [38] This would mean that Khrushchev's mind was preoccupied with matters of a personal nature rather than with
large-scale revolutionary tasks. Like many other workers throughout Russia who did not yet cut their ties entirely with their
peasant origin, he rushed to his native village to secure for
himself and his family land parcels at the expense of the big
landowners. Though no Soviet publication has ever reported
this "revolutionary" act of Khrushchev, it cannot be disregarded,
not only because it was published in a Communist paper, but
also because the author of the article, Mieczyslaw F. Rakowski,
is a high-ranking Polish Communist. In addition to being editor-
in-chief of *Polityka*, he occupies the positions of chairman of the
Press Committee attached to the Central Committee of the
Polish (Communist) United Workers' Party and President of
the Association of Polish Journalists. *Polityka* is considered the
mouthpiece of the Polish Premier, Wladyslaw Gomulka, and
Rakowski is known to be Gomulka's main spokesman.

The first date of Khrushchev's political activity cited by the
Soviet biographies is 1918, when, at the age of twenty-four, he
joined the Communist Party. The month is not mentioned, al-

though that would be of importance. The Bolshevik upheaval took place in November, 1917. Every month thereafter, the new regime had to go through severe contests with the defeated but still struggling forces of the opposition. Those who did not make up their minds which side to join during that period were regarded as philistines or waverers. Here again, Gomulka's organ, *Polityka*, is more precise than the Soviet sources. It reveals that when Khrushchev was admitted to the Party, he had "already finished the twenty-fourth year of his life." [39] This would indicate that he did not become a member of the Party before April 17, 1918, or at least six months after the November Bolshevik Revolution. Yet one official account of Khrushchev's life, published in 1939, when he became a full-fledged member of the Politburo, says that he was an "active fighter" in the November Revolution "from its first days." [40] But the 1940 version reduced his role from "active fighter" to "active participant," [41] and subsequent versions omit this claim altogether and count his revolutionary merits only from the year 1918, when he joined the Party and enlisted in the Red Army.

Unlike his former associate Malenkov, the Khrushchev of the Civil War period, 1918-20, is as shadowy as the Khrushchev of the prewar Doniets turmoil. In January, 1938, the Ukrainian press asserted that he had "participated for three years in the Civil War as a *politrabotnik* (a political worker) in Red Army units at the Southern Front." [42] A similar duty was attributed to him in the *Short Course of the History of the Communist Party of the Soviet Union*, also published in 1938. There he was included in a list of Soviet leaders who contributed to the "political education of the Red Army" during the Civil War.

When a Soviet leader has really given effective service in the capacity of a political officer it usually emerges in his biographies very clearly. Malenkov, for instance, is a typical example of the successful political worker in the Red Army. Having started as a political worker in a squadron, he moved up to serve in the same capacity in a regiment, in a brigade, and, finally, in the political administration of the Eastern and Turkestan Front. All this information was faithfully included in every biographic account of his life.

In Khrushchev's case the opposite is true. Contrary to the 1938

version of his career, the 1939 and 1940 versions merely describe
him as an "active participant" in the Civil War, adding that for
three years he performed "large-scale work." [43] Even the reference
to "large-scale work" is omitted in later versions, including the
1960 version, which states simply that he was an "active participant" in the Civil War and secretary of his regiment's Party cell.

From these accounts, and from the facts of his life prior to
entering the Army, it is logical to conclude that Khrushchev was
probably not a *politrabotnik*. This term was applied to carefully
screened Communists, most of whom had been selected by the
Central Committee of the Party to serve in political sections of
the Red Army. The functions of these sections were manifold.
They included political education of men and officers; surveillance, prosecution, and liquidation of politically unstable elements; Cheka-style mopping-up operations in the rear after the
fighting front moved forward; subversive activity in areas occupied by the enemy; and organization of local Soviet and Party
authorities in "liberated" areas. It is improbable that a young
man who had in no way distinguished himself during the struggle
for power prior to 1918 would have been entrusted with such an
important position.

But if Khrushchev was not a *politrabotnik* during the Civil
War, as the Ukrainian press has claimed, it was still necessary in
the Soviet scheme to identify his stature. During the period
after 1938, when he was in charge of the Ukraine, the Central
Committee of the Ukrainian Communist Party announced plans
for a book on "Noteworthy Places in the Ukraine." This book
was designed, among other things, to describe places "connected
with the Civil War of 1917-21 and the great Stalin era . . . where
the wise and beloved *vozhd*° and friend of the Ukrainian people,
Comrade Stalin, and his closest companions-in-arms Molotov,
Voroshilov, Kaganovich, and Khrushchev had conducted their
activities." [44] Unfortunately, the book, which was to reveal
Khrushchev's role in the Civil War and present him, along with
other acknowledged old Communists, among the "closest com-
rades-in-arms" of the great Stalin, does not exist. Planned for
publication in 1942, on the twenty-fifth anniversary of the Bol-

---

° *Vozhd* is the Russian equivalent for *duce* in Italian and *Führer* in German.

shevik Revolution, its preparation was discontinued as a result of the outbreak of World War II.

The effort at upgrading Khrushchev was continued, however, when he became First Secretary of the Soviet Communist Party after Stalin's death. In 1954, the Soviet historian A. V. Likholat wrote on the events of 1918 that "in the district of Yuzovka, where N. S. Khrushchev and other Bolsheviks guided the organization of armed detachments, four workers' detachments and the First Proletarian Regiment of the Doniets Basin were formed." [45] It seems that this new role in the Civil War ascribed to Khrushchev is now accepted by Soviet Civil War historians as a fact, since the third volume of the official *History of the Civil War*, published in 1957, repeats Likholat's claim. The only change made is that Khrushchev did not "guide" but "took part" in the organization of armed detachments.[46] In both versions, this claim is in conflict with earlier works of Soviet history, and the first and second editions of the *Large Soviet Encyclopedia*,[47] which make it clear that it was Kliment Voroshilov who organized these units in the Doniets basin as a whole, including the town of Yuzovka where Khrushchev lived.

Particularly indicative of the inaccuracy of Likholat's assertion that Khrushchev played a major role in the organization of armed detachments in the Ukraine during the Civil War is an episode that took place in 1929. In March of that year, the Institute of History of the Ukrainian Communist Party invited forty-one members who had been active in Red Army detachments in the Doniets basin to participate in an evening of celebrations and recollections. Khrushchev was not among those invited.[48]

Other vague attempts to fortify Khrushchev's record during the Civil War were to follow. The 1959 "revised" version of the *History of the Communist Party of the Soviet Union*, in its Civil War chapter, carries the names of leaders described as "old cadres of Party leaders, companions-in-arms and disciples of Lenin, organizers of the victory of the Great Revolution, new cadres of leaders who carried the burden of liquidating the consequences of the war and building a socialist society."[49] Khrushchev is among them, but since the names are placed in alphabetical order and not according to merit, it is difficult to ascertain to which category he was assigned.

It would seem that the last word about Khrushchev's role in the Civil War has not yet been spoken. In 1958, in a brochure published by the Soviet Defense Ministry, the Soviet Civil War historian S. F. Nayda pointed out that in the past Stalin's role in the Civil War had been greatly exaggerated and that now, when his role has been cut according to his actual merits, there is nothing in the way to "work out thoroughly and to elucidate widely" the activity of the "political commissars" who were the "actual organizers of the Red Army and the political leaders of the Red Army masses." [50] Nayda mentions by name only eight such political commissars, and Khrushchev is among them. In addition to "many, many others," who remain unidentified, these eight men are described as "the best party cadres of the Party" whom the Central Committee selected to fulfill the complicated duties of political commissars at the Civil War fronts.

Another attempt to enhance Khrushchev's role in the Civil War was made on February 6, 1961, by V. P. Mzhavanadze. "The Georgian people," *Pravda* quotes him, "know that Nikita Sergeyevich came to Georgia for the first time in the memorable year of 1921, together with the legendary 11th Army which . . . rendered aid to the toilers who rose against the Menshevik Government." Since it is a matter of record that Soviet forces seized Georgia, Khrushchev's present anticolonialism ill becomes him.

Before proceeding with the description of Khrushchev's political career after his discharge from the Red Army, it is appropriate to relate here some data about his personal life. During her visit to the United States in 1959, Nina Petrovna Khrushcheva, Khrushchev's wife, said that he married her in 1924 and brought into his new family a daughter and son, six and eight years old, from his first marriage. His first wife died "during the famine," Nina Petrovna reported. This would indicate that Khrushchev married for the first time around 1915, at the age of twenty-one, and that the two children were born in 1916 and 1918. To what extent the change in his personal life influenced his interest and participation in the revolutionary turmoil is not known, but it would be logical to conjecture that it was not an easy task for a worker to take care of a family of three in times of revolution, food shortage, and inflation.

2

The Rise of a Political Star

The end of the Civil War found Russia a devastated country, its population exhausted by famine and disease. In some areas cannibalism was reported to be a common occurrence. Typhus killed thousands daily, and corpses lay in rows awaiting burial. A short railroad trip was the surest way of becoming infected with the typhus carrier, the louse. "Either the louse will conquer socialism, or socialism will conquer the louse!" So spoke Lenin at the time. Industry slowed virtually to a halt. Farmers refused to sell their produce in exchange for worthless banknotes, demanding consumer goods instead. Leather transmission belts, taken off the machines, were divided among workers to be exchanged for food. Fuel was as scarce as bread. Transportation, power stations, and factories worked only with great interruptions. Hospitals, schools, and dwellings were unheated.

Amid conditions such as these, Khrushchev, now twenty-seven and discharged from the Red Army, returned to Yuzovka to resume work in a mine. All of Russia was waiting for coal from the Doniets basin, which in 1920 had delivered less than 15 per cent of prewar annual production. But Khrushchev, a Party member, was not there to work as a miner. The latest Soviet official biography does mention Khrushchev's duties in the mine, thus supporting information about Khrushchev released by the Soviet Embassy in the United States in 1959, that he "was employed for a time as assistant manager of a mine."[1] In addition, he was "elected Secretary of the Party unit" and "mobilized the miners" to speed up the restoration of coal production.[2] While men with

15

technical and organizational talents were urgently needed to
start coal flowing from the pits again, the Party also needed
reliable Party members who could "mobilize" the miners to
increase production. It was for this Party work that Khrushchev
was sent to the Yuzovka mine.

Work in the mines, even in this new capacity, must have
seemed no future for a man of Khrushchev's ambitions. Great
changes were taking place in the Soviet Union under the direction of the Communist Party. With three years' membership in
the Party and service in the Red Army, he had qualifications
which could advance his future within the Party machine. He
was handicapped, however, by his lack of general education. To
gain the training he would need, he enrolled in a Workers'
Faculty.

The Workers' Faculties were established in 1918 in Moscow
and Leningrad and thereafter in the provinces to prepare new
cadres of Communist specialists for "socialist construction." Despite the Bolshevik upheaval, the overwhelming majority of
teachers and students in the universities and higher technical
schools remained opposed to the new regime. To replace these
anti-Communists with workers who belonged to the Party or who
sympathized with it was not an easy task. The educational level
of prospective student candidates was extremely low. The
Workers' Faculties were designed to provide the usual eight
years of pre-university education in a course crowded into three
or four years. Requirements for admission to these faculties were
minimal: elementary literacy, knowledge of the first four rules
of arithmetic, and some political notions.

The Workers' Faculty which Khrushchev attended was part
of the Doniets Mining Technical School established in May,
1921. (In 1941, the school, an Industrial Institute since 1935,
was named after "N. S. Khrushchev" to commemorate the fact
that he once studied there.)

The exact date of his admission is not known, there being
conflicting reports as to whether he worked in the mines first
and then enrolled, or worked and studied simultaneously.
Khrushchev has volunteered that "When the Civil War was over
and we had expelled all enemies from our land, I, a former
miner, entered the Workers' Faculty. At that time . . . I was

already twenty-seven." [3] But in 1946, a Soviet Ukrainian paper reported that he enrolled in the autumn of 1922,[4] at which time he was over twenty-eight years old. Unaccountably, ten of the twelve official biographic sketches are divided as to the date of his admission. Five state that he worked and studied simultaneously, thus supporting Khrushchev's own statement; five other versions maintain that he worked in the mines first and then entered the school, thus confirming the report in the Ukrainian paper. The other versions of his biography are silent on the matter.

A Soviet source[5] describes the Doniets Mining Technical School as occupying the two-story building of a former commerce high school of Czarist times. Students were lodged in "nearby empty, half-destroyed barracks." It is doubtful that Khrushchev shared these quarters, since he was more than a regular student at the school. As soon as he enrolled he became secretary of the Party cell, with the assignment of "strengthening the political leadership of the Party." In 1923, he was promoted to the position of a *politruk* (political guide), which function he performed until his graduation in 1925. Under his leadership, the source states, "the political-educational work among the students reached a high level." They acquired a "feeling of responsibility and high discipline." After school hours, "they were mobilized for large-scale creative work in construction and equipping the school." Khrushchev also used them as political agitators "in the mines and the pits" and in the workers' barracks, where they carried on "large-scale social work."

Burdened with responsible political functions, Khrushchev could hardly have devoted himself seriously to the crowded high-school curriculum of the Workers' Faculty. His attendance at the school gave him, however, the opportunity to gain experience as an agitator, experience indispensable to a Communist Party worker. In this field he certainly showed a far greater talent than in physics, algebra, or languages. In fact, after completing his "studies" in 1925, he was not interested in continuing them, as thousands of Workers' Faculty graduates were encouraged to do. Instead, he became engaged in Party work on a larger scale.

While Khrushchev attended school, the Party was involved in

a major crisis of leadership. Lenin fell gravely ill and died,
Stalin was seeking to extend his control through the Party's
Secretariat, and Trotsky, the organizer and leader of the Red
Army in the Civil War, led the opposition to him. The first
phase of their struggle began while Lenin, having suffered
three strokes, was still alive. The third stroke, on the night of
March 9, 1923, impaired his speech, and for ten months he lay
mutely awaiting death, which did not come until January 21,
1924. His heirs, however, did not wait that long; the fight among
them broke out in the autumn of 1923.

All over Russia, at Communist cells of factories and educational institutions, at meetings of Party Committees in cities
and districts, heated debate took place; resolutions, presented
by both sides, were discussed late into the night, and votes "for"
and "against" were taken. The Opposition, led by Trotsky and
others, was vigorously protesting Stalinist manipulation of the
Party machine in the elections of Party officials, punitive trans-
fers of dissenters, discriminatory appointments, and other trans-
gressions of "intra-Party democracy," or freedom of speech
inside the Party.

Demanding "intra-Party democracy," Trotsky and his associates became, quite unintentionally, the spokesmen for those
who demanded political democracy for all, including non-Com-
munists. Kamenev, who sided with Stalin, pointed this out as a
reason why democracy even within the Party was dangerous:

> Today one says: democracy within the Party; tomorrow
> one will say: democracy in the trade unions; the day after
> tomorrow, the workers may say: give us the same kind of
> democracy you introduced for yourselves. And can one
> be in doubt that the multitude of the farmers may also
> say to us: give us democracy? Therefore, I do not attach
> my seal to it.[6]

Although there is no record of Khrushchev's position on this
struggle, as secretary of the Party cell at his school he could not
have remained neutral. The fact that his political star rose steadily during this period indicates the political position he must
have taken. Only Stalinists were progressing in the Party machinery.

Not only the struggle for power between Stalin and Trotsky, but also the crisis of Lenin's New Economic Policy (NEP) were reflected in this controversy. The NEP had conceded to the farmers the right to dispose of their produce freely, but this concession could bear fruit only if industry was able to offer the farmers in return sufficient consumer goods at acceptable prices. The NEP could not solve this problem. Having somewhat relieved the economic situation of the farmers, the NEP had an adverse effect on that of the workers and employees in nationalized industry. Real wages fell from day to day; workers were frequently paid only once in two or three months. On the free market, where goods were available in limited quantities, inflation raged. The situation deteriorated still further when a so-called "regime of economy" was set in operation, for this meant further shrinkage of wages and increased unemployment. The Soviet press reluctantly admitted that as of September 1, 1923, the "conservative" number of unemployed had reached one million,[7] and that was only the beginning of the tide of unemployment.

Particularly miserable were the economic conditions of the miners, despite the fact that, to encourage them to produce more coal, they were promised preferential treatment regarding food and other incentives. Their housing situation was especially critical, as can be seen from the speech of a delegate from the Doniets basin, a certain Portenko, delivered at the Ninth All-Ukrainian Congress of the Soviets:

> Certain [investigating] commissions . . . were filled with indignation that [in some suburbs] one can see small workers' houses that have straw roofs. What would these commissions say if they came to the Doniets basin, to Stalino [Yuzovka], and saw that, on the main street, with its three-story buildings, workers live in houses that have no roofs at all, and that workers and their families live beneath open-hearth furnaces and coke ovens?[8]

The deep discontent of the workers took the form of demonstrations and strikes, and was answered with bloody reprisals and mass arrests. Particularly brutal was the treatment of peacefully striking miners in the Shakhty area in November, 1923.

The strikers' demands included: payment on time and not after
months of delay; an end to deductions allegedly agreed to by
the workers; improvement of living conditions; dismissal of
some Party members against whom the workers had grievances;
the right to elect representatives the workers wanted rather
than those the Party designated. When the spokesman for the
miners, Kapustin, was arrested, ten thousand of them demonstrated for his release. The Government replied with bullets and
whips.[9]

What was Khrushchev's attitude toward these events in the
Doniets basin? Was he, the former shepherd, fitter, and cage
operator in the mines, on the side of the striking miners who
demanded better living conditions? Was he shocked when he
heard of the bloody reprisals against peacefully demonstrating
workers? "There had been strikes in the first years after the
October Revolution, and I used to talk to the strikers," [10] Khrushchev said at a meeting with American labor leaders. There can
be no doubt about the nature of the talks Khrushchev had with
the strikers; as a Party member assigned to speeding up production, he must have taken an active part in suppressing the
strikes. Had he manifested sympathy for the plight of the miners,
he would not have remained in this position. Not even a neutral
attitude could have been maintained.

K. V. Moyseenko, Party boss of the Stalino region, was evidently satisfied with Khrushchev's Party work at the mining
school. Immediately after his graduation in 1925, Khrushchev
was made Party secretary in one of the region's districts. Mar'-
inka, the capital of the Petrovsko-Mar'inski district to which he
was assigned, was a city-like settlement nine miles from the
Mandrykino railroad station. The district contained a territory
of about 400 square miles within which one city, three large
towns, and eleven villages were located. Here Khrushchev
obtained his first experiences as a local Party leader, occupying
this position until 1927. None of the versions of his political life
report any facts about his activity during this period, except for
vague statements released abroad in 1959 to the effect that at
this post "he had to handle questions relating to mining and
agriculture," [11] or that "he made a thorough study of the work
at the coal mines and on the farms." [12] Reminiscing in a speech

delivered at Kiev in 1940, Khrushchev related: "When I worked as Secretary of a District Party Committee in the Doniets basin, I used to go to the villages, and I would get into a sleigh—at that time instead of automobiles there were sleighs—and I would put on a *kozhukh*,* and the frost would not bite me." [13] In these first years of his political career, he was apparently already demonstrating his talent for moving about, talking to people, investigating, agitating—important characteristics of his approach in later years.

At the end of 1925, Khrushchev was elected delegate from the Petrovsko-Mar'inski district to the Ninth All-Ukrainian Party Congress. Lazar M. Kaganovich occupied the position of Secretary General of the Ukrainian Communist Party and chaired the Congress.† Khrushchev's immediate boss, Moyseenko, was one of the speakers furiously attacking those delegates who refused to sing the praises of the Party leadership. There is no record that Khrushchev spoke at this Congress, but he was subsequently included in the list of delegates to the Fourteenth All-Union Party Congress (December, 1925)—an indication that his performance did not meet with disfavor among the Stalinists.

The Fourteenth Congress was an important step on the road to power for Stalin, and also for those who chose to stake their fortunes on Stalin's success. Officially, the issue for discussion at the Congress was the Party's policy toward the middle-class farmers and the poor peasants. Should the Party, in its struggle against the more prosperous farmers, the so-called kulaks, rely solely on the poor peasants and farm laborers, or should it also adjust its policy to the interests of the middle-class farmers and thus detach them from the influence of the kulaks?

In reality, the Fourteenth Congress was the scene of a power struggle between Stalin and Bukharin who advocated the more "liberal" agricultural policy, and Kamenev and Zinoviev, once Stalin's close associates in the triumvirate which controlled the Party after Lenin's death. Their growing political distance from

---

* A coat made of coarse sheepskins, the wool turned inside.

† In its March, 1960, issue, *Kommunist Ukrainy*, the authoritative organ of the Ukrainian Communist Party, carried an "historical" article about this Congress. Fourteen delegates, including Khrushchev, are mentioned by name, but the name of Kaganovich, whom Khrushchev purged in 1957, is not among them.

Stalin was exemplified by their support of the opposite view on
the kulak question. But the main issue was the concentration of
power in the hands of Stalin who, as Secretary General of the
Central Committee, headed both the Organization Bureau
(Orgburo) and the Secretariat. The struggle centered around
the implementation of Lenin's testament, which stated that
Stalin was too "crude" and proposed "to the Comrades to consider a way of transferring Stalin from that position [of Secretary
General] and to appoint to that position another man who differs
from Stalin in that he should have, above all, only one superior
quality, namely, greater tolerance, greater loyalty, greater polite-
ness, and a more considerate attitude toward Comrades, a less
capricious character, and so on." [14]

The will had been completed by Lenin in January, 1923, and
became known to the free world in the summer of 1924. It was
officially ignored in the Soviet Union, however, until the summer of 1956, when it was suddenly published in *Kommunist,*
the theoretical organ of the Party. It took the Kremlin more
than three decades to transmit to the people a message which
Khrushchev characterized in his secret speech to the Twentieth
Party Congress of February 25, 1956, as of "tremendous importance." Indeed, the importance of Lenin's testament was truly
tremendous, for one can only speculate on the shape of the
world today had Lenin's desire to see Stalin hold less power
materialized.

According to Khrushchev, the "text of the testament was
distributed to the delegates to the Twentieth Party Congress." [15]
Actually, the question arises, why was it necessary to distribute
the testament in 1956 at all, when in the same speech he also
stated: "This document of Lenin's was made known to the
delegates of the Thirteenth Party Congress, who discussed the
question of transferring Stalin from the position of Secretary
General." [16]

In actual fact, the testament was not distributed at the
Thirteenth Congress, held in May, 1924, but was read only as
a top-secret document to separate delegations. Therefore it
could not have been discussed at any plenary session of this or
any other Congress during the Stalin era. The document was
distributed, however, in printed form at the Fifteenth Party

Congress (December, 1927), in the Bulletin of that Congress designated "for delegates only." Khrushchev personally could not have missed this Bulletin and, in it, the document of "tremendous importance," because he participated in the work of that Congress as a full-fledged delegate from the Stalino region. Khrushchev did not reveal the fact of the 1927 distribution, perhaps because he was reluctant to admit that he had had firsthand knowledge of this document since that time. He was not present at the 1924 Congress at which he reports it was discussed; he was present at the 1927 Congress.

In any event, at the Fourteenth Party Congress, for Stalin and his close associates the concealment of the testament was one of the tactics in the pursuit of their objectives. Another tactic was the organized prevention of debate. The majority of the delegates, controlled by Stalin, behaved like an organized gang of hecklers, interrupting and shouting down speakers who attempted to criticize the policies of Stalin's Party machine. The Ukrainian delegation headed by Kaganovich was particularly noisy, and Khrushchev's boss, Moyseenko, proved himself to be a heckler par excellence.[17] Presumably the expansive Khrushchev was just as noisy as the rest of the delegation, although he was still too insignificant on the political scene to earn special mention in the records.

The Congress ended with Stalin's triumph: the Opposition was beaten by an overwhelming vote of 599 to 65. This vote surprised no one, least of all Stalin. Through the Secretariat and the Orgburo, he had taken firm control of the Party machine in all parts of the country except Leningrad before the Congress opened. This last stronghold of Zinoviev was undermined while the Congress was still in session; Stalin's emissaries seized the editorial offices of the *Leningradskaya Pravda* and began to purge the Party organization of Zinovievites. Zinoviev himself was replaced by Sergei M. Kirov.

Khrushchev returned to Mar'inka after the Congress and resumed his work as district Party secretary. In October, 1926, he was chosen to represent the district at the First All-Ukrainian Party Conference convened in Kharkov. In 1927, he left Mar'inka for a "leading Party job" in Stalino. His position is not described in any of the Soviet official biographies. However, in 1959, a

Ukrainian historical journal, in a review of a booklet on the
"struggle of the Donbas Party organization for the fulfillment
of the industrialization plan in 1926-29," praises the author for
"introducing into scientific circulation valuable material about
the activity of Comrade N. S. Khrushchev, who was in 1927
one of the leaders of the Stalino regional Party organization.[18]
Also in 1959, in an article released for the press by the Soviet
Embassy in the United States on the occasion of Khrushchev's
sixty-fifth birthday, he is described as Chief of the Organizational
Department of a larger *district* Party Committee.[19] A few months
later, on the occasion of Khrushchev's visit to the United States,
the same Embassy identified him as the head of the Organizational Department of the Stalino *Regional* Party Committee,[20]
thus considerably enhancing his position. Whatever may be the
reason for this discrepancy, Khrushchev's position was significant enough for him to be chosen as a delegate to the Tenth
All-Ukrainian Party Congress convened at Kharkov in 1927.
Moreover, at the Congress he was named a member of the
fourteen-man Credentials Commission and held second place
in the list of that body. The Congress in turn elected fourteen
delegates from the Stalino region to the upcoming Fifteenth
All-Union Party Congress (December, 1927), and Khrushchev
was one of eleven delegates to attend the latter with a full vote;
at the Fourteenth Congress he had held only a deliberative vote.

Although the exact stature of Khrushchev's Party position at
Stalino can only be conjectured, Soviet records present an interesting picture of the condition of the regional Party Committee during this period. The end of 1927 and early 1928
witnessed a crisis in the Stalino leadership that necessitated a
purge on the part of the Ukrainian Communist Party. Georgi
M. Malenkov, who at the time held an important job in the
apparatus of the Party's Central Committee in Moscow, wrote
in *Partiynoye stroitelstvo* (Party Construction), No. 2, 1930:

> About two years ago the organization of the Stalino
> region experienced a deep and difficult crisis in its Party
> leadership. At the end of 1927 and the beginning of 1928,
> the Central Committee and the Central Control Commis-
> sion of the Ukrainian Communist Party (Bolshevik)

brought to light the rottenness of the leadership of the region and part of its cadres. In its resolution of March, 1928, the Central Control Commission of the Ukrainian Communist Party (Bolshevik) noted the systematic drinking bouts among the upper strata of the regional Party organization, "self-provisioning," the ineffective struggle of the Bureau of the Regional Committee against squandering, bad management, and the whitewashing of individual responsible [Party] workers, the use of methods of oppression by the Bureau of the Regional Committee with regard to comrades who protested against shameful conduct, and several other unwholesome occurrences.

Malenkov went on to describe the purge of this leadership:

Mention should be made of the positive work of the new improved leadership (which came to replace the corrupt) for restoring health to the Party organization. The merit of the Regional Committee lies in the fact that, for a period of two years, it systematically exposed the unhealthy conditions in the organization, thereby eradicating the roots and consequences of the corruption of the old leadership. The Regional Committee carried out the purification of the active cadres. This process of purification cannot yet be considered as entirely completed, but unquestionably much has already been done in this respect. The purge will help to finish the process of purification.

Thus, when Malenkov wrote the article, in 1930, the purge still continued. He explained that the "extirpation of the roots of the corruption" was taking so much time because the "unhealthy symptoms had penetrated deep into the organization as a result of bad leadership in the region in the past." But there was also an additional reason for the delay, namely: "the inadequate engagement of the masses into the process of purification."

Until the end of 1927 the Party boss of the Stalino region was K. V. Moyseenko, mentioned earlier for excelling as a heckler of the Opposition at the Fourteenth Congress. There is no doubt that Moyseenko was the "directing upper strata" of the Stalino region that Malenkov had in mind. Moyseenko's political merits as a Stalinist prevailed, however, over his low moral standing. Instead of being numbered among the purged, he was merely transferred from the Stalino region, an important coal production center, to the far less important agricultural region of Poltava.

Khrushchev was transferred in 1928 to a position at Kiev identified only as a "responsible Party job." Although the reasons for the transfer are not known, it did occur during the purge and meant, significantly perhaps, that the Party did not consider his presence and participation during the period of "purification" of the organization to be necessary. It may also be assumed that he did not belong to the "Comrades who protested against shameful conduct," since there are no indications that the "methods of oppression," which Malenkov reported the Bureau of the Regional Party Committee used against such comrades, were used against him.

Khrushchev's role in and attitude toward the moral corruption at Stalino remains unclear. His presence there during this period, and the timing of his transfer, make any assumption possible, including the assumption that he was shifted from Stalino for the same reasons as his boss, Moyseenko. Whatever his relationship to the events at Stalino, his transfer in 1928 could have been, at worst, no more than a minor chastisement. The following year, 1929, he was a delegate to the Second All-Ukrainian Party Conference at Kharkov.

3

Impatient Gravedigger of Democracy

No single event can be identified as the moment that the Bolshevik regime changed into a totalitarian dictatorship—a system where all life, whether spiritual or physical, national or personal, is tightly controlled by a few or by one—a system where all channels of free expression are firmly sealed off, and an atmosphere of primitive fear reigns, destroying everything a human being cherishes—freedom, love, friendship, and trust—a system where human efforts are rewarded only if accompanied by songs of glory for the Party and the *vozhd*. Actually, there was no particular event exclusively responsible for the establishment of this terrifying edifice. Its cornerstones were laid in 1903, when Lenin argued that the Party should consist of professional revolutionaries ruled from above. Its foundation was built in December, 1917, when the Cheka, which destroyed all principles of legality, was established. Its walls were constructed in January, 1918, when Lenin dissolved by force the All-Russian Constituent Assembly, the first legislative group freely elected by all peoples of Russia in their history. Its style was chosen in 1922, when Lenin selected Stalin as Secretary General of the Party. And its finishing touches were added in 1929, when Trotsky, whom Lenin had described in his testament as the "most able man in the present Central Committee," was forced into exile, and in the 'thirties, when the last vestiges of free discussion within the Party were washed away in the blood of the Kamenevs, Zinovievs, Bukharins, and Rykovs. All the dates marked indispensable links in the chains which shackle the

27

peoples of the Soviet empire. What can be easily determined, however, is the period from 1923 to 1929, in which Stalin's personal rule developed.

The defeat of the Kamenev-Zinoviev opposition in 1925 was the most important event leading to Stalin's dictatorship. Having politically isolated these dangerous rivals, he could now cope readily with the so-called Oppositionist Bloc formed in the spring of 1926 by Trotsky, on the one hand, and Kamenev and Zinoviev on the other. It took Stalin only a few months to defeat this new coalition.

Shouts, insults, and systematic heckling, used for the first time with great success at the Fourteenth Congress, now became a basic tactic. Opposition leaders were simply shouted down; squads of trained hecklers and muscle-men were dispatched wherever they made their appearance. Those who witnessed Fascist or Nazi methods at public meetings while the *Duce* or the *Führer* were still struggling for power, would have found a resemblance between the behavior of the Black Shirts and the Brown Shirts and that of Stalin's squads. For example, Trotsky, whose fiery oratory could dominate any audience to which he spoke, was forced from the rostrum by a din which made it impossible for him to be heard. "For Party unity!" "Against discussion!" were the slogans advocated in *Pravda,* which gave the Stalinist reason for rejecting discussions on Party policy:

> Discussion is impermissible . . . because it shakes the very foundation of the dictatorship of the proletariat, the unity of the Party, and its dominant position in the country; because it serves the cause of various groups which crave political democracy . . . and sprouts of political democracy might get through the cracks opened by discussion.[1]

Opposition attempts to appeal to the Party membership for support failed, and the Opposition leaders were faced with a dilemma: either to capitulate or to carry their struggle beyond the Party limits and appeal to the broad masses of the people. In so doing they would have had to raise the banner of political democracy for all. Such a position was untenable for men who had themselves been advocates of the Party dictatorship and taken part, in Lenin's day, in the elimination of non-Communist elements. Thus, only one road was open to them: capitulation to Stalin and betrayal of those who believed in them. On October 4, 1926, the Opposition leaders entered "peace" negotiations with the Politburo. On October 16, Trotsky, Kamenev, Zinoviev, Piatakov, Sokolnikov, and Yevdokimov signed a declaration of submission. They admitted having violated the decisions of the Party, and promised to "unconditionally abide by and unreservedly put into practice" the decisions of the Fourteenth Congress. They were allowed to keep their convictions temporarily.

On October 17, 1926, the declaration of submission of the six Opposition leaders was published. On that same day, the First All-Ukrainian Party Conference convened in Kharkov, with Khrushchev participating as a delegate from the Stalino region. Kaganovich, Secretary General of the Ukrainian Party, delivered the main report on Party policy. He bitterly attacked the complaint of the Opposition that intra-Party democracy had been destroyed and that minority rights of dissenting Party members had not been observed. Minority rights, according to Kaganovich, were not the issue.

The Stalinist logic ran like this: minority rights to disagree with the majority and to persuade it to accept the views of the minority are unnecessary, since the majority is always right, and the minority wrong. Hence, the minority never has a chance to become a majority. When Lenin's widow, Krupskaya, had dared to remind the Fourteenth Party Congress that at the Stockholm Congress of the Russian Social Democratic Labor Party in 1906 the Bolshevik faction had been themselves in the minority and that, therefore, the majority was not always right, she was viciously attacked, and even Opposition leaders were forced to disavow her publicly.

Kaganovich explained that he had an entirely different concept of intra-Party democracy than the Opposition. He said that he considered it "a tool, a means of raising the political activity of the masses." [2] This, he said, had been accomplished in the Ukraine by a sharp increase in Party membership. To prove his point, he adduced figures to the effect that in the preceding two years the membership of the Ukrainian Party had almost tripled. These new members, he told the Opposition, "are joining us and don't accept your platform. Is that not the reason why you are wailing?" [3]

Kaganovich's line of reasoning is one of innumerable examples of how a Soviet leader, trampling upon logic, facts, and the intelligence of his listeners, bends a clear and simple term and gives it a totally alien meaning in order not to be hampered by it in the pursuit of his power politics. The meaning of intra-Party democracy is obvious: within the Communist Party, members should be free to disagree with each other, discuss matters freely, and nominate and elect delegates freely. Instead, Kaganovich insisted that intra-Party democracy—a term which he would not have dreamt of discarding or attacking head-on—was something else, something designed to increase membership and "raise the political activity of the masses."

When a dissenter by the name of Golubenko challenged Kaganovich's observations as well as the figures which he had adduced to prove them, Khrushchev took the floor to make his first recorded speech. He said:

> We just heard the speech of Comrade Golubenko of Odessa. It is entirely clear to me that Comrade Golubenko intentionally slandered the Party and that he lied about the situation in our Party organization. If Comrade Golubenko says that the changes in the Party organs were achieved through padding, then this is the sheerest calumny. . . . New secretaries are being elected on the basis of intra-Party democracy. The changes in the composition of the [Party] cell bureaus were carried out on the basis of intra-Party democracy, and not through enlarging their composition, as Comrade Golubenko said. [4]

Like Kaganovich, Khrushchev insisted that "intra-Party democracy" was observed as long as local Party officials were "elected" rather than appointed from above. Both remained silent, however, about how the elections were carried out. The term "free elections" disappeared from their vocabulary, and Kaganovich introduced instead nebulous terms such as "electiveness" (*vybornost*).

Khrushchev did not limit his speech to an assault on Golubenko. He used the occasion to question the sincerity of the October 16 declaration with which Stalin's enemies had surrendered. Moreover, he demanded, by implication, "repressive measures" against Trotsky, Kamenev, Zinoviev, and other old Bolsheviks who had signed the declaration. He said:

> In my opinion, today's speech of the oppositionist Golubenko entirely confirms the unscrupulous and superficial nature of the declaration of our Opposition. Our Party organizations demand from the Opposition that they totally submit to the decisions of the Fourteenth Congress and the Central Committee of the All-Union Communist Party. I believe that the declaration written by the Opposition is not a sincere declaration. Unless the Opposition entirely recognizes the decisions of the Fourteenth Party Congress, there can be no question of collaborating with them. Should this not be the case, then we ought to demand from the highest Party organs that they apply repressive measures against the incorrigible members of the Opposition, regardless of their former merits and positions.[5] *

At the very moment that he delivered this speech, the "highest Party organs," the Central Committee and the Central Control Commission of the Party, took a different and much more conciliatory line. In their announcement, published simultaneously with the Opposition's declaration, they stated: "Now the Central Committee has the opportunity to state with satisfaction that the Opposition on the whole has accepted the conditions presented on them."[6] On October 20, 1926, *Pravda* editorially pointed out that the declaration of the six Opposition leaders "must be considered a significant historical document."

Thus Khrushchev's intolerant attitude toward the Opposition surpassed at this point even that of Stalin. While the Opposition

---

* The May, 1960, issue of *Kommunist Ukrainy* summarizes Khrushchev's speech as follows: "I believe that the declaration written by the Opposition is not sincere. . . . Their declarations are only a maneuver; they make believe now that they are against a split, that they accept a *rapprochement* with the majority of the Central Committee, with our Party. But, while they admit their mistakes, they try to create for themselves possibilities to carry on a schismatic policy in the future."

not only abided by the decisions of the Fourteenth Party Congress but also promised to put them into practice, and while
Stalin accepted the declaration "with satisfaction," Khrushchev
searched the souls of the old Leninists and demanded total surrender. His position soon became the policy of the Party, but it
is a mark of a successfully rising politician that he could anticipate the trend before Stalin had expressed it. When surrender
was demanded, which Khrushchev must not have doubted
would happen, he would be in good standing.

The speech is also significant for the clarity with which it
reveals Khrushchev's approach to political debate. It contains
all the elements of the kind of verbal assault which is characteristic of a Stalinist: the fierce, insulting style; the unfounded, un-
proved assertions; and the ultimatum-like demands.

Golubenko, who had made factual remarks to answer Kaganovich's distortions, was called a liar, a slanderer, a man engaging
in the "sheerest calumny"; the possibility that he might have
spoken sincerely was not considered. Proof was not offered in
refutation of his claims; he was answered instead with a counter-
claim ("the changes . . . were carried out on the basis of intra-
Party democracy and not . . . as Comrade Golubenko has said").
And finally, having defamed Golubenko and the entire Opposition as unscrupulous and insincere, Khrushchev demanded their
unconditional surrender, and threatened that unless they yielded
completely there would be no question of "collaborating with
them."

At the Tenth Ukrainian Party Congress held in November, 1927,
Khrushchev again pulled ahead of the other speakers, who were
mostly concerned with dealing the final blow to the Opposition
which he had anticipated earlier. Speaking on November 24,
he developed some original ideas concerning organizational
policy of the Party. He said:

> As we carry on the struggle against the Opposition, we
> should not overlook practical questions of Party construc-
> tion. I consider it necessary to raise at this Congress a series
> of organizational problems of Party construction. In the
> first place, I propose that secretariats of the regional [*okrug*,
> now *oblast*] Party committees be created in important

industrial areas and districts [*rayons*]. It might be argued
that the creation of such secretariats could lead to a re-
striction of intra-Party democracy, and thus prevent the
district committees from solving certain problems, and
so on. Nevertheless, I believe that by introducing this organizational innovation we do not violate the basic principles of intra-Party democracy.

At the same time, the creation of secretariats will make
it possible to free the district Party committees from petty,
less important questions and concentrate their attention on
basic questions.

My second proposal deals with the necessity of chang-
ing the intervals between the elections of the Party cell
bureaus and the convocation of district conferences. The
Stalino region believes that elections to the cell bureaus
should be held only once in six months and that the district
Party conferences should be called once a year. Such
changes are required from the viewpoint of making our
work really businesslike.[7]

Khrushchev made his proposals in the name of the "Stalino
region." This would confirm the conjecture that in 1927 he occupied the position of Chief of the Organizational Department
of the Stalino Regional Party Committee. His motions were not
discussed, which would suggest that they had not been inspired
from above. This circumstance increases the significance of
his proposals, as they show the direction in which his mind
worked in the mid-'twenties so far as questions of Party organization were concerned. He anticipated a much stricter authori-
tarian control, at the expense of local elections, measures which
were in part realized in 1934, and further developed in 1952
and 1956.

It was still possible in 1927 for Party members to criticize the
Party leadership and its decisions to a limited extent. *Pravda*
was still publishing "Discussion Sheets," and the Stalinists insisted that they were not guilty of suppressing freedom of
expression within the Party. Party meetings were, however, well
prepared in advance by the Party machine, and, through noisy
interruptions, members of the Opposition were prevented from

expressing themselves. Khrushchev was a promoter of the new concept of intra-Party democracy, who considered even limited freedom of speech dangerous for the dictatorship of the Party bureaucracy. He therefore advocated, for the time being, that the number of occasions where courageous Party members could speak up be reduced. The remedy he suggested was to lengthen the intervals between elections and conferences.

The Party Statutes adopted in 1925 had specified that district Party conferences should be called "at least once in six months." Khrushchev proposed to increase the periods between conferences to a year. This would have meant a further strengthening of the local Party bosses.

The central Party machine, however, was not yet ready for such a measure, because the low-level Party organs were still full of "doubtful elements." It must be remembered that Stalin's rise to absolute power within the Party was accomplished in stages. First it had been necessary to create a "popular" movement against Trotsky and other Oppositionists. This was done by admitting to the Party politically inexperienced "workers from the bench" who, in return for having been granted entrance to the ruling Party, readily supported the Party bureaucracy in its fight against the more sophisticated opposition which consisted mostly of intellectuals. Also, newcomers had to be admitted to the lower Party organs in order to replace purged oppositionists. This had resulted in the padding of these lower Party organs with opportunists and morally unstable elements, who engaged in "drinking bouts" and "self-provisioning" much like the men in the Stalino regional organization. Khrushchev's proposal, if accepted, would have meant a stabilization and perpetuation in office of these undesirable low-level Party bureaucrats. But, with the Opposition already beaten, this was not in the interests of the Party as a whole. The "workers from the bench" had done their job, and many of them had become dangerous ballast which had to be jettisoned eventually.

Nevertheless, the "organizational innovations" proposed by Khrushchev were fully compatible with the general desire of the Kremlin to limit debate and elections as much as possible. The sole difference between his line of thinking and that of the Moscow planners was that he, a low-echelon local Party bureaucrat, thought in terms of his limited area, while Stalin was interested in strengthening the independence of his central Party machine. In fact, at the time Khrushchev made his suggestions to limit the prerogatives of local Party organizations, the Party machine in Moscow was preparing an amendment to the Party Statutes limiting its responsibility to the All-Union Party Congress. This amendment, adopted in 1927 at the Fifteenth Party Congress, increased the period between All-Union Congresses from one year to two years. The Seventeenth Congress in 1934 adopted new Statutes which increased the intervals between the Congresses from two to three years. These Statutes also specified that district Party conferences should be convened only once a year, as Khrushchev had proposed in 1927.

Actually not even these reduced schedules were observed. The All-Union Congress, which was scheduled for 1937, was called in 1939, and the Nineteenth All-Union Congress, scheduled for 1942, took place in 1952. The 1939 Party Statutes reintroduced All-Union Party Conferences, which had been abolished in 1934, and provided that these conferences be called "at least once a year." But this provision was also violated; between 1939 and 1952, only one All-Union Party Conference was called.

In view of the "organizational innovations" he proposed in 1927, it was not surprising that it was Khrushchev who introduced additional changes in the Party Statutes at the Nineteenth and Twentieth Party Congresses in 1952 and 1956, changes which went further in the direction of limiting the prerogatives of the All-Union Party Congress and the local Party organs. Thus, Khrushchev's idea of strengthening the grip on the Party membership, an idea which found expression in his speech in 1927, remained prominent throughout his political career.

In his secret speech to the Twentieth Party Congress charging the late dictator with "brutal violation" of "our Party's holy Leninist principles" regarding the convocation of Party Congresses, Khrushchev said:

Whereas, during the first few years after Lenin's death, Party congresses and Central Committee plenums took place more or less regularly, later, when Stalin began increasingly to abuse his power, these principles were bru-

tally violated. This was especially evident during the last
fifteen years of his life.[8]

Since Stalin died in 1953, the violation of the Party Statutes
became, according to Khrushchev, "especially evident" only
after 1938. But the following table (see below) shows that the
violations began as early as 1926, two years after Lenin's death.
Khrushchev was, of course, aware of these violations, having
participated in Party congresses since 1925.

In Lenin's time, the Bolshevik Party could by no means have
been called a democratic party as far as the rights of its members
were concerned. But only by comparing the provisions of the
Party Statutes of 1919, when Lenin was still alive, with the
Statutory changes introduced after his death (as shown in
Tables 2 and 3), can one evaluate how the Party separated itself
even from "Lenin's rules of Party life." By being among the first
to propose such changes, Khrushchev was not so much a blind
follower of Stalin as a promoter of conditions necessary for the
development of Stalin's dictatorial control.

TABLE 1.

*Violation of the Party Statutes Regarding Party Congresses
and Conferences*

Party Bodies	Due	Called
All-Union Party Congresses:		
Fifteenth	1926	1927
Sixteenth	1929	1930
Seventeenth	1932	1934
Eighteenth	1937	1939
Nineteenth	1942	1952
All-Union Conferences:		
Sixteenth	1927	1929
Seventeenth	1930	1932
Eighteenth	1933	1941

Table 2.

Frequency of Convocation of Party Congresses and Conferences

Party Bodies	Statutes of 1919	Statutes of 1922	Statutes of 1925	Statutes Changed in 1927	Statutes of 1934	Statutes of 1939	Statutes of 1952	Statutes Changed in 1956
All-Union Level:								
1. Congresses	1 yr.	1 yr.	1 yr.	2 yrs.	3 yrs.	3 yrs.	4 yrs.	—
2. Conferences	3 mos.	1 yr.	1 yr.	—	abolished	1 yr.	abolished	—
Republic, Krai, Oblast Level:								
1. Congresses	—	—	—	—	1½ yrs.	1½ yrs.	1½ yrs.	2 or 4 yrs.[a]
2. Conferences	6 mos.	6 mos.	6 mos.	—	abolished	abolished	abolished	—
Okrug Level:								
Conferences	3 mos.[b]	6 mos.[b]	6 mos.[b]	—	—	1½ yrs.	1½ yrs.	—
City, Rayon Level:								
Conferences	3 mos.[c]	6 mos.[c]	6 mos.[c]	—	1 yr.	1 yr.	1 yr.	2 yrs.[d]

[a] The four-year term was established for the Ukrainian, Belorussian, Kazakh, and Uzbek S.S.R.
[b] These terms were established for organizations on the *gubernia* level.
[c] These terms were established for organizations on *uyezd* level, where no *rayons* existed.
[d] For larger cities divided into *rayons*.

TABLE 3.

Frequency of Plenary Sessions of Party Committees and Elections
of Bureaus of Primary Party Organizations (Cells)

Party Bodies	Statutes of 1919	Statutes of 1922	Statutes of 1925	Statutes of 1934	Statutes of 1939	Statutes of 1952	Statutes Changed in 1956
All-Union Central Committees	14 days	2 mos.	2 mos.	4 mos.	4 mos.	6 mos.	—
Republic, Krai, *Oblast* Committees	14 days	1 mo.	2 mos.	3 mos.	3 mos.	2 mos.	4 mos.
Okrug Committees	14 days[a]	1 mo.[a]	1 mo.	1 mo.	—	1½ mos.	3 mos.
Elections to Party Cell Bureaus	1 mo.	3 mos.	6 mos.	1 yr.	1 yr.	1 yr.	—

[a] These terms were established for organizations on the *gubernia* level.

4

The Soviet Countryside Becomes a Colony

The "repressive measures" against the Opposition which Khrushchev had advocated in October, 1926, at the First All-Ukrainian Party Conference became a reality on December 18, 1927. At that time the Fifteenth Party Congress ousted from the Party those in opposition at the Fourteenth Party Congress who had not been expelled or jailed between the Congresses. Among the group were Kamenev, Piatakov, Radek, and Rakovsky—Trotsky and Zinoviev had been ousted one month earlier. The stenographic report of the Congress does not contain any evidence of Khrushchev's moves during the sessions; he was not elected to any Congress or Party body, nor was he among the speakers. But one thing is certain: he belonged to the Stalinists who voted for the expulsion of the Opposition.

After this Congress, Khrushchev returned to Stalino for a short time, and then went to Kiev. Kiev was then the second most important city in the Ukraine after Kharkov, the latter being the capital where the Central Committee of the Ukrainian Party and Kaganovich, its Secretary General, were located. Soviet sources do not disclose the nature of Khrushchev's work in Kiev, but it may be assumed that he worked as an active whip in the Kiev regional Party machine. This assumption is supported by the content of a speech which he delivered at the Second All-Ukrainian Party Conference in April, 1929, at Kharkov. In this speech, which deserves careful attention, Khrushchev said:

Comrades, the work performed under the guidance of our Central Committee on the basis of the decisions of the Party congresses and subsequent plenary sessions of the Central Committee, has fully justified the course taken at the Fifteenth Party Congress with regard to the development of industry and agriculture.

In spite of the resolutions unanimously adopted at the Fifteenth Party Congress, there are *some leading comrades* who, admitting by word of mouth the correctness of those decisions, *sabotage the work of the Central Committee* and do not carry out assignments given by the Party. They want to cover up their deviation from the Leninist line by various slanders about oppression allegedly existing in the Party; they want to deceive some Communists, using the same pattern as Trotsky did. The same comrades who in their time brilliantly repulsed the Trotskyites now use the rusty weapon of Trotskyism in their struggle against the Party and its Central Committee.

Our organization condemned the behavior of the Right deviationists. The entire organization unanimously voted against the Rightists and against reconciliation with them. *But one should not deceive oneself by unanimous decisions.* Some comrades, under the influence of difficulties, begin to waver. We do not always know how to harmonize fundamental policy decisions with our daily work.

I believe that, at the present time, when we witness a considerable weakening of labor discipline and nonfulfillment of our plans and tasks, it is necessary to explain to each Party cell the responsibility for fulfillment of the tasks of which each cell is in charge. Speaking of the necessity to fight the Rightists, we sometimes overlook vital questions whose solution would help the Party to cope with its basic difficulties and overcome the hesitations and vacillations which some unsteady Party members display. I believe that we should strive for a more precise organization of the work, check on whether everybody does his work, ensure correct conduct of affairs, and thus help the Party to master all difficulties and to fight the rightist deviations which spring from those difficulties.[1]

In all, this speech was a typical expression of the official Party line of the day, but it contains a few interesting points of its own. First, it indicates that Khrushchev's functions in the Kiev organization were those of an organizer and propagandist. This is also clear from a statement in *Stalinskoye Plemia*, November 18, 1939, according to which some time in 1929 Khrushchev participated in a *subbotnik*—a gathering on rest days to perform additional work without pay—at which he distinguished himself by turning out some metal part almost twice as fast as "highly skilled workers." This information was volunteered by a certain Burdakov, an "old Bolshevik," who "supported" Khrushchev's candidacy for the Kiev *oblast* Soviet in 1939. Evidently Khrushchev was engaged in organizing the "socialist-competition" movement which was launched in the spring of the same year, and which was to become one of the principal devices of labor exploitation in the entire Soviet bloc in the decades to come.

Another interesting remark in the speech is that "one should not deceive oneself by unanimous decisions." This remark implies that "unanimous decisions" were the result of some kind of pressure from above. Such was actually always the case under the Communist regime, but by making the statement Khrushchev contradicted himself when he attacked the Rightists for their complaints about "oppression allegedly existing in the Party." In other words, he admitted indirectly that this "alleged" oppression really existed.

The most interesting remark, however, is that "some leading comrades" had sabotaged the work of the Central Committee and not carried out the assignments of the Party. There can be no doubt that Khrushchev was thinking of Bukharin's group in this connection. Bukharin was the actual leader of the "Right deviation," although he was not identified as such until August 24, 1929, in a *Pravda* editorial, "About the Errors and Deviation of Comrade Bukharin."

At this point a few words are in order on the Stalin-Bukharin controversy. This conflict, seemingly extinguished together with the lives of Bukharin, Rykov, and Tomsky, never came to an end and is still alive after three decades. It emerged again and again in one form or another during the Stalin era. The post-Stalin

period was full of conflicts which were the logical continuation
of the Stalin-Bukharin struggle. It was this controversy which
helped to push Malenkov out of the premiership in February,
1955, led Imre Nagy into exile and death, and ignited the flames
of the rebellions in Berlin, Poznan, Warsaw, and Budapest.
Ideologically, the rebelling Communists in Communist countries
are the heirs of Bukharin's ideas, while Khrushchev and the
Khrushchevites are the faithful apostles of the general policy
line laid down by Stalin and his followers in 1928-29. The conflict is virtually one over consumer goods versus heavy industry.

On July 13, 1928, Stalin assailed "some comrades" who thought
that "in order to strengthen the bond (between workers and
peasants) the main stress must be shifted from heavy industry
to light industry . . ." [2] Twenty-seven years later, on January 25,
1955, Khrushchev attacked "some comrades" who "are trying to
prove that at a certain stage of socialist construction the development of heavy industry . . . ceases to be the main task and that
light industry can and should take the lead. . ."[3] Both Stalin
and Khrushchev ascribed these beliefs to the Rightists led by
Bukharin. It seems that the bullet which killed Bukharin in
1938 could not destroy the belief of "some comrades" that the
daily needs of the people should not be sacrificed altogether to
"socialist construction." This conflict of opinion has always been
at the root of the most important deviations from the Party's
general line.

The conflict flared up almost immediately after the Fifteenth
Party Congress (in 1927), at which, allegedly, a more solid
unity had been exhibited between Stalin and the remaining big
leaders: Bukharin, foremost Party theoretician, editor-in-chief
of *Pravda*, successor to Zinoviev in the Comintern; Rykov,
Lenin's successor as Chairman of the Council of People's Commissars; Tomsky, Chairman of the All-Union Council of Trade
Unions; and Voroshilov, People's Commissar of the Army and
Navy. Bukharin, Rykov, and Tomsky were dissatisfied with
the "emergency measures" taken against the farmers, which in
plain language meant the forcible expropriation of the farmers'
produce, begun in the first months of 1928 in clear violation of
Lenin's NEP. The turn in policy was motivated by the fact that
between January, 1927, and January, 1928, the procurement of

grain had dropped by 30 per cent, because the farmers preferred to store their grain rather than sell it to the state at low prices without getting equivalent compensation in the form of manufactured goods, particularly textiles, leather goods, etc. It became clear that the farmers were not willing to contribute to the "construction of socialism," as the rapid industrialization drive was called, by sacrificing their labor and produce in favor of a government not responsible to anybody. The following dilemma arose: either a slower rate of industrialization had to be adopted, in favor of the production of more consumer goods, in order to reduce the enormous disproportion between the prices of farm products and consumer goods (gradual closing of the "scissors"); or an all-out industrialization had to be launched and carried out by following the alleged capitalist practice of "sucking the peasant's blood from his heart and the brains from his head," * and throwing it all on the altar of "socialist construction." Stalin chose the latter solution, while Bukharin and his colleagues insisted on an honest continuation of Lenin's NEP and on an industrialization policy which would take into account the daily needs of the population.

What the new line held in store for the farmers was stated with utmost clarity by Stalin himself on July 9, 1928:

> The way matters stand with the peasants . . . is as follows: they not only pay the state the usual direct and indirect taxes; in the first place, they also *overpay* for the relatively expensive manufactured goods, and, in the second place, they are more or less *underpaid* for their agricultural products.
>
> This is an additional tax levied on the peasants for the sake of promoting industry, which works for the whole country, the peasants included. It is something in the nature of a "tribute," a supertax, which we are compelled to levy for the time being in order to preserve and accelerate the present rate of industrial development.[4]

---

* This is part of a quotation from Marx used by Molotov at the Fifteenth Party Congress, to the effect that: "The bourgeois society sucks the blood from the farmer's heart and the brains from his head and throws all this into the furnace of capitalism—this new alchemist."

Stalin made this speech at a plenary session of the Central Committee. Apparently even some members of the Committee could not accept the frank admission that in a Communist country the peasantry must pay a tribute to the state. This prompted Stalin to make a second speech on July 11, 1928, in which he explained:

> There are some people who do not like this [supertax]. These comrades apparently fear the truth. Well, this is a matter of taste. Some think that it is not advisable to tell the truth at a plenary session of the Central Committee. But I think that at a plenary session of the Central Committee of our Party it is our duty to tell the whole truth. It should not be forgotten that the plenary session of the Central Committee cannot be regarded as a mass meeting. Of course, "supertax," "additional tax" are unpleasant words, for they hit hard. But . . . [these] words fully correspond to the facts.[5]

On April 22, 1929, at another session of the Central Committee, Stalin again elaborated on the question of the "so-called tribute" and severely attacked Bukharin for calling it "military-feudal exploitation of the peasantry." [6]

It is noteworthy that the "whole truth" which Stalin told the members of the Central Committee in July, 1928, was kept secret for more than two decades: Stalin's speeches on the subject of the "tribute" were published in full for the first time only in 1949, in volume 11 of his *Works*. The disclosure of the real meaning of the collectivization of agriculture as a method of "squeezing" the tribute from the farmers reached the Soviet peoples too late. But nothing has changed since Stalin's death in this regard. Even in his de-Stalinization speech at the Twentieth Party Congress in 1956, Khrushchev endorsed Stalin's "squeezing" policy, saying:

> We must affirm that the Party had fought a serious ideological fight against the Trotskyites, the Rightists, and the bourgeois nationalists, and that it disarmed ideologically all the enemies of Leninism. This ideological fight was carried on successfully, as a result of which the Party became strengthened and tempered. *Here Stalin played a*

positive role. . . . Let us consider for a moment what would have happened if, in 1928-29, the political line of Right deviation had prevailed among us, or the orientation toward "cotton-dress industrialization" [This was an allusion to Bukharin's proposal to increase the production of textiles so badly needed in the countryside.], or toward the kulak, etc. We would not have a powerful heavy industry to-day . . .[7]

The methods by which Stalin, assisted by his leading lieutenants, fought the Bukharin group are typical of Communist strategy and tactics. His struggle against the "Right deviationists," as the Bukharin group was called, was a masterpiece of duplicity and subversion. At the beginning Stalin's chances of overcoming the new opposition were slim, and a straight attack against Bukharin might have ended in Stalin's defeat. For this reason, Stalin tried to avoid an open showdown until the ground for victory was prepared. At sessions of the Politburo, Stalin, always supported by his inseparable companion-in-arms, Molotov, showed willingness to compromise, allegedly for the sake of Party unity. Thus he marked time. "When the fruit does not fall from the tree when you shake it, it means that the fruit is not yet ripe. Stalin can wait." [8] This is how one of Stalin's followers described his tactics toward the Bukharin group. But outside the Politburo Stalin engaged in the most vigorous activity. In his capacity as Secretary General of the Party, he used his authority to oust actual and potential supporters of Bukharin from influential positions in the Party. Molotov and Kaganovich, who at this crucial period were secretaries of the Central Committee, controlled by Stalin, helped him to design his strategy and stepped in wherever a strong hand was needed. In addition to keeping the secretaryship in the Central Committee, Molotov in 1928 became First Secretary of the Moscow Party Committee after Uglanov, a sympathizer of Bukharin's, had been ousted, while Kaganovich was "elected" a member of the Presidium of the All-Union Council of Trade Unions so that he could serve as a watchdog over Politburo member Tomsky.

For more than eighteen months the Party propaganda machine kept firing at the "Right deviation" and the "conciliatory atti-

tude" toward it, without mentioning the names of the leaders of
this deviation—Bukharin, Rykov, and Tomsky. During this time,
moreover, Stalin claimed on several occasions that there was
absolute unanimity in the Politburo. In a speech delivered on
October 19, 1928, at the plenary session of the Moscow Committee and the Moscow Control Commissior of the Party, he
criticized various people—but not Bukharin. Having stated that
"a victory of the Right deviation in our Party would mean a
development of conditions necessary for the restoration of capitalism in our country," [9] and that this deviation in the lower
Party organizations should be fought at all cost, Stalin added:

> Well, and what about the Politburo? Are there any devi-
> ations in the Politburo? In the Politburo there are neither
> Right nor Left deviations, nor conciliators toward those
> deviations. This must be said quite categorically. It is time
> to put a stop to tittle-tattle spread by enemies of the Party
> and by the opportunists of all kinds about there being a
> Right deviation or a conciliatory attitude toward the Right
> deviation in the Politburo of the Central Committee. [10]

These were Stalin's words in October, 1928, more than three
months after Bukharin had secretly visited Kamenev on July 11,
1928, and had for a whole hour spoken of the deep split in the
Politburo which had begun to show months before. A description of his visit was given in a leaflet dated January 20, 1929,
illegally disseminated by the Trotskyites. In it Bukharin described the situation in the Politburo as follows:

> "The differences of opinion between us [Bukharin, Rykov,
> and Tomsky] and Stalin are deeper, much deeper than
> those between him and you [Kamenev]. I, Rykov, and
> Tomsky evaluate the situation this way: it would be much
> better to have Zinoviev and Kamenev in the Politburo
> instead of Stalin. For several weeks I have not been on
> speaking terms with Stalin. He is an unscrupulous intriguer
> and subordinates everything to his desire to retain power
> for himself. In order to eliminate somebody at a given
> moment, he changes his theories. . . . Now he has begun
> to retreat in order to finish us off. . .[11]

On January 30 and February 9, 1929, at the joint session of the Politburo and the Presidium of the Central Control Commission, the secret talks between Bukharin and Kamenev were discussed and a strong resolution of reprimand was passed. A plenary session of the two bodies held in the second half of April, 1929, approved this resolution, after Stalin had made his famous speech "On the Rightist Deviation in the All-Union Communist Party." In it he had informed the members of the Central Committee for the first time that Bukharin was a "deviationist." The resolution was approved on the following day, but was kept under lock in the Party archives for three years.* Stalin spoke on April 22, 1929, and the important question arising from this fact is: where did Khrushchev obtain his information that "some leading Comrades sabotage the work of the Central Committee and do not carry out assignments given by the Party," as he had stated in his speech published on April 12, 1929? It was almost two weeks before Stalin made this charge before the members of the Central Committee and stated that the Bukharin group "is not only not helping its Central Committee, but, on the contrary, is hampering it in every possible way. . . ."[12] Khrushchev's knowledge of what was taking place in the highest body of the Party can be explained only by the assumption that at that time he, a comparatively small Party functionary, must already have had intimate connections with high Party officials who informed him of the details of the Stalin-Bukharin struggle in the Politburo. This would also explain his transfer to Moscow which took place in the summer or early fall of 1929, and which should be considered a decisive step in his career. Khrushchev, once again, was ahead even of Stalin, and ahead on the right track. While Stalin still maintained that there was unity in the

---

* Resolutions and decisions of congresses, conferences, and plenary sessions of the Party have been published in seven editions, the latest having appeared in 1954. The April, 1929, resolution was published in the fourth edition (1932). A comparison of different editions shows that the Party documents, omitted in previous editions, suddenly appear in newer editions and vice versa.

At the Twentieth Party Congress in 1956, Khrushchev solemnly announced the intention of the Soviet Government gradually to introduce the seven-hour work day beginning in 1957. A 1929 resolution to the same effect was not reprinted in the latest edition, probably in order to increase the impact of Khrushchev's promise.

highest echelon of the Party, Khrushchev spoke of discord,
which was confirmed two weeks later by Stalin himself. It cannot be assumed that this anticipation of a change in line was
meant by Khrushchev to impress Stalin, who certainly was not
even interested in Khrushchev at that time. Rather, it probably
was designed to impress his equals and immediate superiors,
and he was probably quite successful on that score.

The Stalin-Bukharin struggle practically ceased at the end of
1929, with Stalin's complete victory. The Soviet countryside
actually became a colony. It paid tribute to the Communist
regime engaged in "socialist construction" which was neither
socialist nor constructive. It would be a fascinating task to
compare the tribute of sweat, tears, and blood which subjugated
colonial peoples have paid to their mother countries, with the
tribute the Soviet people have paid to their "own" government
so that it could develop its industries in order to "surpass the
world," a slogan used by the Communist regime from the first
day of its existence. The price paid so far by the people has
been high, certainly much higher than a subjugated people ever
paid to a conqueror. This explains why a totalitarian form of
dictatorship had to be set up at the end of the 'twenties and
why Khrushchev and his colleagues still employ Stalinist repression whenever peoples of the Communist empire rebel against
the "squeezing" policy. It took a decade until the Communist
regime threw off its mask as a "defender" of the working people
and showed the face of a state entrepreneur endowed with
means of oppression of which no "bourgeois class" has ever
even dreamed.

The contours of the totalitarian dictatorship were already
clearly visible in the late 'twenties. On December 21, 1929, its
creator celebrated both his fiftieth birthday and his decisive
victory over all dangerous rivals whose intellectual superiority
he had so much feared. Now he was surrounded by a crowd of
men who were insignificant compared with the early giants of
the Revolution, and who were in the most servile fashion expressing their love and admiration for the victor. Khrushchev was
not yet among them, but in the controversies which had been
the by-play of Stalin's internecine struggles and victories, he
had built up a most enviable record.

II

The Moscow Act

5

The Formation of a Stalinist

Sometime in the early fall of 1929, Khrushchev, an unknown, low-echelon Party worker, moved from Kiev to Moscow. Eight and one half years later he returned to the Ukraine as a Politburo member and Stalin's vicar and ruler over forty million Ukrainians. Moscow of the 'thirties had a political climate in which the Khrushchev characteristics—shrewdness and versatility, combined with roughness and impetuousness—could flourish.

The swiftness of his rise is truly impressive: September, 1929 —student of the Industrial Academy; January, 1931—First Secretary of the Party in one of the ten Moscow districts; July, 1931— the same position in the largest Moscow city district; January, 1932—Second Secretary of the Moscow City Party Committee; January, 1934—First Secretary of the Moscow City Committee and Second Secretary of the Moscow Province Party Committee; March, 1935—First Secretary of both Moscow Party Committees. In addition he was elected a member of the Party's Central Committee in February, 1934; in 1938, an alternate member of the Politburo, and in 1939, a full-fledged member of that supreme policy-making body.

One of the most important reasons for this rapid advancement was the urgent need of the Bolsheviks for new cadres capable of learning, applying and developing the "Stalinist style of work." Once they had taken over this vast country they were forced by virtue of their doctrine to establish a dictatorship not bound by moral or human feelings. Mercy and Bolshevism are incompatible. The most difficult problem facing the regime was to find "crusaders" who could comply with this axiom. A score of old Bolsheviks had been eliminated in the course of the establishment of Stalin's rule—partly for being "soft," but largely because of their personal superiority to Stalin. The new cadres who had joined the Revolution in its first stages by and large regarded Lenin's doctrine as a well-intentioned social philosophy which needed to be "pushed" into minds in order to bear fruits. They had not resented taking up arms to carry out this operation; they voluntarily took part in the Civil War to destroy the remnants of the old regime and those few and badly organized democratic elements who for many reasons were unable to establish a stable democratic system. After the Civil War ended, however, not all of these new Bolshevik cadres were willing to participate in continuing a revolution which demanded further sacrifices. As the Kronstadt rebellion of 1921 had shown, they preferred a change in the doctrine rather than to bring the Revolution to its logical end—a totalitarian dictatorship.

Mass purges in the 'twenties and the 'thirties disposed of these shaky, apathetic, and even, in some cases, hostile elements. Tens of thousands were ousted from the Party in the 'twenties and the early 'thirties and were liquidated or perished in prisons and camps during and after the Great Purge of 1935-38. A large proportion of those who remained in the Party, fearing persecution, bowed to Stalin and in this way bought some kind of tranquillity—paying for it with their consciences. And only a small part of these postrevolutionary cadres fully and conscientiously accepted the Stalinist interpretation of the doctrine and its total amorality. They were the men in the commanding strata of the Party, the secret police, and all other organs of the dictatorship. They manned the Party machine and, together with Stalin, created the new style of work. All members of the post-Stalin ruling circle in its first composition, including Khrushchev, belonged to this group.

Four members of this group—Molotov, Kaganovich, Voroshilov, and Mikoyan—played important roles from the very beginning of the Stalinization of the Party and the government machine. In the 'twenties three newcomers—Bulganin, Malenkov, and Khrushchev—made their debuts on the Moscow political scene. The other three senior Stalinists having become engaged in governmental work at the time the newcomers began moving up—Mikoyan and Voroshilov as People's Commissars, and Molotov as Chairman of the Council of People's Commissars—Lazar M. Kaganovich remained in the Party machine and was responsible for training and supervising Malenkov, Khrushchev, and Bulganin.

In his youth, Kaganovich is reported to have been a worker in the leather industry, but as far as his social origin is concerned there is no claim that his father was also a worker. Reliable sources assert that his father had a small shoe shop, which, in Marxian terms, would mean that he belonged to the "petty bourgeoisie." Before the Revolution, Kaganovich distinguished himself as a "professional revolutionary" who fought not only the Czarist regime, but also the "Zionists, Bundists [members of the Jewish Workers' Alliance "Bund"], Mensheviks, and Social-Revolutionaries." [1] A man without formal education, he has been, perhaps, the ablest Stalin-type Bolshevik. Usually he was merely called the Kremlin's best "troubleshooter," but actually he was the most talented Communist organizer and administrator in all branches of the "proletarian dictatorship," particularly in the period of reconstruction of the Bolshevik Party and the national economy on a totalitarian basis.

From 1918 to 1921, Kaganovich worked successively as organizer of the first Red Army detachments, leading agitator, front-line fighter in the Civil War, special envoy of the Party's Central Committee to Central Asia, and trade union secretary in Moscow. From 1922 to 1939, he was one of the secretaries of the Central Committee, and simultaneously occupied the following positions: Secretary General of the Ukrainian Communist Party (1925-28), Secretary of the Moscow Party Committee (1930-35), Chief of the Central Committee's Agricultural Department (1933), Chief of the same Committee's Transportation Department (1934), Chairman of the Party Control Commission (1934), People's Commissar of Transportation (1935-44), People's Commissar of Heavy Industry (1937), and People's Commissar of Fuel Industry (1939-40). In 1930, he was already one of the most influential figures in the Politburo and the leader of those who insisted on the harshest measures against the peasantry. At that time he was described as a "wicked, vindictive man,

whose love for mankind is very questionable." [2] In 1937, an
old Bolshevik characterized him as a "very outstanding man
. . . able to catch quickly the thoughts of his interlocutors, extremely industrious, with an excellent memory and organizational
talents." Then the old Bolshevik went on: "It is a pity that such
a talented head belongs to a man about whose moral qualities
there can hardly be two opinions. . . . One cannot rely on his
word: he is as facile in making promises as in backing out. . . .
Maybe circumstances are to blame for that: he began his Party
career at a time when perfidy was very much in demand. . . .
But, on the other hand, was he not one of those who most of all
contributed to the increase of that demand?" [3] The moral outlook of Kaganovich is clear: he survived the execution, on Stalin's
orders, of his two brothers Mikhail and Yuri, and continued to
support their executioner.

Kaganovich had occasion to meet his three apprentices in
the early stages of his career. In 1918, he headed the Party and
government organizations in Nizhni Novgorod, where Bulganin worked as a Chekist. He could have met Bulganin again
in 1921-22 in Tashkent, where the latter continued his secret
police work. There, Kaganovich, in the capacity of "one of the
leaders of the Revolutionary Military Council of the Turkestan
Front," probably also met Malenkov, who was working in the
Political Administration of that front. Kaganovich and Khrushchev met in the Ukraine, and Khrushchev's transfer to Moscow
was probably the result of Kaganovich's observance of his Party
work and his Stalinist performance at congresses and conferences. All three had worked for five years in increasingly responsible positions under the direct supervision of Kaganovich,
and were then left on their own while Kaganovich was transferred to important governmental work.

All three of the men were postrevolutionary Communists:
Bulganin joined the Party in 1917, Khrushchev in 1918, and
Malenkov in 1920. Bulganin and Malenkov had an additional
handicap—their nonproletarian origin. This partly explains the
varied speeds with which the three reached top Party positions.
Khrushchev, a worker, became a member of the Central Committee in 1934, while Bulganin and Malenkov were not admitted
to that body as full-fledged members until 1939. Khrushchev was

made a full-fledged member of the Politburo in 1939, while Malenkov joined this highest Party body in 1946, and Bulganin in 1948.

In addition to his proletarian origin, Khrushchev had another advantage over Malenkov and Bulganin. For Soviet propagandists "work among the masses" has always been a difficult problem, or, as Khrushchev once put it, "the most complicated job." He engaged in practical work of this type during the 'twenties and 'thirties, and his approach to people in general is apparently based on this experience. Despite his abundant oratory, he does not consider public speeches as the main weapon for influencing people. "A speech is good," he once said, "if it is supported by subsequent individual heart-to-heart talks." People should be approached differently, depending on their age, background, and the like. If a worker "does not grasp our agitation as quickly as is desirable . . . one should find a key to his soul and open it up, expose the enemy who whispers in his ear, and win him over to our side."

Malenkov and Bulganin, both of "bourgeois" origin, lacked Khrushchev's experience as an agitator. During the Civil War Malenkov worked in the Political Administration of the Eastern and Turkestan Fronts, which means that his duties were in the domain of secret police work rather than of propaganda and agitation. During the same period Bulganin was engaged in direct Cheka work in Nizhni Novgorod and in Tashkent. After the Civil War, Malenkov worked for five years "behind closed doors" in Stalin's personal secretariat, while Bulganin was engaged in office work in economic organizations, and later as manager of a plant. Both were far removed from the masses.

It is likely that Malenkov had still another blemish on his political reputation: he had not blindly accepted Stalin's policies in the early 'twenties. During the open discussion between the forces of Stalin and Trotsky at the end of 1923 and the beginning of 1924, Malenkov appears to have sympathized with the Trotskyites.*

---

* The following facts support this supposition: In 1923, 25 per cent of the Moscow Party organization were students, and practically all of them participated in the debate along the lines presented by the Party machine, headed by Stalin, and the Opposition, led by Trotsky. Following the dis-

In spite of their different backgrounds, each of the newcomers was a valuable Party asset. The industrious Malenkov, with his extraordinary memory, specialized in organizational Party problems and particularly in questions concerning Party cadres. His work in that field was of enormous value to the regime during the Great Purge, when the terror machine was responsible for a significant increase in the turnover of the Party cadres. Bulganin, having gained some administrative experience while working in economic organizations, emerged as a government worker (Chairman of the Moscow Soviet). The energetic, vivid, and impetuous Khrushchev became engaged in open Party activity, purging recalcitrant dissenters, encouraging and wooing the Stalin followers, and initiating new practical ways of mobilizing the non-Party masses for the execution of Party decisions. Only by keeping the above considerations in mind can one fully appreciate the frank statement *Pravda* published on March 3, 1935, on the occasion of Khrushchev's appointment to the highest Party position in Moscow city and province:

"Comrade Khrushchev, having gone through a school of struggle and Party work all the way from the bottom, is an outstanding representative of the postrevolutionary generation of Party workers educated by Stalin."

---

cussions Party cell members voted on resolutions. The results were: 70 per cent of the students cast 6,594 votes for the Opposition, while only 2,790 students either voted for Stalin's Party line or abstained. The Communist cell of the Moscow Higher Technical School, of which Malenkov was Secretary, also took part in the discussion, and, according to *Pravda*, January 4, 1924, the cell of the Workers' Faculty of that school voted in favor of Trotsky. If Malenkov, the highest Party authority of the school, had dissented from Trotsky, he surely had opportunities to so declare publicly. One of these opportunities presented itself to Malenkov when the Party machine inspired a letter criticizing Trotsky to be signed by students who supported Stalin. This letter was published in *Pravda* in two installments on January 9 and 11, 1924, and signed by 404 Communist students (*Pravda*, January 11-19, 1924). There can be no doubt that all pro-Stalin Party cell secretaries, and especially those whose cells supported Trotsky, signed the letter. The total number of Communist cells in the Moscow higher schools was at the time only seventy-two. In other words the total number of cell secretaries was about one sixth of the number of students who signed the *Pravda* letter. If Malenkov, one of the seventy-two cell secretaries, had been a supporter of the Stalin line, he would have signed the anti-Trotsky letter. His name, however, cannot be found among the signatories.

Khrushchev's Moscow career began with study at the Industrial Academy. After he had finished his studies at the Workers' Faculty in Stalino he did not take advantage of his right to enter a higher technical school, preferring Party work. Now, in 1929, at the age of thirty-five, he interrupted his Party activity in Kiev and went to Moscow to continue his studies at the Industrial Academy.

This institution had been established for the technical and economic training of leading administrative personnel, such as directors of industrial trusts and large enterprises, chairmen of provincial councils of the national economy, and the like.[4] In 1930, while Khrushchev was at the Academy, there were 410 students divided into small groups for specialized training. The curriculum included thirty specialties, covering practically all branches of industry.[5] The importance which the Kremlin attached to the Industrial Academy was expressed by Stalin in a special address in April, 1930, in which he greeted the first graduates as the "new Bolshevik detachment of leaders for our socialist industry." [6] In 1929, only 100 freshmen,[7] chosen from all parts of the country, were admitted. Khrushchev was one of them.

It is doubtful that Khrushchev's transfer to Moscow was caused by his thirst for higher education. There are no indications what specialty Khrushchev had chosen, if any. It is true that if he had actually wanted to continue his studies in the Ukraine he would have encountered difficulties because of his age; thirty was the age limit in Ukrainian colleges and universities at the time.[8] The age limit at the Academy, which was designed for selected Party members with prior experience in industry, was higher, probably thirty-five—Khrushchev's age in April, 1929. This circumstance would seem to have had some bearing on Khrushchev's going to Moscow. There are some factors, however, which do not support the assumption that he suddenly decided to give up Party work and become a "technocrat." The most important is that he never graduated from the Academy; he discontinued his studies at the end of 1930, after he had been a student for only one year and three months, including vacation time; the regular course was three years. This fact, and the fact that none of the official Soviet accounts of

Khrushchev's life claim that he finished the studies at the
Academy are sufficient justification to disregard a thirty-four-
word "biographic" note published in *Pravda,* July 26, 1931,
which stated that he did graduate. The improbability of this
statement is even more evident if one considers that, during half
of his fifteen months at the Academy, he was occupied with
Party work as secretary of the Academy's Party organization. His
subsequent rapid advancement in the Party is additional evidence that he did not concentrate on becoming a "leader of
socialist industry," and that his admission to the Academy was
probably a pretext for his transfer to Moscow and a spring-
board to his political career.

Lazar M. Kaganovich supported this move. He had returned
from the Ukraine to Moscow in the summer of 1928, to resume
his work as one of the secretaries of the Party's Central Committee. Here his duties were manifold, and among them the
preparation of new "reliable cadres" to meet the demands of
the First Five-Year Plan occupied an important place. Some of
these cadres were to be trained at the Moscow Industrial Academy. As stated before, in 1929 only 100 highly recommended
Party members from all parts of the Soviet Union were selected
to study there. Ukrainian Party boss from 1925 to 1928, Kaganovich was certainly consulted about the few candidates who were
to fill the Ukrainian quota. It seems likely that his support of
Khrushchev's candidacy would have been necessary.

Soviet official biographic notes on Khrushchev's life published
between 1938 and 1941, describe his activity as a student at the
Industrial Academy in Moscow in greater detail than the postwar
versions. The version published in January, 1938, states: "In
1929, Comrade Khrushchev was sent to study at the Industrial
Academy where he was elected Secretary of the Party Committee and where he carried on an active struggle against the Right
Uglanovist elements." [9] (Uglanov had been First Secretary of
the Moscow Party Committee until October, 1928, when he had
been ousted as a Bukharin follower). The version published in
May, 1938, states that "In 1929, the Central Committee of the
All-Union Communist Party (Bolshevik) sent Comrade Khrushchev to study in the Stalin Industrial Academy where he, working in the capacity of secretary of the Party Committee, carried

on an active struggle against the Trotskyite-Bukharinite mercenaries and traitors of the Fatherland." [10] The same account is given in the Historical Revolutionary Calendar for 1941, except that the Central Committee is not mentioned as the sponsor of Khrushchev's transfer.[11] These earlier versions furnished more information about Khrushchev's activities as a purger in the Academy than later versions, because they were published during or immediately after the Great Purge, when such activities were very creditable. In later versions, published during and after World War II, it was considered unnecessary to recall Khrushchev's participation in the Purge—a chapter which the Kremlin rulers are now intent on relegating to oblivion.

The purge of the Communist Party cells at the Moscow Industrial Academy and other higher educational institutions coincided with Stalin's intensified collectivization drive in the countryside. It was mostly this ruthless policy which caused opposition to the Kremlin among the students. When Khrushchev arrived in Moscow, the "decisive attack against the kulaks" was well under way. It had been launched in the summer of 1929, and was gaining momentum in the winter of 1929-30.

The term "kulak" has never been clearly defined—purposely—in order to give the local authorities more leeway. The number of farmers physically liquidated, driven from their small holdings of land, or deported like cattle to concentration camps was far larger than the small number of well-to-do peasants who had "flourished" under Lenin's NEP. The Kremlin was intent not only on the elimination of a tiny group of landowners, but on compelling the bulk of the Soviet peasantry to give up private farming and join the government-sponsored collective farms falsely presented as a voluntary form of cooperative farming. The organs of the "proletarian dictatorship" were instructed to use the most barbarous methods of suppression in carrying out this "socialization" of agriculture. This was known in the Soviet Union long before it was known in the West; the Soviet correspondent of *Sotsialisticheskii Vestnik* wrote in March, 1930:

It is a veritable nightmare in which we live. The story cannot be told. It is impossible to describe in words the frightful hopelessness which has gripped the minds of the

majority of the Soviet population. In my last letter I wrote
to you about executions, suicides, starvation, and ruin of
the peasants. Now there are also epidemics of the grippe
and typhus. The peasants die by the thousands. It has
been reported from circles of Soviet employees that Stalin
has cynically expressed the opinion on several occasions
that there are too many peasants in the Soviet Union. Here
are his words: "The Revolution demands victims; even if
the achievement of full-scale socialization of the countryside should demand 20 million peasant lives, we would not
hesitate." [12]

The peasants resisted as best they could. Under the conditions of totalitarian dictatorship, which had begun to solidify,
any organized resistance was, of course, impossible. The slightest attempt to resist was met with most brutal acts of violence:
entire villages were burned down and the inhabitants deported;
churches and mosques were closed or destroyed, and the clergy
arrested, executed, or exiled; markets where the farmers had
sold their produce were invaded and the merchandise confis-
cated. The official Communist doctrine referred to this organized
form of manslaughter and robbery as "class struggle." The only
weapon remaining to the peasants was passive resistance:
slaughter of their livestock and cutting down of the sowing area.
When the Kremlin finally realized that the collectivization drive
could not be forced through at this accelerated pace, there
appeared, on March 2, 1930, in all Soviet newspapers, Stalin's
famous article "Dizzy With Success." In it, he admitted that the
Party line had been carried out with "infractions and distortions"
—for which he blamed the local executives.

Was it actually possible that the local executives had exceeded Party orders? Did not Kaganovich, Stalin's closest associate, make trips to the provinces to "organize the struggle . . .
against the sabotage of the kulaks?" [13] Had not Stalin himself,
in a speech delivered on December 27, 1929, declared that "the
liquidation of the kulaks as a class" should be carried out not
by "mere scratching" or "empty noise," but by delivering a real
Bolshevik blow "from which they could not recover"? [14] These
questions were in the minds and on the lips of many Party mem-

bers, but to ask them openly was "Right deviationism," and even those who failed to rebuff their comrades for their doubts in the infallibility of Stalin and the Kaganoviches and Molotovs were suspect and called "conciliators towards the Right deviationists." Both categories were treated in the same fashion.

Stalin's retreat in 1930 was probably prompted by an event which occurred shortly before his article appeared in the papers. One K. Y. Bauman, at the time First Secretary of the Moscow city and province Party organizations, had distinguished himself by excessive zeal in carrying out the Party's directives. Together with Kaganovich, he had set the early spring of 1930 as a deadline for the completion of the collectivization in the Moscow province. The distress and hopelessness of the peasants had reached such proportions that, unafraid of the consequences, tens of thousands of them, with their wives and children, on sleighs, by train, and on foot, invaded the Moscow streets near the office of Mikhail I. Kalinin, then head of the Central Executive Committe of the Soviets, to plead with him for help from ruin and arbitrariness.[15]

This unprecedented spectacle had impressed not only the Kremlin, but also the rank and file in the Party. Politically minded students of the Moscow higher educational institutions, just like the rest of the population, were shocked by the events in the countryside, and, as soon as Stalin announced the temporary retreat, they became even more critical of the Party line. And such criticism ran higher at the All-Union Industrial Academy—the school which Khrushchev attended—than at other Moscow educational institutions.

The Party cell at the Industrial Academy had been purged of "Right deviationists" in the fall of 1929; on October 20, 1929, *Pravda* had stated that a group of Rightists "closely connected with the Bukharin group of young professors" had been uncovered in the Industrial Academy, and on November 21, 1929, Kaganovich had disclosed that "the people [at the Industrial Academy] were taken, so to say, red-handed." [16] During this purge, the purgers came to the conclusion that the cell bureau "had connived with the Rightists and shown an obviously conciliatory attitude toward them." For that reason, in November, 1929, the cell bureau was dissolved and a new one was "elected."

At this time, Khrushchev had just arrived in Moscow. There can be no doubt that he was occupied with settling down in the crowded capital, which was not an easy task.

In 1929, Khrushchev's family consisted of four members—himself, his second wife, Nina Petrovna, and two children from his first marriage: a son of about thirteen and a daughter eleven years old. His third child, Rada, was to be born around this time. The housing shortage in Moscow was extremely acute, and married freshmen from the provinces were warned that no living quarters for their families could be provided. Under these conditions it was unlikely that Khrushchev had already begun to participate in Party affairs at the Academy in the fall of 1929, when the Party cell was purged. Khrushchev's election to the post of secretary of the Party cell—a post mentioned in the official accounts of his life—must have taken place toward the end of May, 1930. This was exactly the time when the new cell bureau, elected in the fall of 1929, was accused of tolerance towards the Rightists and dissolved.

Pravda on May 26, 1930, specified the "crimes" committed by the cell between November, 1929, and May, 1930, in the following fashion: "In the last six months the cell bureau has not even put before the cell members the question of the need to struggle against the right-wing danger in the Party"; the cell had "created a favorable climate for an increase of the activity of the Rightists and conciliators who had used this opportunity for spreading their activity in the Industrial Academy"; "some cell members . . . disseminated slanderous anti-Party rumors concerning the leadership of the Party," and the like.

It is noteworthy that these "crimes" of the Party cell which was eventually headed by Khrushchev had been committed before May, 1930, over a period of six months. How was it possible that the higher Party organs had not been informed about what was going on in the Party cell of the Academy? Was Khrushchev so absorbed in his studies that he had overlooked these happenings, or was he also among the "conciliators"? His previous Party record and the fact that after the discovery of the "crimes" he was elected secretary of the Party cell make this very improbable.

There must have been other reasons why these "crimes,"

committed by the cell of which Khrushchev was a member, had not been reported to higher authorities at the time they had been committed. In order to come to some understanding of this riddle it is necessary to consider the fact that Nadezhda S. Alliluyeva, Stalin's wife, had been an active member of the Academy's Party cell.

There are rumors to the effect that it was through Alliluyeva that Khrushchev came into contact with Stalin. However, nothing is definitely known about the role which she played in Khrushchev's career, or about the influence Khrushchev might have had on the events which brought about her death. Yet there is incontrovertible evidence that there was some relationship between Khrushchev's actions as a member of the Academy's Party cell during the fateful six months from November, 1929, to May, 1930, and Alliluyeva's growing disagreement with her husband's ruthless policy (which is believed to have been the reason for her sudden death). Before looking at this evidence, a few words about Alliluyeva.

Nadezhda Alliluyeva was born in 1901, the daughter of a metal worker who had joined the revolutionary movement at the end of the last century in Tiflis, where he met Stalin for the first time. In 1917, the Alliluyevs lived in Petrograd (now Leningrad), and for a short time harbored Lenin when he was in hiding. In 1918, at the age of seventeen, Nadezhda joined the Communist Party. In 1919, she worked in Lenin's secretariat, "where she was assigned to the most responsible secret work." Lenin "highly appreciated her energy, attentiveness, and limitless devotion to the cause." [17] During the Civil War she was dispatched to the Tsaritsyn (now Stalingrad) front, where Stalin was a political commissar.

There, the forty-year-old Stalin fell in love with the eighteen-year-old Nadia and they were married. After the end of the Civil War, she worked for *Revolutsia i Kultura* (Revolution and Culture), a magazine sponsored by *Pravda*. In 1929, already the mother of two children, she decided to prepare herself for an independent career and enrolled in the Chemical Faculty of the Industrial Academy and the Mendeleyev Institute of Artificial Fiber, from which she was to graduate as an industrial engineer on December 1, 1932. Three weeks before graduation she suddenly died. The official announcement did not disclose the cause of her death. There are two versions circulating regarding her death: suicide and murder, the first version being the most widely accepted.

The concealment from the public of the real reason for Alliluyeva's tragic end at the age of thirty-one, "still young and full of strength," [18] gave rise to wild rumors in the Soviet Union and abroad. Leaving speculation aside, there are two facts: first, the description of her character given by her sister Anna and, second, testimony from several independent sources to the effect that Alliluyeva was greatly disturbed over Stalin's terroristic policy.

In her memoirs, Anna Alliluyeva-Redens, wife of Stanislav Frantsevich Redens, a high-placed official of the Soviet secret police who was liquidated in 1937 as an "enemy of the people," described her sister Nadezhda as having had "always a lively, straightforward and open nature," and as having been "unable to conceal her opinions." [19] And there is sufficient evidence that Nadezhda Alliluyeva was a frequent critic of her husband's policy of mass terror. Victor Kravchenko relates that the brutal collectivization drive which began in 1929 horrified her, and that she repeatedly assailed the official policy line at Party meetings at the Academy,[20] which means, in official terminology, that she joined the "Rightists," or at least sympathized with their views. Nadezhda Alliluyeva's opposition to the new Party line certainly had some bearing on the political atmosphere at the Academy, particularly at the first stage of the intensified collectivization drive (1929-30). Her influence in Party affairs was significant. At the time of her death Soviet sources stated that she had been a "leader of a Party group" and member of the Party cell of the Chemical Faculty, a position which she had held during the three years of her studies at the Academy.[21] Thus she must have been aware of Party affairs at the Academy, including the fact that, despite the purge in the fall of 1929, discontent with her husband's policy had not subsided "even for one minute," to use *Pravda's* phrase.[22] If Alliluyeva had been a faithful follower of Stalin's policy she would have informed him about the "dangerous" situation at the Academy and particularly about the "slanderous anti-Party rumors concerning the leadership of the

Party"—that is, Stalin himself.* Apparently she did not so inform him.

On the other hand, having Stalin's wife in their midst as a dissenter from his policy, the oppositionists and their sympathizers might have felt more secure. Since Khrushchev did not belong to either group, he found himself faced with a most intricate situation. Stalin's wife, a student at the Academy, was among those who expressed criticism of the extreme features of her husband's collectivization policy and apparently consorted and sympathized with other students who held similar views. This was known to the Party cell which had already been purged once for not exposing the dissenters. Khrushchev was a member of this cell. What was he to do?

If he had fought the dissenters in the customary fashion, by denouncing them by name to higher Party organs, he would have had to denounce, among others, Stalin's wife, Alliluyeva. It was impossible to know how Stalin would react to such a denunciation—whether he would be favorably impressed with the fearless pursuit of duty by the zealous subordinate, or whether he would be enraged, for purely emotional reasons. If Khrushchev kept silent, it would become apparent to Stalin—who probably knew that Alliluyeva was expressing certain impermissible views at the Academy—that he was willing to sacrifice his vigilance under certain delicate conditions. This, in turn, might be considered worthy of a Party stalwart, or unworthy—it was impossible to foretell.

Clearly, the dangers facing Khrushchev were great. The situation which seemed to permit neither action nor inaction, was tantalizing. But Khrushchev found his way out. How did he do it?

To some extent the account of his victory over the distressing impasse must rest on speculation. It is likely that instead of reporting officially to higher-ups on the subversive climate at the Academy, in which Nadezhda Alliluyeva was involved, he reported unofficially on them to some of the top officials—Kaganovich, for instance, whom he knew well from the Ukraine, and

---

* One subject of these rumors was possibly the strained relations between Stalin and his wife.

who apparently was sure of Khrushchev's loyalty to the Stalin line. In this way he actually did his duty of informing the top leadership, and, at the same time, passed the dilemma on up the line to Kaganovich; it was now Kaganovich who had to decide what to report about the dissenters. Secondly, Khrushchev was building up, in this fashion, an alibi for himself against the day when the dissenters would be eliminated and when those who failed to denounce them would be purged for lack of vigilance; he could then prove that he had been vigilant.

Thus Khrushchev insured himself against the possibilities of calamity. At the same time he apparently gathered around himself a few hard-boiled Stalinists of the Party cell in order to strike a blow for himself at the appropriate moment. This assumption is largely supported by the following course of events.

When at the end of May, 1930, delegates to the local Party conferences were elected, the plenary meeting of the Industrial Academy's Party cell took a shocking course; the dissenters actually spoke up openly, criticized the Party leadership, attacked the prevailing collectivization policy, and one of the speakers, a certain Tveritinov, even went so far as to defend "organized capitalism." [23] When the time came to elect the delegates to the forthcoming conference, the dissenters "pulled their candidates through in an organized manner."

All this took place at the time when one A. P. Shirin was Secretary of Moscow's Bauman District Committee, where the Industrial Academy was located. Shirin, who was indirectly responsible for the events, as they had happened in his domain, tried to save his position by officially complaining that "not even one protesting voice was raised against the nominated candidates. Of those comrades who during the long struggle against the Rightist deviationists and their sympathizers had occupied the proper position and actually opposed them, not even one took the floor to refute the impudent onslaught of these Rightists." [24]

In brief, Shirin accused the entire Party cell, including Khrushchev, of having stood idly by while the dissenters were elected as delegates. Shirin apparently thought that he could absolve himself of all personal responsibility merely by expressing his disapproval. But *Pravda* thought differently. It criticized Shirin for noninterference in the critical situation at the Academy, especially for his neglecting the demand made the day after the election by "a number of Party members . . . that another meeting be held that would revoke the elected delegates . . ."[25]

Who were those Party members who had kept silent during the shocking proceedings, but demanded a new meeting for the purpose of recalling the unsuitable delegates and of electing others? It was doubtless Khrushchev and his associates; the results of the new meeting, convoked after *Pravda's* attack, showed this clearly. Shirin, frightened by the attack on him, called a meeting of the Party cell. The meeting was in session for two days. The cell "admitted its errors," and revoked the eight delegates elected to the district conference six days before. The cell bureau was dissolved and a new one elected. Khrushchev was elected its Secretary.

The resolution "unanimously" adopted at this meeting instructed the new bureau to begin investigating immediately the political posture of those already exposed during the 1929 purge and to "unmask [those] who are not yet uncovered" with the purpose of expelling them from the Party. Paragraph ten of the resolution, which Khrushchev as head of the new bureau had to carry out, read: "In view of the fact that, within the cell of the Industrial Academy, a factional group of Rightists and an organized group of conciliators leaning towards the Rightists have existed for a long time, the Party cell considers it impossible that some comrades remain in the Academy, since after their graduation these comrades would be in no position to ensure the carrying out of the general line of the Party. The bureau is assigned to carry out this decision in the shortest time, bringing up the question before the Central Committee."[26]

This paragraph is interesting for two reasons: first, it implies that the Central Committee, and consequently Stalin personally, paid special attention to the daring sortie of the Bukharinites in the Academy, and second, it paved the way for Khrushchev to obtain access to the highest Party organ, for the matter was taken up by the Central Committee itself.

One official biographical note on Khrushchev's life says that he was elected Secretary of the Academy's Party cell because of his "organizational abilities."[27] The circumstances under which his election took place make it clear that he used his "organizational abilities" for organizing the "struggle against the Trotsky-ite-Bukharinite mercenaries and traitors of the Fatherland," [28] rather than for standard-type Party work. Only highly recommended Party members were admitted to the Academy. Thirty to 35 per cent of the students were old Bolsheviks who had distinguished themselves as underground agitators before the Revolution. [29] In other words, as head of the Party organization of the Academy, Khrushchev was not burdened with problems of agitation and propaganda among non-Party people; his function was to investigate, expose, and denounce the "traitors" among Party people to the proper authorities. As a general rule, primarily old Bolsheviks were under suspicion of being followers of Trotsky and Bukharin, and Khrushchev, a Party member only since 1918, must have enjoyed this job. In addition to being a test of Khrushchev's organizational abilities, the Academy affair was good experience for him. He used this experience later, when he operated as a purger on a larger scale in the Ukraine and elsewhere, and millions of people, rather than a few hundred students, were involved.

How successfully Khrushchev passed the test follows from the fact that six months later Shirin himself was relieved of his duties, and Khrushchev took over the secretaryship in the Bauman district. After this first big step, other successes soon followed.

What Khrushchev's attitude towards Alliluyeva's political behavior was after he became the leader of the Party cell at the Academy is not known. He still found himself in a difficult situation. He still could not act against Alliluyeva with the same harshness as against other dissenters. On the other hand, Alliluyeva's straightforward dissent from some official policy lines undoubtedly imposed upon him the duty to keep her under strict surveillance and to report his observations to some high Party official, in all probability again to Kaganovich. All reports concerning Alliluyeva's death concur that deep political differences with her husband's policy were the main reason for it. Whether or not Khrushchev's reports contributed to an intensification of these differences, and thus helped to precipitate events, will probably never be known.

6

The Setting of the Moscow Act

The swiftness of Khrushchev's rise on the Moscow political scene of the 'thirties was due to his fitness for the jobs to which he had been assigned. As Secretary of a Communist Party organization he was responsible for all aspects of the economic, political, and cultural life in the region entrusted to him. Of course, the first responsibility was always to keep his Communist parish and the population fully obedient to the regime, to eradicate every vestige of opposition to the Party line, and to see to it that all curves and zigzags of the line were followed, no matter how contradictory they were. The second responsibility was to ensure the fulfillment or, even better, the overfulfillment of the economic plan. To achieve these two primary objectives, the Party, and consequently the government, provided the necessary tools: laws and decrees, propaganda material, and means of oppression. This arrangement has never ceased to exist in the Soviet Union, but it was particularly fierce in the 'thirties, when the all-out collectivization and industrialization drives were pressed with unprecedented vigor.

When Khrushchev came to Moscow in 1929, the first Five-Year Plan was to be accomplished in four years. The local Party organs, industry managers, and trade unions were ordered to work out counterplans exceeding the goals of the regular plan—which the "enthusiastic" workers allegedly considered to be insufficient. If such enthusiasm had really existed, no enforcement measures would have been necessary. That this was not the case is evident from the fact that in the early 'thirties laws, decrees, ordinances, and decisions followed in rapid order, restricting and repealing whatever theoretical rights the workers had and introducing newly refined methods of exploitation.

On December 17, 1930, reasons justifying absence from work were substantially narrowed, and on November 15, 1932, a new decree was issued prescribing dismissal of workers from employment and even eviction from their dwellings for being late to work or for absence without "valid reason." How stringent the new regulations were can be seen from an article in *Pravda*, January 4, 1933, attacking plant managers and trade unionists who considered "giving birth by a worker's wife in the hospital" or "moving to new living quarters" as valid reasons for absence from work for a day or two.

Unemployment was simply abolished by the decree of October 9, 1930, which suspended payment of unemployment insurance benefits and made sickness the only valid reason for refusing job offers. Also in 1930, wage books were issued and the plant managers were made to enter into these books the "real" reasons for discharge. A decree of December 27, 1932, forced every Soviet citizen to carry a passport and to present it when applying for a job. These measures helped to establish tighter control over workers' migrations and to tie them to their places of work.

In addition to legislation restricting the workers' freedom to choose where to work or live, the Party and government issued decrees and ordinances "regulating" the supply of food and other necessities in such a manner that preference was to be given to the "shock-brigade workers"—mostly physically strong young people able to cope with the demands of the newly introduced sweatshop system based on the so-called progressive piecework remuneration. The scarcity of food made these decrees particularly effective.

The consumer cooperatives—the principal channel through which the population was supplied with food and manufactured goods—became an additional weapon in forcing the workers to fulfill the high output norms. "The main task of the consumer cooperatives consists in the subordination of their entire work to the task of fulfillment of the Five-Year Plan in four years . . ." editorialized *Izvestia* on May 13, 1931. The cooperatives were to serve above all the "enthusiasts and the advanced workers of socialist construction." The order of the day was the abolition of equalitarianism. Such an arrangement is not harmful in itself, if the better worker can get additional goods *beyond* the bare necessities of life. But in the 'thirties, the abolition of equalitarianism meant literally less bread for those who for one reason or another were physically unable to absorb their full share in the race for more production.

In June, 1931, the trade unions called a special conference to remind the factory workers' committees of their duty to give preferential treatment to the shock brigades, and on January 4, 1933, *Pravda* plainly stated in an editorial: "Beginning January 1, the enterprises have adopted a new system of supplying the workers. Now the ration cards are entirely and fully in the hands of the plant director. This is the best weapon in the struggle against shirkers and shirking." As shown above, the same issue of *Pravda* branded as shirkers those whose absence from work for as little as a day was due to such reasons as the birth of a child or moving from one dwelling to another.

Another reason for reorganizing the consumer cooperatives was to increase their share in financing the industrialization. This meant an increase in prices and, consequently, a preferential treatment for consumers with higher earnings. *Izvestia* illustrated this trend with a quotation from a speech by Sergei M. Kirov, the Leningrad Party boss: "A worker with *sufficient earnings* can buy a meal for sixty kopeks, while the cooperative charges him thirty kopeks, but the meal is bad." [1] Thus the cooperatives were urged to double the price for a somewhat improved meal which workers with "sufficient earnings" probably would enjoy, but which workers with insufficient income could not buy.

A further device in accelerating the industrialization drive was the revision of the wage policy. In the first years after the Revolution the Soviet trade unions pursued a policy of leveling wages. In the NEP years, however, the leveling of wages was no longer favored. But the really drastic step along this road was taken in 1931, when the abolition of "equalitarianism" was declared to be the cornerstone of "socialist" wage policy and the leveling trends were decried as a "petty bourgeois remnant." The fact that in 1931 inflation raged and the standard of living reached its lowest point, was ignored. An analysis of the wage trends made by

Solomon M. Schwarz reveals that, during the first three years of
the First Five-Year Plan (1929-31), living costs rose at least by 150
and perhaps 200 per cent, while the nominal earnings in industry
increased by only 33.4 per cent. This meant an average decline
of about 50 per cent in real wages.[2] There can be no doubt that
the real wages of the majority of Soviet workers had fallen even
far below this average figure. This did not stop the government
from revising the "wage scales" which deliberately favored the
highest brackets. In the metallurgical departments of the iron and
steel industries, for example, "the daily wages (without over-
time, progressive piecework premium, or bonuses) of the highest
paid worker were 450 per cent above those of the lowest paid
worker."[3]

Yet this was only the beginning. The second step was the
introduction of an incentive system which brought about still
more drastic inequality in workers' earnings. The fundamental
idea of this system was a progressive increase of basic pay
relative to the increase of a worker's output above an established
work quota. The previous piecework system, under which the
basic pay for a produced unit remained unchanged regardless of
the number of pieces turned out by an individual worker, was
declared insufficient to whet the worker's appetite for a higher
daily wage. Some trade union leaders went so far as to promote
the so-called progressive piecework and premium pay system
under which the basic pay for a produced unit progressively increased if the worker produced more pieces than required by
the work quota. Thus, for example, if the basic pay for each unit
was ten kopeks and a worker attained the prescribed norm of
fifty pieces, he received five rubles; if he overfulfilled the norm
by ten pieces he would be paid not ten, but twelve kopeks per
piece; having produced seventy pieces the basic pay for a unit
would be fourteen kopeks, and so on. But if the daily work norm
was not fulfilled, the basic unit rate would be reduced accordingly.[4]

The progressive piecework system was accompanied by a general increase in the output norms, which made the race for a
higher daily wage more difficult, particularly for workers lacking
the necessary physical strength. Soviet workers, thrown into this
race during a period of extreme food shortage, were trapped in

a vicious circle: in order to be able physically to participate in the race for an additional ruble, they needed more food, which was scarce and available only at soaring prices; and in order to be able to buy the bare necessities of life they were forced to join the race by entering the shock brigades. But only physically strong young people were admitted to these brigades, because their members were being paid according to the total production turned out by the brigade as a whole, and a weak member was a handicap.

"In comparison with the direct piecework system the progressive piecework system creates additional material stimuli for the increase of labor productivity." [5]

This dry definition of the progressive piecework system given by the *Large Soviet Encyclopedia* is an attempt to disguise the continuous physical and nervous stress of those who "succeeded" in earning their daily bread and the starvation and loss of moral strength of those falling behind in the race, whom the Soviet official terminology placed in the category of shirkers and loafers.

All reforms cited had a common objective—to squeeze more production out of a starving population. But the energy which the people threw on the altar of the Five-Year Plans did not return to them in the form of more consumer goods, for the largest part of this energy was "invested" in heavy industry. The most profit-thirsty capitalist has never dreamed of the possibility of creating such a fine system of "accumulation of capital" as that practised by a Party which claimed to have abolished forever man's exploitation by man. The truth is that exploitation of man by man was supplanted by the exploitation of man by the State which used all the powers of its dictatorship to keep the workers under constant pressure.

Hand in hand with this economic exploitation went political repression. Those who dared to express the slightest disagreement with Communist policy were persecuted as "Right-wing opportunists," "Left-wing deviationists," "rotten liberals," or just plain counterrevolutionaries.

Such was the setting within which Khrushchev developed his talents when he left the Industrial Academy after fifteen months of nominal study.

7

Improving the Stalinist Style of Work

Khrushchev's first Party job in Moscow was the secretaryship in the Industrial Academy which he held from May 27, 1930, to January 8, 1931, when he became First Secretary of the Bauman district,[1] as stated before. Three weeks later the students of the Academy "elected" Khrushchev deputy to the Moscow City Soviet,[2] and on February 23, 1931, he and Bulganin became members of the city Party Committee and its fifteen-man bureau under Kaganovich, who was First Secretary.[3]

Although all visible opposition within the Party had been knocked out, Khrushchev used the first occasion which presented itself, when Moscow city became administratively separated from Moscow province, to stress in a resolution of the Bauman District Party organization, that "the battle for the Leninist general Party line against Right-wing opposition which is the main danger at this stage; against Left-wing infractions; and against tolerant attitudes towards all deviations from the Party line will be fought even more energetically and with Bolshevik impetuousness."[4]

Khrushchev remained in the Bauman district for only six months. In July, 1931, Kaganovich appointed him First Party Secretary of the Krasnopresnensky (Red Presnya) district, the largest district of the capital. Officially Khrushchev was elected to that post on July 25 at the plenary meeting of the district Party Committee.[5] The reason for the dismissal of Khrushchev's predecessor, A. N. Kozlov, was his "political susceptibility to the Right-wing opportunist acts" of the consumer cooperative

"Kommunar." What had happened was that this cooperative, which supplied a quarter of a million working people in the district with food and manufactured goods, had experienced financial difficulties and not shown much enthusiasm in reorganizing itself on the basis of "business accounting" *(khrozraschet)*, that is, raising the prices. "Several products (including wine) are being sold at a loss, and the commercial expenses are not fully included in the prices," *Pravda* complained on July 16, 1931.* The management of "Kommunar" had preferred to cover its deficit through a State Bank loan rather than by raising prices, because it considered such a raise an additional burden on its low-paid members. Therefore, Kozlov was dismissed and the "Right-wing opportunist" management of the "Kommunar" and its Party bureau were purged. But the difficulties did not disappear: the food supply shrank and the "queues in front of the cooperative stores increased," *Pravda* reported.[6] The reason for the crisis in "Kommunar" was, of course, the general food shortage. Judging from the unusual attention *Pravda* paid to the difficulties in the district, it can be assumed that the population, weary of the food shortage, vigorously showed its dissatisfaction. On July 16, 1931, *Pravda* came out with two articles blasting the District Party Bureau for "political shortsightedness, inability to guide and to work in the new fashion, the actual ignoring of the Right-wing opportunist practice of the former management of the 'Kommunar.' " That same day the District Party Bureau met,

---

* Mention of wine is not accidental, because liquor—and particularly vodka—was an important source of revenue. The monopoly of vodka was abolished after the Revolution. On December 26, 1922, Stalin declared: "Comrades, it must be bluntly stated that our financial position now, in the sixth year of existence of the Soviet Government, has far less opportunities for large-scale [economic] development than, for instance, under the old regime which had vodka, which we will not have, that yielded 500 million rubles per annum" (*Sochineniya*, V, 147). However, five years later, on November 5, 1927, Stalin reversed himself when he told foreign workers' delegations: "At present the revenue from vodka is over 500 million rubles. To give up the vodka monopoly now would mean giving up this revenue." (*Ibid.*, X, 232). Since the introduction of the vodka monopoly, there has never been a shortage of that liquor in the Soviet Union, and it is still an important source of revenue of the Soviet Government. Under the Soviet circumstances, vodka should be considered as a drug helping to distract the Soviet people from the hardships of their lives and keep their minds in a condition under which clear political thinking becomes impossible. Thus, in the Soviet Union, vodka became the real "opium of the people."

but in its decision it tried to justify itself and even to deny *Pravda's* accusations. Secretary Kozlov evidently underestimated the political aspect of *Pravda's* attack, which was meant to find a scapegoat for the difficulties created by the Party itself. Kozlov had to make room for Khrushchev, who already had some experience in "working in the new fashion."

It is questionable whether the cooperative "Kommunar" under Khrushchev's control improved the food situation in the Red Presnya district, but there is no doubt that he weeded out all "opportunists" from the management of the cooperative. After months had passed, the Soviet press reported that, following the disclosures in *Pravda*, the new District Party Committee headed by Khrushchev "fights in a Leninist way against all distortions of the general Party line,"[7] and that "it has overcome the errors of its former leadership which had failed to ensure a decisive struggle against the Right-wing opportunist practice in the consumer cooperative 'Kommunar.'"[8]

During the short period that Khrushchev worked in the Red Presnya district he not only faithfully followed Kaganovich's orders and the Party decisions in general, but also displayed initiative in inventing new methods and devices for better and speedier fulfillment of these orders and decisions. Khrushchev's district was the first to introduce "days" and "ten-day" periods during which the entire district organization was mobilized to achieve one or several tasks. At the end of October, 1931, Khrushchev mobilized his district for a ten-day period to determine the work done by all Party cells with regard to the political training of Party candidates before their admittance as full-fledged members.

This "ten-day" period had another purpose: to speed up the fulfillment of the economic plan for the last quarter of the year and to carry out the so-called Stalin Estafette.* This Stalin Estafette was Khrushchev's innovation. After it had proved its efficiency, it was introduced in all other Party organizations of

---

* "In the U.S.S.R., the term *estafette* is used as a method of checking the results achieved in one or another sector of work performed on the basis of the shock method (*udarnichestvo*) and emulation; it is one of the forms of organization of the masses in the struggle for tempo and quality of construction" (*Bolshaya Sovetskaya Entsiklopedia* [*Large Soviet Encyclopedia*, 1st ed.; Moscow, 1934], LXIV, 651).

the Moscow city and province. The Stalin Estafette was so called because its purpose was to implement Stalin's new methods of work which had to be observed in order to fulfill the industrial plan. These methods were: "recruiting labor in an organized way" (that is, compulsory recruiting); to "put an end to the heavy turnover of labor power" (which meant abolishing the workers' freedom to choose their places of work); to "put an end to lack of personal responsibility" (which meant making the workers responsible for the condition of the machines and tools); to "introduce and reinforce business accounting, increase the accumulation of capital within industry itself" (which meant the reduction of production costs which, under the circumstances, could only be achieved by keeping wages down and norms of output high).

Praising the initiative of the "Party and working masses" of the Red Presnya district, *Pravda* pointed out that the Stalin Estafette was such a success in that district that "workers of advanced factories had appealed to all Moscow proletarians to prolong the Stalin Estafette until January 1, 1932, turning it into a forty-day Bolshevist campaign for the advance fulfillment of the industrial and financial plan . . ." [9]

The Stalin Estafette was a well thought-out, concrete plan. Khrushchev divided the Estafette into nine "routes," each "route" being a special device to force upon the workers one or several of Stalin's new forms of labor exploitation. One of the "routes" was "the preparation for a new counterplan for 1932" exceeding the goals of the regular plan; another "route" was concerned with "the mobilization of monetary resources," that is, squeezing subscriptions to state loans out of the workers and employees. The most important "route" was the creation of new types of shock brigades—a better term would be sweat brigades: shock brigades "based on the progressive and premium piecework system" and shock brigades engaged in outstripping the regular plan by a "counterplan." In a short period Khrushchev succeeded in forming 2,250 new brigades comprising more than 12,000 men of the first and an unknown number of brigades of the second type (about 4,000 men). It seems that the Stalin Estafette was not particularly popular among the workers. *Pravda* pointed out that "further development of the Stalin Estafette demands more

careful control," because, in some places, "all kinds of opportunists try to distort, to vulgarize, to ignore, or even actively to
resist [the Estafette]. It is necessary to deal a decisive Bolshevist
blow at the Right-wing and Left-wing attacks against the new
mass movement, at all disorganizers and killers of the workers'
initiative." [10]

The "progressive and premium piecework system," described
in the preceding chapter, was only one of the tools that the
Party had put into the hands of its secretaries. Khrushchev used
these tools with skill and ingenuity. His attention was fixed on
figures, percentages; he concentrated on discovering the best
means to increase them. Perhaps the only limits he respected
were shortages of raw materials and machines. The working men
and women who used them counted only as far as they could
contribute another percentage point or a fraction of a percentage
point to the Plan.

Khrushchev's devotion to the general Party line and its creators
—Stalin and his two closest companions-in-arms at the time, Kaga-
novich and Molotov—was not the result of conviction alone, but
also of his increasing readiness to please the *vozhd*, at all costs.
In that connection, Khrushchev's behavior in the so-called
Slutsky case is of special interest.

In November, 1931, in a letter to the editors of *Proletarskaya
Revolutsia* (Proletarian Revolution), the then official historical
journal of the Communist Party, Stalin scolded the editors for
the publication of an article by a certain Slutsky, who had expressed the opinion that Lenin had underestimated the danger of
the middle-of-the-road position of the German and other social
democratic parties before World War I. Stalin himself disagreed
and angrily insisted upon the need "to raise the questions concerning the history of Bolshevism to the proper level, to put the
study of the history of our Party on scientific, Bolshevik lines, and
concentrate attention against the Trotskyites and all other falsifiers of the history of our Party by systematically ripping off
their masks." [11]

This letter was the initial signal for revising the history of the
Bolshevik Party for one particular purpose: to elevate Stalin's
past role, to place him at least on the same level as Lenin. In

other words, the revision of the history of the Party meant revision of Stalin's biography. Stalin's letter was immediately reprinted in all Soviet newspapers and magazines, and all Party cells were directed to promulgate the "historical" letter in detail and to take measures "to rip the masks" off the "falsifiers" of history.

It so happened that Slutsky lived in the Red Presnya district, where Khrushchev was First Party Secretary. Khrushchev acted promptly. In a special resolution, Slutsky's article was described as a "deliberate utilization of Party literature for propaganda of Trotskyism, the spearhead of the counterrevolutionary bourgeoisie."[12] By virtue of this resolution Slutsky was thrown out of the Party and disappeared forever. Prompt action of this sort was considered one of Khrushchev's major merits. In January, 1932, the "Bolsheviks of Red Presnya," i.e., Khrushchev and his close associates, were praised for having dealt "a decisive rebuff to the attempts of the Trotskyite contrabandists to falsify the history of our Party. They threw out from their ranks the Trotskyite Slutsky who had disguised himself."[13]

This passage is taken from an editorial in *Rabochaya Moskva,* organ of the Moscow Party organization, devoted to the opening of the Red Presnya district conference. It can be assumed that the editorial was inspired by Khrushchev himself.

From the viewpoint of evaluation of the moral aspect of Khrushchev's personality, the question arises as to whether he was acting in good faith when he ousted Slutsky from the Party for having expressed a different opinion from that of Stalin on a historical matter of no practical significance. This question is not merely academic, because, twenty-five years later, at the Twentieth Party Congress, Khrushchev made the following statement:

> Stalin acted not through persuasion, explanation, and patient cooperation with people, but by imposing his concepts and demanding absolute submission to his opinion. Whoever opposed this concept or tried to prove his viewpoint and the correctness of his position was doomed to removal from the leading collective and to subsequent moral and physical annihilation.[14]

Having ousted Slutsky, Khrushchev was certainly aware of the fact that he had paved the way for Slutsky's moral and physical annihilation. Did Khrushchev act as a blind tool in Stalin's hands? This is not likely, for at the time Khrushchev was thirty-eight years old and experienced enough to understand what was at stake. Thus he either acted in good faith, believing in the necessity of eliminating those who dissented from Stalin, or he acted in bad faith, as did the *vozhd* himself in using Slutsky's article as a pretext for preparing the ground for a general assault against historical truth. The second assumption is more probable, for reasons to be discussed later in detail.

Khrushchev's assignment to the Red Presnya district was of short duration. Exactly six months later, on January 30, 1932, he became Second Secretary of the Moscow City Party Committee, while Kaganovich was its First Secretary. At this time "the liquidation of the kulaks as a class, on the basis of total collectivization" was the order of the day. The farmers' resistance in the principal grain-growing areas reached a new peak. By autumn of 1932, in these areas alone, over 240,000 "kulak" families had been evicted from their homes and deported to Siberia and Kazakhstan for "re-education." This official figure, published in the 1959 version of the *History of the Communist Party of the Soviet Union*,[15] does not include the number of those who were executed without trial and those who were "tried" and sentenced to death or long terms of slave labor for violation of the so-called "law of preserving socialist property" issued on August 7, 1932. The exact number of the "kulaks" liquidated "as a class" and those liquidated as human beings will never be known.

After the principal grain-growing regions had been "socialized," the turn came for the remaining vast areas of the Soviet Union, including the Moscow province. Kaganovich mobilized 2,000 "leading Party workers" of the Moscow Party machine to organize "total collectivization" of that province. In March, 1933, when more help was needed to curb the farmers, he assigned three of his best trainees—Khrushchev, Bulganin, and Malenkov—to supervise and guide the collectivization drive in three districts.[16] Here they learned how to apply the Stalinist method of "building socialism" in the countryside. In 1940 and in the first postwar years, Khrushchev had occasion to use the experience, gained under Kaganovich's guidance, on a far larger scale in the newly acquired regions of the Ukraine.

Khrushchev's promotion to the post of Second Secretary of the Moscow City Party Committee was the first important step in his political career and should be regarded as a reward for his persistent struggle against the remnants of the Opposition, and his successful conquest of problems connected with the fulfillment of the economic plan. The significance of this promotion is apparent from the fact that Kaganovich, overburdened with work in the Central Committee and the Moscow Provincial Party Committee, could not personally guide the daily work of the Moscow City Party Committee, and this circumstance helped Khrushchev to rise from the position of first Party official in one of Moscow's ten districts to the post of acting Party boss of the capital as a whole.

Thus the period of Khrushchev's closest collaboration with Kaganovich began, and it lasted for more than three years. In 1947, for a short period, they again worked together in the Ukraine—Kaganovich as Party boss and Khrushchev as Chairman of the Ukrainian Council of Ministers. This "cooperation" must have been less agreeable to Khrushchev, because Kaganovich had been sent to Kiev by Stalin to take away from Khrushchev the secretaryship of the Ukrainian Party. While the Ukrainian encounter was an affair in which rivalry was involved, the Khrushchev-Kaganovich contact in the early 'thirties was a harmonious relationship between one of the most powerful personalities in the Kremlin and a rising political "star."

Khrushchev showed real devotion to Kaganovich, under whom he worked during this period. In his speeches, he praised Kaganovich's instructions "which we receive in our everyday work," his brilliant proposals to "plow virgin land and grow wheat in the Moscow province," [17] his "direct militant guidance," [18] and so on. Even in 1935, when Khrushchev, having replaced Kaganovich as Moscow's Party boss, worked on his own while Kaganovich became People's Commissar of Transportation, he continued to sing the praises of Kaganovich. On June 10, 1935, in a speech before active Moscow Party workers, Khrushchev referred several times to his predecessor's merits. Speaking of the necessity of "combating the *laissez-faire* frame of mind" and applying "Bolshevist will power, impetuousness, and organized preparedness in solving the urgent tasks" in the field of procurement of agricultural products, Khrushchev made the following remarks: "It is our duty to do so especially because, in the course of several years, the Moscow province, under the guidance of Comrade Kaganovich, occupied one of the first places in all agricultural campaigns." Then he added that for this "successful Bolshevist work, which was carried on under the guidance of Comrade Kaganovich, the government and the Party awarded the Moscow province the Order of Lenin," and that this award, being a "great honor," "imposes upon us great obligations."

This appraisal of Kaganovich was probably sincere. By his nature, Khrushchev resembles the Kaganovich of the 'thirties: the same liveliness, mobility, persistence in solving problems by not shying away from the smallest details, shrewdness, and unlimited ruthlessness if the problem cannot be solved by gentler means. What Khrushchev originally lacked was Kaganovich's ability to concentrate simultaneously on many problems. In four years of close contact with Kaganovich, Khrushchev benefited not only from promotions, but also from the many opportunities to learn the "new style of work." Although the latter has always been connected with Stalin's name and called the "Stalinist style of work," it is not accurate to say that Stalin alone was responsible for it; it seems that some, if not all, of the post-Stalin "collective leadership" men contributed greatly to the creation of this style, and this is particularly true with regard to Lazar M. Kaganovich.

When Khrushchev became secretary of the Moscow City Party Committee, Moscow had 3.6 million inhabitants. Although Bulganin was the "mayor" of Moscow, it was the Moscow City Party Committee, rather than the Moscow Soviet, which decided all principal municipal problems, and particularly the reconstruction of Moscow's municipal economy. In discussing these problems and in solving them, Khrushchev showed himself to be a man with a tight fist. In this respect the speech he delivered in August, 1933,[19] on construction matters, in which he took up some questions of management and labor relations, is of considerable interest.

"At the construction sites," Khrushchev said, "as everywhere, mere words are not enough. We need a Bolshevist organized system, clearness of purpose, knowledge of the matter and ability to fulfill without fail the plan assigned by the Party and Government."

Khrushchev criticized construction managers relying on time-keepers and standardizers, who became the principal figures on construction sites and "turned into lawmakers." He urged the construction chiefs to take off their "white gloves" and exercise the authority given to them, particularly in handling labor:

"The success of construction depends on the workers' fulfillment of the norm. If you are a chief of a construction site, encourage the better worker, help him, let him earn more, but at the same time carry on a decisive struggle against the self-seeker and the 'runner' who comes to the construction site to snatch wages and run away."

Khrushchev accepted no valid reasons for non-fulfillment of a plan, not even faulty raw materials. If the timber was bad, its suppliers were to be prosecuted. In this connection, Khrushchev asked the construction chiefs whether they had "instituted court proceedings against the negligent timber suppliers," adding menacingly, "no such trials have been heard of lately."

In the same speech Khrushchev revealed his attitude toward workers' demands to lower the norms of output. He said:

Under the influence of self-seekers who have wormed themselves into our construction sites some workers have begun to think along the following lines: well, would it not be a good idea to revise the norms of output? These harmful disorganizing aspirations should be met with a severe rebuff. It is necessary to fight in a Bolshevist way so that every bricklayer, plasterer, and painter fulfills his norm of output. All kinds of opportunistic whisperers who attempt to revise the norms should be repulsed with all resoluteness, for they reflect the pressure of the petty bourgeois element and sometimes even that of real kulak counterrevolutionary groups . . .

This was the language of an entrepreneur whose words are law and whose opinion is an order. With the ease of a skilled juggler, Khrushchev turned the simple demand by workers to reduce the pressure of high output norms into a political question, which meant that further discussion of such a demand would lead to a knock on the door at midnight. . . . Two decades later, in June, 1953, German construction workers on the Stalin Allee in East Berlin, having put forward a similar demand, had occasion to convince themselves that this Bolshevist language was backed up by Soviet tanks.

As Moscow's Party secretary, Khrushchev was also active in other realms. In 1934, Khrushchev had an opportunity to contribute to the tightening of the remaining gaps through which information on events in the non-Communist world occasionally penetrated into the Soviet Union. *Vechernyaya Moskva* (*Evening Moscow*) of March 16, 1934, published an article by the Soviet writer Boris Lavrenyev in which he described his impressions of a visit to Italy and reported that "all of northern Italy is an area where industrial and economic life is in full swing," and that "all of Italy is becoming modernized." On March 27, in an unsigned article, *Pravda* ironically accused Lavrenyev of "having discovered a capitalistic country where the economic crisis is gone." The flourishing of industry in northern Italy in 1934 was, of course, an actual fact, but this fact did not fit into the official line at that time; hence *Pravda's* assault against Lavrenyev. The editors of *Vechernyaya Moskva* were criticized for having published his article. This was one of the "errors" of the evening paper. The second fault was the paper's reporting, on March 20, that "new discoveries in the field of radium" had been made in France, Poland, England, and "even in Austria and Germany" (under Hitler). *Pravda* showed particular dissatisfaction with the paper's assertion that "1896, the year of the discovery of the phenomenon of radioactivity by Antoine Henri Becquerel in Paris, can be regarded as the initial year of a new scientific world perception—the world outlook of the twentieth century." What the author had in mind was that the discovery of radioactivity might have been the beginning of a new perception of the universe. *Pravda* interpreted this thought, which proved to be true, as an attempt to persuade the readers that "Marxism-Leninism is not at all the only scientific world outlook of the twentieth century." As far as scientific discoveries in other countries were concerned, *Pravda* attacked the evening paper for its attempt to impress readers with "alleged" large-scale scientific research going on in capitalist, and even fascist, countries while every "honest Soviet citizen" knows that such possibilities existed only in the Soviet Union.

Khrushchev reacted to the whole affair personally by swiftly firing the evening paper's deputy editor-in-chief, A. Deyev. He also warned the editor-in-chief, Rzhanov, that he too would be dismissed in the event that "political errors continue to be tolerated." As reason for his action Khrushchev gave "Lavrenyev's sketch about Italy and the article 'New Discoveries in the Field of Radium.'" [20]

Incidentally, at the time the odious article on radium appeared, Khrushchev could have looked up volume five of the first edition of the *Large Soviet Encyclopedia,* on page 270 of which was an article on Antoine Henri Becquerel, stating that his "discovery had an enormous significance for contemporary science and gave Becquerel wide fame," and that in 1903 he had shared the Nobel Prize with Pierre and Marie Curie.

8

The Party Builds a Subway

At the time Khrushchev was elevated to the position of Moscow City Party Secretary, the plan for the rebuilding of the capital, adopted in a resolution of the Party Central Committee in June, 1931, was in the first stage of its acccmplishment. The transportation problem in Moscow was acute, but there were still sufficient surface possibilities which could have been developed. There was no immediate need for an extremely costly project at a time when the most essential needs of the population, such as housing, were neglected. It is true that the Party decision took this problem into consideration, and small-scale housing construction was begun, but the Moscow subway, which was to become so famous, had priority over all other projects. The reason was not so much the urgent need to improve the transportation network, as the desire to construct in record-breaking time the best and most beautiful subway in the world. The Moscow subway was to become a prize exhibit for foreign delegations, journalists, and tourists, a visible proof of the superiority of the "socialist" planned economy over the free enterprise system, and tangible evidence that at least in one respect the Communist state had already "caught up with and surpassed" the capitalist world. With no experience in constructing tunnels under a crowded city, under constant strain and fear of disastrous landslides, of crumbling buildings, of breaking sewers and gas mains, under enormous pressure to finish the project in record time unprecedented in the history of subway building, over 70,000 men and women worked steadily in three shifts supervised and rushed by Party

86

officials, foremen, brigadiers, and engineers.

Officially, the Moscow subway was built by the construction organization "Metrostroi." In reality, however, all major and most minor decisions, even of a technical nature, were made by the Moscow Party Committee headed by Kaganovich and Khrushchev. Although the construction of the subway has always been considered a major accomplishment of Kaganovich, Khrushchev's role in this enterprise was most important. In March, 1935, a book appeared in Moscow entitled *Accounts of the Subway Builders*, in which construction chiefs, engineers, and shock brigadiers described their experiences. Full of superlative praise for Kaganovich, this book also contains flattering references to Khrushchev's role in the construction of the subway. In fact, the bounds of ordinary flattery were far surpassed in the statement of a certain I. D. Gotseridze:

"In the life of every man there are especially memorable days. On such days one suddenly begins to understand in a new way the simple things which seemed to be well known long ago. On such days one becomes inspired with love for things and phenomena with which one was only slightly concerned heretofore. Exactly such a day was the day when my conversation with Comrade Khrushchev took place."[1] It is also somewhat surprising to read what Y. T. Abakumov, deputy chief of the subway construction, said in connection with a difficult technical problem: "And it was he [Khrushchev] who showed us how one should apply here socialist methods of work which had a tremendous effect,"[2] There was good reason for this kind of talk. Gotseridze, who could not forget the day he first met Khrushchev, was on that very day made chief of one of the tunnel shafts after Khrushchev had talked to him for almost an hour and "thoroughly examined me as an engineer, person, and Communist." As far as Abakumov's statement is concerned, there is an indication that what he wrote must have been heavily edited. This can be seen from the following fact.

For unexplained reasons the *Accounts of the Subway Builders* was published in two versions. According to information given on the last page of both versions, they allegedly appeared the same day—March 7, 1935. The versions differ in size; one contains 505 pages and the other 452 pages. Since the longer version contains more accurate data, it can be assumed that it was a corrected version. Both versions carry Abakumov's article, but the wording of the sentence quoted above is different; while the short version claims that Khrushchev showed how "socialist methods of work" should be applied in solving technical problems, the corrected version added Bulganin's name, so that the sentence reads: "And it was they [Khrushchev and Bulganin] who showed us how one should apply the socialist methods of work which had a tremendous effect." Along with Khrushchev, Bulganin was also given credit in another sentence of Abakumov's article. This fact suggests that, after the short version had left the printing plant, Moscow's Mayor, Bulganin, complained about the omission of his name, while that of Khrushchev had been given prominence. The "mistake" was partly corrected, but Bulganin still remained heavily overshadowed by Khrushchev, and both— Khrushchev and Bulganin—by Kaganovich. Khrushchev's role in the subway construction is described in the following fashion:

> Comrade Kaganovich's closest assistant in the subway construction was Comrade N. S. Khrushchev. All engineers, all brigadiers, and shock workers of the construction know Nikita Sergeyevich. They know him because he visits the construction sites every day, gives daily instructions, checks, criticizes, encourages, advises one or the other shaft chief, one or the other Party organizer, on concrete urgent questions.
>
> Comrade Khrushchev's office turned into an office similar to that of a "Metrostroi" manager where Party organizers and shaft chiefs and engineers and individual brigadiers work out measures for the fulfillment of the daring, urgent assignments of their tested leader, L. M. Kaganovich.[3]

What was meant under "daring" assignments was partially clarified by G. Lomov, a chief engineer, who frankly stated: "When we constructed the subway we were, of course, aware of the fact that we were digging under an enormous city, that every disturbance of the foundations might lead to a disaster, but, nevertheless, during the first period of construction, we did not show particular vigilance."[4]

What a choice of words! If in a civilized country a construction

manager, responsible for the lives of his crews working underground and for the lives of people living on the surface, had
not shown "particular vigilance," he would have been subject
to criminal prosecution. But under a Communist regime he might
receive an award, as Lomov did, if his work without safety devices
helped in the fulfillment of the plan.

There is sufficient evidence to the effect that, not only during
"the first period" but also at later stages of the construction,
Kaganovich and particularly Khrushchev ignored precautionary
measures urgently recommended by experts, and took it upon
themselves to issue orders which no responsible specialist would
dare issue.

At the end of October, 1934, in connection with the upcoming
seventeenth anniversary of the October Revolution, the Kitaigorod
wall at the Dzershinsky place was ordered torn down so that
a wide avenue could be built for the marchers in the parade.
In the vicinity of the wall the "Metrostroi" had built a freezing
station which refrigerated the water-soaked silt in order to eliminate the danger of disastrous landslides. In order to clear the
place for the parade, Khrushchev directed the two engineers,
A. F. Denishchenko and N. G. Trupak, who were responsible for
the freezing works, to transfer the freezing station elsewhere.
The engineers were taken aback, since stoppage of refrigeration
meant warming up of the ground and a possibility that "the
shaft might collapse under the weight of water while people
were working there." Another problem with which Khrushchev
burdened the engineers was to assemble the new freezing station
in a few days while four months had been needed to assemble
the units built earlier. It was a miracle that no major disaster
took place.[5]

Another incident in which Khrushchev was involved is told
by A. M. Stepanov, chief of the seventh subway sector. In view
of the excessive speed with which the work had to be done,
the buildings along the excavation line of this and other sectors
had not been properly shored up. One of the houses began to
collapse, and the inhabitants had to be evacuated. A commission
consisting of construction experts examined the situation on the
spot and decided against further excavation until the buildings
could be adequately supported. Then Khrushchev appeared at

the construction site and asked Stepanov: "Why don't you go ahead with your work all along the line? Are you afraid of the buildings?" Answering Khrushchev's question, Stepanov told him about the decision of the experts and his colleagues' hesitation, but he also said that, if ordered, he would not object to continuing the excavation without shoring up the buildings. By saying this, Stepanov anticipated Khrushchev's order. Stepanov described what then happened as follows:

> Nikita Sergeyevich Khrushchev thought for a while and then supported our point of view. This I did not expect, because we ourselves had different views on the subject. Furthermore, I described our doubts in sufficiently vague terms. However it may be, Nikita Sergeyevich's words definitely persuaded us to go ahead with the work along the entire line.[6]

In assessing this incident one has to consider that Stepanov described it for the purpose of showing Khrushchev's merit in taking quick and "courageous" decisions. The fact, however, remains: despite a decision of construction experts and the hesitation of the engineers responsible for the safety of their crews and the inhabitants of the endangered buildings, Party Secretary Khrushchev, with no experience in tunneling, ordered the engineers not to be "afraid of the buildings."

Officially, Khrushchev channeled his "suggestions" through the chief of the subway construction, Rottert, or his deputy, Abakumov, so that he was not formally responsible for mishaps, accidents, and catastrophes which resulted from these "suggestions." And when something happened he used strong language in reprimanding the technical personnel for "negligence."[7]

In the Moscow newspapers of the period under discussion, there are no reports of a major or even a minor accident during the construction of the Moscow subway. Only descriptions of unlimited enthusiasm and devotion of the workers adorned the pages of the press. However, careful reading of Soviet books about the subway construction—published for the purpose of describing, first, the merits of Kaganovich and Khrushchev (Bulganin was mentioned only in rare instances) and then the heroic deeds of the brigadiers and their shock brigades, reveals that not all was quiet on the subway front. Desiring to impress the readers with an act of heroism of a brigadier, one of the builders related this story:

> Let us take the brigadier of excavators, Kholod. Having worked through the night, he dropped into the room of the Party organizer and laid down on the bench for a rest. Suddenly, shouts reached him: "Kholod, your heading is flooded!" Kholod leaped to his feet, descended into the shaft, and saw the workers in water up to their necks. The crew chief, also submerged to his neck, without batting an eye, calmly explained what had happened. Then Kholod also got into the stinking water, looked for the cause of the accident, and found that a sewage pipe had burst. To stop the torrent it was necessary to reach the well and to close the pipe. Kholod did it, and so the heading was saved.[8]

And what about the workers? This question apparently did not interest the teller of the story.

Describing a catastrophe in the eighteenth tunnel heading, E. D. Reznichenko, editor-in-chief of the newspaper *Udarnik Metrostroya (The Shock Worker of the Subway Construction)*, remarked: "This catastrophe was the result of the fact that safety measures were applied wretchedly."[9] Only when excavating took place under a building where foreigners lived were precautionary measures rigorously applied. For example, Kaganovich, who never limited the initiative of the construction managers in taking chances, remarked, regarding one of the buildings under which digging had to be done: "In the house above us live Americans, and political considerations do not permit this house to fall down."[10] In other words, chances could be taken under buildings where Soviet citizens lived, since no political complications could arise for the Party and the Government if these buildings were to collapse.

There was no time to take precautionary measures: Kaganovich and Khrushchev worked out an extremely tight time schedule. Chief engineer P. P. Zarembo, responsible for track-laying in the tunnels, called his contribution to one of the above-mentioned books as follows: "The Time Schedule Grabbed Us by the Throat."[11] It seems that the editors overlooked this honest title.

An excerpt from a speech delivered by Kaganovich on December 29, 1933, to construction managers and shock brigadiers sheds light on the working speed expected from them. Kaganovich said:

"We must declare with the utmost sharpness that the present stand of the construction works cannot ensure the completion of the first subway section by November 7 [1934]. The main task is to speed up the construction tempo . . . In the shortest possible time we must increase the speed of excavating five times and the speed of the tunnel building eight to nine times." [12] Khrushchev, Kaganovich's right hand in supervising the subway construction, was in charge of carrying out Kaganovich's decision. How Khrushchev drove the construction engineers and the shock brigades is illustrated by the following case. During a visit to one of the construction sites, Khrushchev said to its chief:

> "Comrade Kuzmin, you promised to clear away the scaffolding by the twelfth of the month and let the assemblers begin working. But it seems that you deceived the Moscow Party Committee. Today is the tenth, and see for yourself what it looks like around here."
>
> The chief of the sector looked around and replied: "No, Nikita Sergeyevich, we promised, and our crews will keep the promise."
>
> A talk with Comrade Khrushchev inspired the workers. Nobody wanted to lose face before the Moscow Party Committee. The entire entrance hall of the station was filled with scaffolding and timbering. Everywhere there were mountains of rubbish. The engineers, mechanics, technicians, and foremen did not leave the underground for two days. They vied with one another for the speediest completion of the clearing of their sectors. Woman-engineer Leonova had been on duty for five shifts without interruption. [13]

On the twelfth Khrushchev appeared again to check whether or not the work was done. It was.

On another occasion Kaganovich and Khrushchev visited a subway station, and Kaganovich expressed doubts whether the work would be finished according to schedule. He commissioned Khrushchev to see to it that things would get done. A meeting was called at which Khrushchev spoke. The shock brigadiers promised him to complete the work on time.

Next day, under the guidance of Comrade Khrushchev, we discussed and adopted a new work schedule. Not a single day passed without Comrade Khrushchev's visiting the station, and after each visit we worked better, wrote one of the engineers.

"May I tell Lazar Moiseyevich [Kaganovich]"—Comrade Khrushchev asked us all the time—"that the station will be finished according to schedule?"

After the work was done the chief of the construction site remarked:

"We achieved this victory because the work . . . was directly guided and organized, not by me, despite the fact that officially I am in charge, but by Nikita Sergeyevich Khrushchev." [14]

Another witness stated that Khrushchev issued "slogans" which actually were orders, such as that "the English shield * should lay one tunnel ring per shift and the Soviet shield should catch up with the English shield in July." Foreign specialists, experienced in shield tunneling, were of the opinion that the shield should not move faster than three-quarters of a meter in twenty-four hours. Khrushchev's "slogan" about increasing the shield movement to one tunnel ring per shift meant tripling the speed recommended by the specialists. Even this speed was soon considered too low, and Khrushchev came out with a new "slogan" demanding one linear meter of tunnel per shift. Each of these orders "inspired" the brigadiers, who "enthusiastically" entered into "socialist competition" in order to execute Khrushchev's slogans. [15] The same witness stated:

Comrade Khrushchev constantly kept his eye on our work; every day the surveyor marked on a chart in

---

* A part of the first section of the Moscow subway was built with two shields: one was purchased in England and the other was copied from it. A shield is a circular steel and cast-iron ring moved forward in excavating to support the ground ahead of the tunnel lining. A tunnel ring (which is a unit of the lining) was 0.75 meter long.

Khrushchev's office the movement of the shields. At the slightest slowdown of the shield movement Khrushchev would immediately call in Comrade Tyagnibeda or Suvorov and demand an explanation as to why the slowdown had taken place and what the difficulties were. This constant vigilance of Comrade Khrushchev always inspired the workers to work even better.[16]

Such speed increase certainly led to several catastrophes. Most of them have never been disclosed. The following description of one case gives an idea of the conditions under which the shield crews worked:

> The shield approached the silt—a brown fluid mass. The caisson* worked under an air pressure of 2.3 atmospheres. With every hour the conditions became more difficult. Sometimes the silt resisted and unprecedented efforts were necessary to stop it, to save the tunnel, the machine, and, chiefly, the people. Once a fire broke out in the caisson. In order to avoid rapid spreading of the fire in compressed air rich in oxygen it became necessary to lower the air pressure, but this opened the way for the silt that poured in torrents into the shaft . . .[17]

The author of this description does not reveal how many people perished in this catastrophe. He only praised the Komsomol members who saved the machine and the shaft. A few days later the same shield was flooded. "Huge torrents poured in from all sides, breaking the crosspieces and knocking down people . . ."[18]

What was behind this drive for speed? Why should people work forty-eight hours without interruption or be on duty for five straight shifts? Why was it necessary to stay in a caisson for eight, ten and eleven hours when working in it for more

---

* A caisson is a watertight chamber used for deep construction under water or ground. A caisson works under increased air pressure and, in the absence of precautions, causes the "caisson disease," sometimes fatal, which is marked by neuralgic pains and paralysis, induced by too rapid decrease in air pressure after a stay in compressed atmosphere.

than four hours endangers human life? Was the "inspiration" generated by Khrushchev for the task dictated by some kind of national emergency?

The answer to this question is simple. The Party had ordered completion of the first section of the subway by November 7, 1934, the seventeenth anniversary of the October Revolution, in order to impress the foreign delegations with this great "socialist" achievement. This was the only reason why Khrushchev had driven the construction workers at such a pace and why he "inspired" them to pay no attention to the warnings of experienced specialists. The tight time schedules, however, were so unrealistic that, despite Khrushchev's "inspirations" and Kaganovich's speeches, the prescribed deadline could not be met. It was not until May 15, 1935, that the doors of the subway were opened.

There are no indications that the first section of the Moscow subway was built with the help of slave labor, like the White Sea and the Moscow-Volga canals.* There is, however, first-hand testimony that slave labor was widely employed in the construction of the subsequent sections. This testimony was given by Valentin Gonzalez, known as "El Campesino," a former Communist general and hero of the Spanish Civil War who was forced to work in the subway construction after he had been tumbled from his pedestal. El Campesino wrote:

"The Russians are extremely proud of the Moscow underground. It is their prize exhibit for foreign delegations, journalists, and tourists. They claim it as a masterpiece of construction, and they are quite right. Only, they forget to explain that it is a monument not only to Soviet engineering but also to the slave labor which went into its construction.

"Almost 90 per cent of the construction workers were in a position similar to mine. They had fallen into disgrace and had been allotted this sort of work which offered them the faint—the very faint—hope that their efforts would in time restore

---

* In its April 16, 1959 press release the Soviet Embassy in the United States said that Khrushchev "was often seen" not only on the construction sites of the Moscow subway but also "on the construction site of the Moscow-Volga Canal." Here he "personally checked construction progress" (*U.S.S.R.*, No. 10 (37), p. 3).

them to their former position in the ruling class. Yet the alternative to this work was Siberia, and so they did all they could to follow the faint ray of hope."[19]

Khrushchev's assistants were, of course, not less zealous than their boss. One, M. I. Olkhovich, the Party secretary of the shaft 7-8, wrote:

"It was a difficult time. People, even Communists, came and asked to be released from work. Party candidate Kozlovski came and brought a certificate issued by the doctors' commission to the effect that it was bad for his health to continue working. I did not release him."[20] Olkhovich's "philosophy" towards physically unfit workers was as follows:

"Where is the point in all this? It is necessary to get used to the work. When you start working, fatigue occurs immediately, but you should not leave your working place: fatigue passes, and working inspiration begins. The doctors' commission does not know it, but we—the Party organization—do know it."[21]

It seems that the "working inspiration" did not grip all the workers. Otherwise, why would G. Lomov, the chief engineer of the Arbat sector, admit that people from the Moscow Military District "established a strict discipline among the ill-assorted mob that worked in this sector?"[22] Or why would chief I. D. Gotseridze—the same Gotseridze who was "enchanted" by Khrushchev's charm when he first met him—boast that in this sector "the discipline was actually similar to that at the battlefront?"[23] In his speech of December 29, 1933, Kaganovich complained that there were hostile elements "which attempt to frustrate the great cause of the construction of the first subway in the U.S.S.R. which was started on the initiative of our great leader, Comrade Stalin."[24] In order to "expose" these elements he appointed I. N. Kuznetsov, whose past experience was "the battlefront and the Cheka, and nothing else,"[25] to the post of Assistant Chief of Construction. As a result of his purge activity, about 2,000 workers were "moved away."[26] For one reason or another some of the purged did not have passports and hid in the dark corners of the tunnel headings. "Then," Kuznetsov wrote, "my people descended into the shafts to look for them. Sometimes it was necessary literally to drag them out from there to the daylight."[27]

"Working inspiration" did not always agree with the wage policy established for the subway workers. During a heart-to-heart conversation with a group of Komsomol members working on excavation, Kaganovich asked the young "enthusiasts" how they were coming along. One of the youths shyly said that the wage rates were too low. Kaganovich replied: "Well, it is possible that the rates are too low. But anyway you should know that the rates were calculated on the assumption that the work will be done at shock speed." [28] The answer was clear: in order to earn a living one had to work at shock speed.

Wherever the management attempted to encourage the workers with a higher wage rate, the attempt was immediately frustrated. For example, Anton Kholod—the same shock-brigade chief who so "heroically" saved his shaft from being flooded—and his brigade were temporarily transferred to another tunnel heading, where the rate was three rubles and ninety kopeks for one cubic meter of excavated dirt. "Each of us," wrote Kholod, "began to earn forty to forty-five rubles from the first day of our work there. I was surprised. I spoke about it with the standardizer. He got in touch with the chief engineer. They checked the rates on the spot, and the rates were cut to almost one third. We explained to the workers that they would earn the same as before if the work were organized as it should be," [29] that is, if the workers would triple their efforts.

As might have been expected, Kholod was not forgotten when the awards were distributed to the heroic builders of the subway. For his slave-driving abilities he received the Order of the Red Banner of Labor.

Lives and health were sacrificed not only to establish a record for speed in subway-building,* but also to construct the "most beautiful subway in the world." In a brochure, *Moscow's Metro*,[30] published in many languages by the Moscow Foreign Publishing House in 1955 and widely disseminated all over the world, a chapter entitled "Underground Palaces" contains this passage:

---

* It is doubtful whether a record was actually established, if one takes into consideration the enormous number of people engaged in the construction of seven miles of the first subway section; at the time this section was finished 75,369 men and women had worked on it (*Metro, sbornik posviashchennyi pusku Moskovskogo metropolitena* [Moscow, 1935], p. 70).

Over 70,000 square meters of marble were required for the stations of the first and second sections alone. This is one and a half times what was used in all the palaces of Czarist Russia during the fifty years preceding the Great October Socialist Revolution. Labradorite, an exceedingly beautiful and durable stone of a dark gray color, with sparkling ultramarine, went to decorate the columns and walls of several stations. Lavish use was made of porphyry, granite, bronze, smalto, and ceramic, as well as glazed panels. Many of the interiors were adorned with gold leaf, statuary, bas-reliefs and mosaics.

The station's panels are done in multicolored stones and smalto, each inlaid with some 300,000 pieces, its eight panels a fancy work of 2.5 million stones. The station is brightly illuminated with artistically wrought chandeliers holding fluorescent lights.

Marble and granite of the finest quality was used to finish the two recently built stations of the Belt line— Kievskaya Koltsevaya and Krasnaya Presnya.

The bases of stainless steel columns are faced in panels of a dark-rose precious Ural stone called *Orlets*. Built in the vaulted ceiling of the central hall are thirty-six oval cupolas with mosaics in multicolored smalto.

In 1933, Kaganovich disclosed that the first section of the Moscow subway alone would cost about half a billion rubles, and that in order to finish this section the Government had appropriated, for 1934 alone, 350 million rubles.[31] This section was not finished as planned in 1934, and more appropriations were certainly needed. The real meaning of an investment of half a billion rubles in the early 'thirties can be understood if one considers the fact that during the four years of the First Five-Year Plan the total investment in consumer goods industries averaged 300 million rubles per year.[32] In 1934, when 350 million rubles were spent for the completion of the first subway section and ornamentation of the underground palaces, only 85.4 million pairs of shoes were produced in the Soviet Union,[33] averaging about one shoe per person. While the underground ornaments were the very best, the quality of the shoes was such that "their durability was one half and sometimes one third of what was prescribed."[34] It is in the light of these facts that the architectural splendor and beauty of the Moscow subway must be evaluated, and that the statement on the last page of the official pamphlet *Moscow's Metro* must be read: "The Moscow Metro is a vivid example of the Communist Party's and the Soviet government's solicitude for the welfare of the Soviet people, for the improvement of their living conditions, of which the Soviet man has daily and hourly evidence."

Khrushchev had not only been aware of the contradiction between the misery on Moscow's surface and the splendor of its underground, but had been responsible for the lavishness with which he, Kaganovich, and Bulganin expended the people's labor, health, and lives. All three of these recent members of the Party Presidium belonged at the time to the Commission of Architecture and Planning (Arplan) which had the last word in deciding on architectural plans and extravagant materials for the palatial stations.[35]

Two decades later, in 1955, Khrushchev and Bulganin signed a "Decree on Eliminating Waste in Building Design" which contains the following passages:

> Completely unjustified tower-like superstructures and numerous decorative colonnades, porticos, and other architectural excesses borrowed from the past have become characteristic of apartment and public buildings, as the result of which state funds have been overexpended on housing construction in the last few years to an extent that would have provided many million square meters of living space for the working people. . . .
>
> An improper architectural trend is also evident in the design and construction of railroad stations, and manifests itself in the erection of palatial stations. In spite of their great cost, these stations do not provide the essential comforts for passengers.[36]

This decree blames several architects, including the architect Vlasov, for "architectural excesses." It is noteworthy that Vlasov, like Khrushchev and Bulganin, had also been in the 'thirties

a member of Arplan, which bore the responsibility for the
extravagant ornaments of the palatial stations of the Moscow
subway. At that time, Vlasov was a young architect and his name
was listed far down, while Kaganovich, Khrushchev, and Bulganin headed the list of Arplan's membership. The responsibility
was primarily theirs. But, after all, why not blame, in the 'fifties,
a man who carried out one's orders in the 'thirties?

9

The Evasive Witness

> We are the men of lofty morals, and we believe that our kind of morality will come to prevail not only in the socialist lands alone but throughout the world as well. —Khrushchev Press Conference, June 3, 1960, Moscow.

The years 1934 to 1938 were the most significant and bloody in the history of the Soviet totalitarian dictatorship. During those years Khrushchev, as head of the Party Committees of Moscow city and province, occupied one of the most important positions in the Party machine. Only a few who preceded him in that position or who worked with and under him survived this period. Most of them became victims of the Great Purge of 1935-38. On the Moscow local political scene Khrushchev was in the forefront, and he left his mark not only in the fields of economics and Party work in the general sense, but also helped to bring about the political atmosphere which made the Great Purge possible. It goes without saying that on the Moscow local level he participated in this unique enterprise with the same energy and ardor which he had displayed in other fields.

On December 1, 1934, began a new phase in the Soviet dictatorship. On that day, at half past four in the afternoon, in the headquarters of the Leningrad Soviet, a young Communist named

Leonid Nikolayev shot and killed Sergei Mironovich Kirov, a prominent member of the Politburo and the Leningrad Party boss. The circumstances under which Kirov was killed, the actual reasons for Nikolayev's act, the names of the real instigators and accomplices, if there were any, remain a mystery. There is, however, sufficient circumstantial evidence that the long list of people executed after the assassination of Kirov did not include those who were actually interested in his death. In his secret speech at the Twentieth Party Congress in 1956, Khrushchev said:

> It must be asserted that to this day the circumstances surrounding Kirov's murder hide many things which are inexplicable and mysterious and demand a most careful examination. There are reasons to suspect that the killer of Kirov, Nikolayev, was assisted by some one of the very people whose duty it was to protect the person of Kirov. A month and a half before the killing, Nikolayev was arrested on the grounds of suspicious behavior, but he was released and not even searched. It is an unusually suspicious circumstance that, when the Chekist assigned to protect Kirov was being brought in for interrogation, on December 2, 1934, he was killed in a car "accident" in which no other occupants of the car were harmed. After the murder of Kirov, top functionaries of the Leningrad NKVD were given very light sentences, but in 1937 they were shot. We can assume that they were shot so as to cover the traces of the organizers of Kirov's killing.[1]

The organizers of Kirov's assassination apparently eliminated later all material witnesses who could have helped clear up the mystery surrounding this affair, but they could not destroy logic. An analysis of the political situation in 1933-34 and Kirov's way of looking at it is helpful in establishing the reasons why Kirov had to die.

At the end of 1936, an "Old Bolshevik," a member of the Party Central Committee, who occupied a responsible job when the Great Purge started, was interviewed privately while abroad on official business. The result of this interview was published as the "Letter of an Old Bolshevik"* in *Sotsialisticheskii Vestnik*, organ of the Russian Social Democrats in exile, in the issues of December 22, 1936, and January 17, 1937. Because of its undoubted authenticity, this letter has since been regarded in the free world as the key to the events preceding and following Kirov's assassination. Today this letter is even more important than it was two decades ago, for it can now be compared with the testimony of Khrushchev, who, at the time of Kirov's death, belonged to Stalin's elite, while the Old Bolshevik did not. It is, therefore, of great interest that Khrushchev's evaluation of the political situation in 1933-34 is similar to that of Kirov's as reported by the Old Bolshevik.

According to the Old Bolshevik, the Party was faced with these alternatives at that time: either to pursue the former policy of crushing all dissenters by tightening the administrative pressure and intensifying the terror, or to try "reconciliation with the people" and gain their voluntary cooperation in the political preparation of the country for the coming war. The most convinced and prominent advocates of the reconciliation policy were Kirov and Maxim Gorky, the writer.

Kirov's line of thought was: the destructive period of the Revolution was at an end; the collectivization of agriculture, which in his view had been necessary to extirpate the small landowners in the villages, provided a new firm basis for future development. Kirov therefore *strongly advocated reconciliation with those Party elements who, during the destructive period, had gone over to the opposition* but might be made to cooperate on this new basis.

Kirov's conclusions from his analysis of the situation in 1933-34 were similar to those Khrushchev made in his secret speech in 1956. Khrushchev blamed Stalin for abandoning "the Leninist method of ideological struggle in exchange for administrative

---

* The author of the "Letter," Boris I. Nicolaevsky, kept silent about the identity of the Old Bolshevik for about a quarter of a century. In December, 1959, on the occasion of the twenty-fifth anniversary of the Kirov assassination, Mr. Nicolaevsky believed that it was then safe to disclose that he had received the information contained in the "Letter" from Nikolai Ivanovich Bukharin. The foremost Bolshevik theoretician after Lenin, Bukharin was "tried" and executed in 1938.

violence, mass repressions, and terror." [2] Stalin's arbitrary behavior "brought about annihilation and the expulsion from the
Party of workers who were loyal but inconvenient to Stalin.[3]

"Had Leninist principles," Khrushchev said, "been observed
during the course of this fight [against the Opposition], had the
Party's devotion to principles been skillfully combined with a
keen and solicitous concern for people, *had they not been re-
pelled and wasted but rather drawn to our side*—we certainly
would not have had such a brutal violation of revolutionary
legality, and many thousands of people would not have fallen
victim to the method of terror." [4]

Thus what Khrushchev preached in 1956, after a lapse of
over two decades, was actually Kirov's political platform
for which he and Maxim Gorky had desperately fought in
1933-34. In his Leningrad domain, Kirov actually practiced
"liberalism"; he insisted on granting all sorts of concessions to
former Oppositionists, and urged that their services be used in
cultural and scientific institutions. Only a few months before
his death he permitted the former head of the Marx-Engels
Institute, the old Bolshevik Ryazanov, a persistent Oppositionist
in the 'twenties, to reside in Leningrad instead of Saratov where
he had lived in exile and without any possibility of working in
the field in which he was interested. Kirov stood for the abolition
of terror, both in general and within the Party. When the question of applying the death penalty to the old Bolshevik Riutin
came up in the Politburo, with Stalin in favor of granting the
OGPU's demand for Riutin's head (in violation of Lenin's
commandment not to resort to the death penalty in the fight
against Party Oppositionists), Kirov vigorously opposed Stalin's
demand and succeeded in winning the Politburo over to his
view.

At that time the struggle within the ranks of the Party's
leading group differed from similar conflicts in the past. There
was no longer any question of Stalin's removal. The groupings
were not for or against Stalin. "It was rather a fight for influence
over Stalin," the Old Bolshevik stated. Supported by Gorky,
who had exercised "a great beneficent influence on Stalin," Kirov
was to some extent successful in his efforts. Early in the summer
of 1933, Kamenev, Zinoviev, and a number of other former

Oppositionists were readmitted to the Party. They even received invitations to speak at the Seventeenth Party Congress (January-February, 1934). Bukharin, who had been in disfavor for some years, was reinstated as editor-in-chief of *Izvestia*.

It was then that Kirov began to gain influence in the Party. An unswerving follower of Stalin's general line during the First Five-Year Plan, Kirov could not be reproached for any kind of "deviations" or softness in carrying out the ruthless measures against the peasants and the elimination of the "kulaks." For this Stalin valued him highly, but at the same time Stalin was annoyed by the fact that there was always a certain independence in Kirov's attitude. In the winter of 1933-34, Kirov had so strengthened his position that he could afford to follow his own line. His influence in the Party had grown swiftly. At the Seventeenth Party Congress in 1934, when he mounted the rostrum to speak, "all rose to their feet and gave Comrade Kirov, the well-tried leader of the Leningrad Bolsheviks who enjoys enormous authority in the Party, a prolonged stormy ovation," *Pravda* wrote on February 1, 1934. On the other hand, the Old Bolshevik related that "during the recesses there was discussion as to who had received the more enthusiastic reception, Kirov or Stalin." Following the Congress Kirov was not only re-elected to the Politburo but was also elected a member of the Organization Bureau (Orgburo) and a secretary of the Central Committee. This would have made it necessary for him to move from Leningrad to Moscow within a short time, and to take over the supervision of a group of departments in the Central Committee which had been under Postyshev and Lazar Kaganovich. His transfer to Moscow was delayed, however. The official reason given was that his presence in Leningrad was indispensable.

"Kirov's success," wrote the Old Bolshevik, "reached its zenith at the plenary session of the Central Committee in November, 1934. This session discussed a number of concrete measures which were to be taken in accordance with the new course. Kirov presented the report on the question and was the hero of the hour. His transfer to Moscow was again discussed, and it was definitely decided that it would occur very shortly."

The plenary session finished its work on November 28, 1934.

Three days later Kirov was assassinated.

As stated above, almost a generation later Khrushchev admitted that "the circumstances surrounding Kirov's murder hide many things which are inexplicable and mysterious." Such had been the opinion of the "Old Bolshevik" and many other private sources since 1935. The question arises: When did Khrushchev discover the Kirov mystery? Was he not informed about the mysterious car accident in which a principal witness was killed? He must have been. The witness was killed on December 2, 1934. Khrushchev was in Leningrad that day, where he had arrived from Moscow, together with Stalin, Molotov, Voroshilov, and Zhdanov, in a double capacity: as head of the delegation of Moscow "workers" and as a member of the official funeral commission.* [5] There can be no doubt that he had knowledge of the "accident," all the more so as the death of the witness and even his name, Borisov, were known in the free world long before Khrushchev confidentially informed the delegates to the Twentieth Party Congress. Khrushchev only confirmed what was known long ago in a number of reports on the Kirov assassination.

The post-Stalin "collective leadership" in its third (July, 1957) composition had in its midst six men who were aware of the fact that the Kirov affair had been deliberately hushed up. These men were: Khrushchev, Bulganin, Voroshilov, Mikoyan, Shvernik, and Pospelov.

In view of Kirov's extraordinary popularity in the Party, a fervent desire to solve the mystery surrounding his assassination was voiced by many of his sympathizers, but the six men mentioned were certainly not among them. This is strongly supported by the fact that during the Great Purge of 1937 not only all possible material witnesses, but also Kirov's immediate associates from the Leningrad Party Organization vanished forever. In his

---

* The other members of this commission were: Avel S. Yenukidze, M. S. Chudov, P. A. Alekseyev, Yan B. Gamarnik, and Nikolai A. Bulganin. Of the six members only two—Khrushchev and Bulganin—are known to be alive. The fate of a third is unknown. The fates of the other three members were as follows: Yenukidze was executed in December, 1937; Gamarnik committed suicide in June, 1937, when secret police agents were about to arrest him; and Chudov was arrested in 1937 and disappeared.

secret speech, Khrushchev mentioned only a few of them: M. S. Chudov, A. I. Ugarov, P. I. Smorodin, B. P. Pozern, and L. K. Shaposhnikova. All five were members of the 157 Leningrad delegates to the Seventeenth Party Congress. Fourteen members of that delegation, including four of the five men mentioned by Khrushchev, had been elected at that Congress to leading Party organs. Three of them died during the period between the Seventeenth and the Eighteenth Party Congress (1934-39): Kirov was killed; Kuibyshev is believed to have died a natural death (a view contested by private sources believing that he, too, was killed); and Ordzhonikidze died in 1937. (The latter's death was then officially called the result of a heart attack, but in his secret speech Khrushchev asserted that Ordzhonikidze had committed suicide, having been driven to it by Beria; there have been, however, numerous accounts that he also was killed.) Of the remaining 154 Leningrad delegates only two were re-elected to the next (Eighteenth) Party Congress in 1939. These two were hard-boiled Stalinists—A. A. Andreyev, at that time a member of the Politburo, and Shkiriatov, member of the Party Control Commission. The fate of the remaining 152 delegates is unknown. It is, however, a matter of record that none of this group was re-elected to the Eighteenth Party Congress. They disappeared from the political scene and, in all probability, became victims of the Great Purge which followed the assassination of Kirov. The above facts were sufficient proof that the organizers of Kirov's killing were interested in the elimination of not only the Leningrad leader, but also of the cream of the Leningrad organization which stood solidly behind Kirov. But there is evidence that Stalin, who ordered the purge, had made his decision only after he was "prepared" by Kaganovich and Yezhov.

If one can assume [the Old Bolshevik stated] that for a time Stalin had been in favor of a complete change in the Party course and of a policy of reconciliation inside the Party, his *immediate circle*, his working staff, was always entirely against it. This was not because members of this staff were in principle opposed to a change in the general policy of the Party, as expressed in the projects of Kirov and his friends, but because questions of general policy were more or less a matter of indifference to this group.... *What they emphatically opposed was any change in internal Party policy*. They realized that, while many were ready to overlook the negative aspects of Stalin's character because of his outstanding positive features, his immediate assistants (who knew precisely how to take advantage of the negative aspects of his character) *could expect no mercy in the event of a change in the intra-Party regime*. For, to repeat, the fight being waged was no longer for or against Stalin, but for *priority of influence over him....* The struggle was being waged around the proposed replacement of the existing working personnel of the Central Committee with new men seeking to introduce new ways and a new attitude toward people. *It was quite natural, therefore, that this old staff should resist any changes by every means in its power.*

Directing this resistance were *Kaganovich* and *Yezhov....* This pair, *Kaganovich and Yezhov, had opposed, from the very beginning, the policy of intra-Party reconciliation.* While Kirov was alive, they did not venture to come forward into the open. Instead, they contented themselves with stirring up Stalin against it, with intensifying Stalin's natural mistrust of those in whom he surmised a foe, and with sabotaging, as the opportunity presented itself, Kirov's transfer to Moscow, for they knew well that this move would reopen the whole question of changes in the personnel of the Party machine which they had assembled with such painful effort. . . . This attempt at sabotage was defeated at the November plenary session; nevertheless, Kirov never came to Moscow. After Kirov's death, *which the pair found very convenient*, they stepped out into the open.

Thus, Kaganovich and Yezhov, and the Party machine—all those whom they had picked and "educated" during the second half of the 'twenties and the first half of the 'thirties—were the instigators and the beneficiaries of Kirov's murder.

It is necessary at this point to dwell briefly on the personality

of Nikolai Ivanovich Yezhov. Born into a poor family, he knew
hunger and poverty in his young days. Perhaps this unhappy
circumstance, combined with his diminutive and frail appearance
and his lack of education, developed in him inferiority feelings
of the highest degree, which expressed themselves in uncon-
trollable hatred of all who were intellectually above him.

Yezhov [the Old Bolshevik related] was the right-hand
man to Kaganovich. While Kaganovich might have been
just as able to make his way by honest means, there can
be no such assumption with respect to Yezhov. In the whole
of my long life, I have never encountered a more repulsive
personality than Yezhov's. When I look at him I am reminded irresistibly of the wicked urchins of the back
alleys of Rasterayeva Street, whose favorite occupation it
was to tie a piece of paper dipped in paraffin to a cat's
tail, set fire to it, and then watch with delight how the
terrified animal would tear down the street trying desperately but in vain to escape the approaching flames. I
do not doubt that in his childhood Yezhov amused himself
in just such a manner, and that he is now continuing to do
so in different forms. It is only necessary to observe with
what ecstasy he badgers any of the old Oppositionists
whenever he has the chance. It seems that, for a long time,
Yezhov had found it difficult to make his way in the Party.
He was disliked and despised. A great store of bitterness
had accumulated in his soul against all those who had
formerly occupied prominent posts in the Party—against
intellectuals who were good speakers (he is a poor orator),
against writers whose books achieved popularity (he could
never write anything except an informer's report), against
old revolutionists proud of their past (he had never worked
in the underground movement). No man could be more
fit to function in this period, when the persecution of Old
Bolsheviks has become the official slogan of the "rejuvenated" Bolshevist Party. The only talent with which nature
has abundantly endowed him is his talent for intrigue
behind the scenes. And he misses no opportunity to use
this talent. Nearly ten years of work in the apparatus of

the Orgburo and the Central Control Committe of the Party have enabled him to acquire extraordinary knowledge of the personal characteristics of the active workers in the Party machine. He congenitally detests all those who evince the slightest measure of independence or steadfastness in their opinions, and systematically removes them from their posts, substituting instead persons ready to execute without question any orders from above. Of course, he is able to pursue this policy because it has the blessing of higher-ups, but to the manner of its enforcement Yezhov adds the stamp of his own character. As a consequence, he has managed in the past ten years to set up a network composed of his trustworthy satellites. There are many of them, in all branches of the Party apparatus, in all Soviet administrative organs, not excluding the NKVD, and in the Army. These persons have proved particularly useful to him now when he has become chief of the NKVD, the governing staff of which he has radically "rejuvenated."

This sketch of Nikolai Yezhov's personality and his style of work was drawn at the end of 1936, when Yezhov wielded enormous power. In his secret speech, made two decades later, Khrushchev referred to Yezhov several times in connection with the Great Purge period of 1937-38, known as the period of the *Yezhovshchina*—the maddest and bloodiest in the history of the Red Terror. Khrushchev did not care to explain how it was possible that this sadistic maniac could have gained almost unlimited control over the population of the "most democratic country of the world," as the Soviet Union has been referred to since 1936 when the so-called Stalinist Constitution was introduced. This reluctance on Khrushchev's part is understandable, for a frank discussion of this question would immediately have shown that the Soviet system itself naturally facilitates the emergence of a Stalin and a Yezhov, a fact which the official line dogmatically denies without presenting proof.

But there was also a personal motive for Khrushchev's refusal to discuss this delicate matter. Khrushchev had met Yezhov in 1931, when he was First Secretary of the Bauman District Party organization, and Yezhov was a member of the Party Committee. The same relationship between the two continued when Khrushchev became First Secretary of the Moscow City Party Committee, and Yezhov one of its members. Thus, on two occasions in his career, Khrushchev was Yezhov's boss.

The events which took place immediately after the shot fired on December 1, 1934, followed each other with kaleidoscopic rapidity. The news was received in Moscow around five o'clock in the afternoon, but, according to Khrushchev, already "on the evening of December 1, 1934, on Stalin's initiative [without the approval of the Politburo—which gave its nominal approval two days later] the Secretary of the Central Executive Committee [Avel S. Yenukidze] signed the following directive:

" '1. Investigative agencies are directed to speed up the cases of those accused of the preparation or execution of acts of terror.

" '2. Judicial organs are directed not to hold up the execution of death sentences pertaining to crimes of this category in order to consider the possibility of pardon, because the Presidium of the Central Executive Committee of the U.S.S.R. does not consider possible the receiving of petitions of this sort.

" '3. The organs of the Commissariat of Internal Affairs [NKVD] are directed to execute the death sentence against criminals of the above mentioned category immediately after the passage of sentence.' " [6]

The "directive" Khrushchev had read to the delegates of the Twentieth Party Congress was actually the text of an unsigned communiqué printed in Soviet newspapers on December 4, 1934. The actual decree, formally signed by the Chairman of the Presidium of the Central Executive Committee of the U.S.S.R., Mikhail I. Kalinin, and its Secretary, Avel S. Yenukidze, appeared in the press the next day, December 5, 1934. The introductory sentence of the communiqué, which Khrushchev omitted citing, reads as follows:

"The Presidium of the Central Executive Committee of the U.S.S.R. at its session of December 1 of the current year adopted a decree by virtue of which it is prescribed . . ." After the introduction followed the text Khrushchev quoted in his report. While the communiqué related the contents of the decree only in general terms, the decree itself is far more important for these details: the investigation period in "cases of terror organizations and terror acts against workers of the Soviet power" was not to exceed ten days; "the act of indictment should be handed over to the defendants twenty-four hours before the court proceedings"; "the court proceedings should be held without the participation of the parties involved"; and "appealing the sentences as well as pleas for pardon should not be permitted."

Khrushchev's version of the Kirov case is confusing, if compared with the official Soviet data published on the subject in the first days of December, 1934. If Khrushchev's account is correct that on the evening of December 1, 1934, Yenukidze signed the decree "on Stalin's initiative," then why was it not published the next day, as decrees of the Central Executive Committee of the U.S.S.R. usually were, and why was it necessary to come out three days later with a preliminary communiqué and to delay the publication of the decree itself for another day? It seems that Khrushchev was, in the first place, interested in blaming Stalin's initiative in issuing what is possibly a unique decree in the history of legislation. This would explain his remark that the Politburo "nominally" approved it only two days later. It is possible that the decree was Stalin's invention prepared in advance by him and his close associates in the Party secretariat—Kaganovich and Zhdanov—but the fact that it was not published until December 5 shows that the delay was necessary to get the approval of the other members of the Politburo. It is very probable that Kalinin, the Chairman of the Presidium of the Central Executive Committee and member of the Politburo, was reluctant to sign the decree unless it was first approved by his Politburo colleagues. Thus the approval was far from "nominal." Khrushchev merely called it so in 1956, in order to attenuate the responsibility which the 1956 ruling group, harboring in its midst three members of the 1934 Politburo, shared with the late dictator for the "Kirov Law," as the decree is often called.

This attitude which runs all the way through Khrushchev's speech explains another otherwise inexplicable point. Blaming Stalin for the decree, Khrushchev called it a "directive." This was perhaps done in order not to publicize the dreadful particulars of the decree with which Khrushchev's relatively young audience in 1956 was hardly familiar. The other, and certainly the most important, reason for hiding the actual decree was the fact that it was still in force when Khrushchev delivered his 1956 report, and, what is even more significant, the "collective" rulers themselves used the decree to do away with their former associate, Lavrenti P. Beria.

The decree of December 1, 1934, gave the green light to the NKVD to exploit Nikolayev's shot and to spread fear and uncertainty all over the country through execution of people who could not have had any connection with the Kirov assassination for the simple reason that they had been imprisoned at the time it happened. On December 5, thirty-seven men were shot in Leningrad and twenty-nine in Moscow;[7] on December 11, nine were executed in Minsk;[8] and on December 15, twenty-eight were shot in the Ukraine.[9] One hundred and three persons in all were executed in two weeks for alleged involvement in the preparation of terror acts against Soviet officials. In the meantime, Andrei Y. Vishinsky fabricated an indictment not only against Nikolayev, but also against thirteen alleged accomplices of whom ten, despite tortures, emphatically denied any relation to the Kirov affair. Vishinsky signed the indictment on December 25, and on December 28-29, all fourteen were "tried" and immediately executed.[10]

The shot fired in Leningrad and the decree of December 1, 1934, were necessary links in the chain of events which started after Lenin's death—events that brought about the gradual development of the cult of Stalin and the establishment of his personal dictatorship. This objective could be achieved only through the elimination of such high-ranking Leninists as Kamenev, Zinoviev, Rykov, Bukharin, Radek, and others who were living witnesses to Stalin's mediocre role in the Bolshevik prerevolutionary movement, and had had far greater ideological and personal ties to Lenin than Stalin and, needless to say, Kaganovich, Molotov, or Mikoyan. Furthermore, it was necessary to liquidate another group of old Bolsheviks—Postyshev, Kosior, Eikhe, Chubar, Antonov-Ovseyenko, Krylenko, Pashukanis, and others, who, in spite of the fact that they never dissented from Stalin's general line and faithfully followed its zigs and zags, attempted to combine this unlimited faithfulness with a limited right to preserve human dignity and not be leveled down to faceless sycophancy. Finally, it was necessary to make room for the post-revolutionary newcomers—the Malenkovs, Khrushchevs, Berias, Bulganins—who, educated by Stalin and his close associates, Kaganovich and Molotov, readily accepted the "Stalinist style of work." These three political aims caused the Great Purge of 1935-38, started by the shot fired in Leningrad and the decree which followed.

Through the Kirov decree Stalin and his close companions-in-arms created the basis on which any case against real or imaginary enemies could be fabricated, or as Khrushchev put it, "the basis for mass acts of abuse against socialist legality," [11] —a formula which, by the way, shows the extreme fragility of this legality where a few men can create an illegal weapon to abuse it. In his speech Khrushchev posed as a pious defender of socialist legality. He went out of his way to show pity for the accused men who were "deprived of any possibility that their cases might be re-examined, even when they stated before the court that their 'confessions' had been secured by force, and when, in a convincing manner, they disproved the accusation against them." [12]

For understandable reasons Khrushchev cautiously avoided making any statements which would imply that some of his colleagues of 1956—Kaganovich, Malenkov, and Molotov—were to some extent involved in the crimes of the Stalin era. Now, however, after the Great (and for the time being, bloodless) Purge of June, 1957, there exists the possibility that at some future time Khrushchev will attempt to establish a closer link between the latter group and Stalin's crimes, and thus obscure his own responsibility.

Lenin's fear that Stalin "accumulated in his hands immeasurable power" and Lenin's doubt whether Stalin would "be always able to use this power with required care" were justified; for some twelve years, Stalin paid attention to Lenin's "serious admonitions," [13] but then extensively abused this power and "often violated all existing forms of morality and Soviet laws";[14] Stalin "originated the concept 'enemy of the people,'" and this term "made possible the use of the most cruel repression";[15] Stalin "put the Party and the NKVD up to the use of mass terror when the exploiting classes had been liquidated and when there were no serious reasons for the use of extraordinary mass terror";[16] and Stalin had sanctioned in the name of the Party "torture and oppression, which led to the slandering and self-accusation of innocent people."[17] Such was, in part, the indictment which Khrushchev hurled against the late dictator. Khrushchev did not explain why and how this sudden change from a good and high-principled Leninist into an amoral tyrant could have taken place. The reason for this omission is obvious. The slightest attempts to explain this mysterious metamorphosis would have implicated him and thus have been tantamount to a false step on the tightrope.

Khrushchev did, however, raise the highly significant question of the distribution of guilt between Stalin and Yezhov.

"We," Khrushchev said, "are justly accusing Yezhov for the degenerate practice of 1937. But we have to answer these questions: Could Yezhov have arrested Kosior, for instance, without the knowledge of Stalin? Was there an exchange of opinion or a Politburo decision concerning this? No, there was not, as there was none regarding other cases of this type. Could Yezhov have decided such important matters as the fate of eminent Party figures? No, it would be a display of naiveté to consider this the work of Yezhov alone. It is clear that these matters were decided by Stalin, and that without his orders and his sanction, Yezhov could not have done this."[18]

An uninformed reader of this passage from Khrushchev's report would be inclined to assume that Khrushchev himself had at the time been a powerless, insignificant Party member and that, because of his inconspicuous position in the Party, he survived the ordeal staged by Stalin and Yezhov. There is, however, sufficient material showing that Khrushchev played a special role in creating the political and psychological climate needed to make Stalin's crimes possible. On January 31, 1934, ten months before the assassination of Kirov and the beginning of the Great Purge of 1935-38, at a mass meeting in Moscow, officially said to have been attended by one million people, Khrushchev declared:

"On the way to the construction of a classless society, no working man, no working woman should forget that a classless society can be won only in struggle. Under no circumstances should vigilance be diminished, Comrades! We must strain all our forces and triple our vigilance!" [19]

Khrushchev repeated this cry for vigilance in almost every speech he made before, during, and after the Great Purge of 1935-38. In June, 1936, Khrushchev urged the Moscow Party workers to practice "more vigilance and revolutionary watchfulness." He caustically ridiculed the "loafers who substitute empty talk for vigilance, who write resolutions about vigilance and do not notice the enemies and double-dealers in their own ranks." [20] On March 16, 1937, in his report to the Moscow Party workers, Khrushchev elaborated on his concept of vigilance:

> Sometimes a man sits, and enemies crawl around him, almost step on his feet, but he does not notice them and puffs himself up: "Among the personnel under my jurisdiction there are no wreckers and strangers." He says so not because of the absence of enemies, but because of his deafness and political blindness caused by the idiotic sickness—heedlessness. [21]

On May 23, 1937, at the Moscow City Party conference, Khrushchev assailed those economic workers who "do not see the ears of counterrevolutionary enemies stick out from their pockets. . . . Not for one minute should we forget that an insignificant group of people sitting next to us and pretending to be our friends, that this group of despicable dregs of mankind do not dare to fight openly, because they know that the masses would immediately raze them to the ground. That is why the enemy goes underground, puts on the mask of a friend in order to destroy our socialist economy and undermine the might of our country," Khrushchev declared. He also pointed out that "enemies of the people" were found even among those Party members whose membership cards had been checked and exchanged only recently, and that the "enemy could have been exposed much sooner had the Party organizations showed greater vigilance." [22]

The last statement is of particular interest with regard to an alleged "enemy of the people," Yan Borisovich Gamarnik. Born in 1894, Gamarnik had joined the Bolshevik Party in 1916, distinguished himself in the Civil War, and risen to the position of Deputy People's Commissar of the Army and Navy (assisting Voroshilov) and chief of the Political Administration of the Army. At four consecutive Party congresses he was elected a member of the Central Committee. On May 28, 1937, he was elected to the Moscow City Party Committee,[23] and there can be no doubt that Gamarnik, like all other candidates to that body, had been previously cleared by Khrushchev himself, since he was its First Secretary. Three days later, Gamarnik committed suicide. The event was reported in the last column of the last page of *Pravda*, June 2, as follows:

"On May 31, former member of the Central Committee of the All-Union Communist Party (Bolshevik) Yan. B. Gamarnik, entangled in connections with anti-Soviet elements and obviously afraid of being exposed, committed suicide."

On June 5, *Pravda* editorially called Gamarnik a "Trotskyite degenerate," and on the same day in a speech delivered before the Fifth Moscow Province Party Conference, Khrushchev assailed Gamarnik as an "enemy of the people" with these words:

Only recently, the Moscow City Party Conference took place, and, on the basis of wide intra-Party democracy, elections to the City Party Committee were carried out, to which reliable [checked] Bolsheviks, faithful to the cause of the Party, have been elected. Nevertheless, a Trotskyite betrayer, a traitor of the Motherland, the enemy of the people, Gamarnik, also got into the City Party Committee. This fact shows again that the enemy foully disguises himself and carries on his subversive activity in the deep underground. . . . But let the enemies know that, no matter how deep they sit in their burrows, we will unmask and annihilate them, and reduce to dust every last one of them, and disperse them to the wind so that not even a trace will remain of these damned betrayers of and traitors to the socialist Motherland.[24]

Six days later it was officially announced that nine Marshals of the Soviet Union, headed by Tukhachevsky and including Gamar-

nik, had allegedly spied for an "unfriendly foreign power." *
Thus, Khrushchev charged Gamarnik with treason even before
the investigation was concluded. After Stalin's death Gamarnik
was posthumously rehabilitated as an "honest Communist."

Khrushchev's cries for vigilance were not so much invitations
to report the "enemies" as to find them under all circumstances
—not because they actually existed, but because theoretically
they *had to* exist and "crawl around and almost step on one's
feet." On the other hand, these admonitions unmistakably prove
that the Party machine, and particularly the First Party Secretaries, worked hand in hand with the NKVD, and, in Khrushchev's case, with Yezhov himself, whom he accused in 1956 of
"degenerate practices," but whom he described in 1938 as "our
Nikolai Ivanovich Yezhov" under whose leadership the enemies
of the people were being annihilated.[25] Khrushchev's statements
made in the 'thirties show that he was not sincere when, in his
1956 speech to the Twentieth Party Congress, he criticized Stalin
for his "attempt at theoretical justification of the mass terror
policy, under the pretext that as we march toward socialism the
class war must allegedly sharpen."[26] Nor is Khrushchev's claim
true that the concept "enemy of the people" was Stalin's own
invention:

> Stalin originated the concept "enemy of the people." This
> term automatically rendered it unnecessary that the ideo-
> logical errors of a man or men engaged in a controversy be
> proved; this term made possible the usage of the most cruel
> repression, violating all norms of revolutionary legality,
> against anyone who in any way disagreed with Stalin,
> against those who were only suspected of hostile intent,
> against those who had bad reputations. This concept, "enemy
> of the people," actually eliminated the possibility of any
> kind of ideological fight or the making of one's views known
> on this or that issue, even those of a practical character.[27]
>
> We must assert that in regard to those persons who in
> their time had opposed the Party line, there were no suffi-

---

* After World War II, reliable German sources disclosed that the case
was fabricated by the Gestapo and transmitted to the Soviet NKVD.

ciently serious reasons for their physical annihilation. The formula, "enemy of the people," was specifically introduced for the purpose of physically annihilating such individuals.[28]

But in his speeches delivered during the Great Purge, Khrushchev himself widely used the term "enemy of the people." It was Khrushchev, Kaganovich, and a few other high-ranking Party officials of the Moscow organization who used this term as early as December 2, 1934, in a letter to the Leningrad Party organization immediately after the Kirov assassination, where they referred to Kirov's murderer as a "rascal secretly sent by the enemies of the people."[29] It is impossible to verify whether Stalin actually was the originator of this concept, but it is established that Khrushchev and Kaganovich used it before the Great Purge started, and that, after the "enemies of the people" who allegedly organized the assassination of Kirov had been tried and executed in August, 1936, this concept became the foundation for "violating all norms of revolutionary legality." It is, therefore, likely that Khrushchev and Kaganovich originated the concept and recommended it to Stalin.

In the second half of the 'thirties the concept, "enemy of the people," was employed wherever it was needed to carry out important campaigns. A case in point were the preparations for the 1937 elections to the Soviets on the basis of the 1936 "Stalinist Constitution." These preparations took place at a time when, as Khrushchev put it in his 1956 speech, "mass arrests and deportations of many thousands of people, execution without trial and without normal investigation created conditions of insecurity, fear and even desperation."[30] In such an atmosphere there certainly was no danger that even the most hard-boiled anti-Communist could and would have challenged the candidates put forward by the Party. Nevertheless, Khrushchev used this campaign in order to intensify the atmosphere of "insecurity, fear, and even desperation" which two decades later he was to ascribe exclusively to the doings of Stalin and Yezhov. In a report which Khrushchev delivered before the Moscow Party workers on July 5, 1937, he urged them to "pull out into the daylight the small roots of the enemies which still remain here and there and to annihilate all of them." And the resolution adopted on Khrush-

chev's report clearly stressed the connection between Khrushchev's appeal and the forthcoming elections:

"Every Party and non-Party Bolshevik ought to remember that
the enemies of the people, the scum of the smashed exploiting
classes—the Japanese and German fascist agents, the Trotskyites,
Zinovievites and Rightists—these spies, diversionists, and murderers will use all means in attempting to exploit the elections for
their hostile counterrevolutionary purposes. The meeting of the
Party activists underlines that the unmasking, extirpation, and
crushing of all enemies of the people is the most important condition for successfully carrying out the elections to the Soviets,
for the realization of the Stalinist Constitution, and, for the
further triumphant progress of our country to Communism." [31]
And in an address to Stalin, the Moscow Party workers pledged
to prepare the elections in such a manner that "no enemies of
the people will be allowed to penetrate into the Soviet organs." [32]

Deeds followed words. On August 23, 1937, at the plenary
session of the Moscow Provincial Soviet, Khrushchev spoke on
"organizational matters." The result of this speech was a radical
shake-up of the leaders of the Moscow Provincial Soviet. Filatov,
its chairman, was "very strongly criticized" for "showing political
carelessness in his work." [33] In 1937, an accusation of "political
carelessness" was only a step short of a charge of being an
"enemy of the people." Filatov disappeared from the political
scene. His fate is unknown.

In his secret speech of 1956, Khrushchev emphasized that
until the 'thirties, Stalin had followed Lenin's method of persuasion and that "even during the progress of the furious ideological
fight against the Trotskyites, the Zinovievites, the Bukharinites,
and others, extreme repressive measures were not used—the fight
was on ideological grounds." But "some years later," Khrushchev
continued, "when socialism in our country was fundamentally
completed, when the exploiting classes had been generally
liquidated, when the Soviet social structure had radically changed,
when the social basis for political movements and groups hostile
to the Party had violently contracted, when the ideological opponents of the Party had long since been defeated politically—
then the repression directed against them began." [34] "It is clear,"
said Khrushchev, "that at the very time of socialist victory there

was no basis for mass terror in the country." [35]

It was precisely during the period of mass terror (1935-38) that Khrushchev rapidly climbed higher and higher in his Party career. In 1935, in addition to the secretaryship of the Moscow City Party Committee, he was given the post of First Party Secretary of the entire Moscow province. In January, 1938, when the Purge reached its peak, he was selected by Stalin as an alternate member of the Politburo, and soon afterward he was sent to the Ukraine and made First Secretary of the Central Committee of the Ukrainian Party to replace Stanislav V. Kosior, who soon became a victim of the Purge and whom Khrushchev posthumously described in 1956 as an "eminent Party and state worker" against whom "a case had been fabricated." [36] In 1939, when Khrushchev had fulfilled Stalin's assignment to complete the purge in the Ukraine, he became a full-fledged member of the Politburo.

It goes without saying that, occupying such important positions in the Party, Khrushchev was aware of the fact that there was no need "to annihilate such people" as his predecessors in the Ukraine, Kosior and Postyshev. Yet, he must have been personally involved in cleaning up their followers from the Ukraine. Furthermore, among all prominent survivors of Stalin, Khrushchev was the most vociferous mouthpiece of Stalin's terror policy. Khrushchev used the most elaborate language, which surpassed that of the General Prosecutor Vishinsky, to whip up hatred against the victims. On June 9, 1936, Khrushchev urged that the workers of the Moscow City Party organization become crusaders of hatred of the "enemies" and promoters of love for Stalin. He said:

"Let us with greater energy and persistence cultivate in the masses hatred against the counterrevolutionary Trotskyites, Zinovievites, and the remnants of the Right-wing deviationists, and let us at the same time cultivate in the masses love for the *vozhd* and teacher, Comrade Stalin." [37] In August, 1936, came the trial and execution of the Zinoviev-Kamenev-Smirnov group of sixteen men. Even before the trial came to an end, Khrushchev demanded death sentences:

"Everybody who rejoices in the successes achieved in our country, the victories of our Party led by the great Stalin, will find only one word for the mercenary fascist dogs of the Trotskyite-Zinovievite gang. This word is execution." It is noteworthy that in the same speech Khrushchev actually predicted the murder of Trotsky which Stalin agents committed in Mexico in 1940.

"Let the ringleader of this gang, the ally of the German Gestapo, Trotsky, be absent at the trial in Moscow—the anger of our people, the sentence of our proletarian court of justice will reach him anywhere." [38]

On November 23, 1936, the day when nine alleged "counterrevolutionary Trotskyites" were executed in Kemerovo, Khrushchev, delivering a speech at the Fourth Extraordinary Congress of Moscow Province Soviets, made the following statement:

> The working people of Moscow city and province . . . fervently approve the fair sentences published today in the press handed down by the Soviet court on the enemies of the people, the foul gang of counterrevolutionary Trotskyites. We draw our proletarian sword to chop off the heads of the loathsome creatures, double-dealers and murderers, agents of fascism. . . . The mad beast must be finished off. [39]

In January, 1937, when the Supreme Court announced thirteen death sentences and long prison terms against the Piatakov-Radek-Sokolnikov group, the Moscow Party Committee, headed by Khrushchev, organized a mass rally in Red Square where, according to *Pravda*, "more than two hundred thousand working people of the capital demonstrated their solidarity with the sentence of the Supreme Court." Khrushchev, "received with stormy applause," delivered the opening speech. This speech is noteworthy for Khrushchev's evil temper, as well as for its vocabulary. Here are some excerpts:

> Comrade workers, men and women, engineers, employees, men of science and art, and all working people of our country! We are gathered here, on Red Square, to raise our proletarian voice in complete support of the sentence passed by the Military Collegium of the Supreme Court against the enemies of the people, the traitors of the Motherland, the betrayers of the workers' cause, the spies, the diversionists, agents of fascism, the vile, despicable Trotskyites.
> Here on Red Square, before all the peoples of the Soviet

land, before the workers of the whole world, we approve this sentence and declare that whatever enemy tries to stop our victorious movement forward to a Communist society will be crushed by us and annihilated!

Judas-Trotsky and his gang intended to turn over the Ukraine, the Maritime, and the Amur regions to the German and Japanese imperialists and to turn our blooming Motherland into a colony of German and Japanese imperialism.

Like their bosses, the Trotskyite serfs counted only on the defeat of the U.S.S.R. in a war with the German and Japanese imperialists; they strove to hasten that war and to prepare for the defeat of the U.S.S.R. They set off explosions in factories; they spied for the fascist secret service. They killed and poisoned workers and Red Army men and they disrupted transport, being paid for this by the Japanese secret service. The Trotskyite murderers trafficked with the blood of the fighters of our valiant Red Army!

The Trotskyite clique was nothing but a gang of spies and mercenary murderers, diversionist wreckers, agents of German and Japanese fascism. There rises a stink of carrion from the vile, base, Trotskyite degenerates!

The sentence passed on these Trotskyite murderers, diversionists, and agents of fascism is a warning to all enemies of the people, to all those who might conceive the idea of lifting their hands against our Stalin, our achievements, our power. . . .

The enemy of mankind, the mad dog, the murderer Trotsky is a true ally of the fascists, an instigator of a world war. The agents of the enemies of peace, the agents of the imperialists, the instigators of war have been caught red-handed by this trial. . . .

The despicable ringleaders and the members of the Trotskyite gang have received deserved punishment for the black betrayal of the Motherland. The loathsome Trotskyite creature has been crushed in the Soviet Union. But this must not dull our vigilance; on the contrary, we should become more vigilant and increase still further our work in all fields of socialist construction in order to finish off and wipe out all remnants of these vile murderers, fascist agents, Trotskyites, Zinovievites, and their right-wing accomplices." [40]

In his 1956 speech to the Twentieth Party Congress, Khrushchev repeatedly stressed that the physical annihilation of the Trotskyites, Zinovievites, Bukharinites, and others had been unnecessary after their political isolation and ideological defeat. He recalled how Lenin had "patiently" handled the Opposition, how he had admitted Kamenev and Zinoviev to "highly responsible Party tasks" in spite of the fact that they "disclosed to the enemy the decision of the Central Committee to stage the [October, 1917] uprising," which was "treason against the Party and against the Revolution." He also recalled that Lenin never considered having them arrested and certainly not having them shot.[41] Furthermore, Khrushchev stated as a matter of fact that "many Party, Soviet, and economic workers who were branded in 1937-38 as 'enemies of the people' had actually never been enemies, spies, wreckers, etc., but always honest Communists; they had only been so stigmatized and, often, no longer able to bear barbaric torture, had charged themselves (at the order of the investigative judges-falsifiers) with all kinds of grave and unlikely crimes."[42] Khrushchev also expressed his "deep conviction" that many of those whom he had called "loathsome Trotskyite creatures" two decades earlier, and whom he had helped to annihilate, would have been alive if Lenin had lived. He said:

> Let us take the example of the Trotskyites. At present, after a sufficiently long historical period, we can speak about the fight with the Trotskyites with complete calm, and can analyze this matter with sufficient objectivity. After all, around Trotsky there were people whose origin cannot be, by any means, traced to a bourgeois society. Part of them belonged to the Party intelligentsia and a certain part were recruited from among the workers. We can name many individuals who, in their time, joined the Trotskyites; however, these same individuals took an active part in the workers' movement before the Revolution, during the Socialist October Revolution itself, and also in the consolida-

tion of the victory of this greatest of revolutions. Many of them broke with Trotskyism and returned to Leninist positions. Was it necessary to annihilate such people? We are deeply convinced that, had Lenin lived, such an extreme method would not have been used against many of them.[43]

It is doubtful that the complete archives of the NKVD and the Party will ever be opened to show just what share any of the Communist leaders had in the bloody purges of the 'thirties. It is, however, easy to prove that Khrushchev topped the "incorrigible" Stalinists—Molotov, Malenkov, and Kaganovich—who are now being accused of having "committed the violations of revolutionary legality during the period of mass repressions,"[44] in propagandizing and popularizing the massacre, and in inciting the basest instincts in the people. While Yezhov, Vishinsky, and Malenkov had been instrumental in the "preparation" of the cases, Khrushchev was the Preacher of Terror. Preaching Stalin's crimes was not, however, Khrushchev's sole role in the Purges. As Party boss in the Soviet capital and its province, he himself successfully "exposed" the "enemies of the people" and urged others to do so. This must have been the reason why, at the time the Purge reached its climax, Stalin selected Khrushchev to complete it in the Ukraine. And this must also have been the reason why Khrushchev became angry when asked at the National Press Club in Washington in September, 1959, to confirm or to deny a rumor that a delegate to the Twentieth Party Congress asked him what he was doing while Stalin was committing his crimes.

10

Faceless Sycophants and Men with a Spark of Honesty

From February 23 to March 5, 1937, a plenary session of the Party Central Committee took place in Moscow. On March 6, Soviet newspapers published a sixty-word announcement informing the Soviet people that the session had discussed the tasks of the Party in connection with the forthcoming elections to the Supreme Soviet on the basis of the new Constitution; questions of "economic and Party construction" followed by "appropriate decisions"; and, finally, the question of the "anti-Party activity" of Bukharin and Rykov, leading to a decision to expel them from the Party. Only one resolution on the first item (preparation for the elections) was added to this communiqué, a resolution that sounded out of key in the light of the Great Purge which, under Yezhov's direction, raged in the country. The resolution pointed out that as a result of the introduction of "universal, equal, and direct election rights with secret voting, the "dictatorship of the proletariat becomes more flexible," its base "wider," and that it is, therefore, necessary to practice "consistent democracy" in the Party, to create conditions under which all Party organs might regain their "electivity," and to give up the practice of having these Party organs selected by local Party leaders. The resolution also cited the "shameful negligence of Party and political work" and mentioned that examples of "wrong leadership" had been discovered in many regional and provincial Party organizations. Two were specifically mentioned: the Kiev provincial organization and the Azov-Black Sea regional organization. The resolution ended with an appeal to Party organs to "carry out fully and unconditionally the principles of intra-Party democracy."

Now, two decades later, the meaning of this resolution becomes clear. Least of all was it intended to loosen the grip on Party membership. It was directed against the local Party leaders who had gained prestige within the Party and had built up their little empires. It was a signal for launching an attack against potential "enemies of the people." The singling out of the Kiev organization was of particular importance for Khrushchev's political career: ten months later he was chosen by Stalin to become his vicar in the Ukraine. No further accounts of what went on at this plenary session were available until February, 1956, when Khrushchev made some interesting statements illuminating the atmosphere which had reigned at this session and the behavior of one of its members, Pavel Petrovich Postyshev, who was at the time First Secretary of the criticized Kiev Party organization and Second Secretary of the Ukrainian Central Committee. A comparison of Khrushchev's statements with facts already known makes it possible to gain more understanding of the events which preceded and followed this historical session.

One of these events which took place practically on the eve of the session was the death of the fifty-year-old Grigori (Sergo) Konstantinovich Ordzhonikidze, a prominent Politburo member and People's Commissar of Heavy Industry. The official medical bulletin stated that on February 18, "during his afternoon rest he suddenly felt ill" and "a few minutes later death occurred as a result of a heart attack." The bulletin was signed by G. Kaminski, the People's Commissar of Health, Dr. I. Khodorovsky, chief of the Medical and Sanitary Administration of the Kremlin, and Dr. L. Levin, a consultant of that Administration.[1] In his February, 1956, speech Khrushchev came out with another version of Ordzhonikidze's death. "Beria," he said, "had cleared from his path all persons who could possibly interfere with him." As "Ordzhonikidze had always been an opponent of Beria," Stalin "permitted the liquidation of Ordzhonikidze's brother and brought Ordzhonikidze himself to such a state that he was forced to commit suicide."[2]

It is, however, doubtful that Beria was involved in Ordzho-

nikidze's death. In 1937, Beria was still Party boss in Transcaucasia, and he came to Moscow only in 1938, to replace Yezhov.
Beria's influence in the Kremlin was probably below that of
Khrushchev, who had become an alternate member of the Politburo one year before Beria, and a full-fledged member seven
years before Beria. Khrushchev's assertion that Ordzhonikidze
was "always an opponent of Beria" is hardly compatible with the
fact that when Ordzhonikidze's fiftieth birthday was widely feted
on October 28, 1936, with *Pravda* devoting five of its six pages
to this event, it was Beria's four-column tribute that was conspic-
uously displayed on the second page of the paper.[3] Whether
suicide was the actual cause of Ordzhonikidze's death remains
uncertain, but Khrushchev's revelation shows how justified were
the many rumors to the effect that Ordzhonikidze did not die
a natural death, but was murdered on Stalin's order. The fact
that the circumstances under which Ordzhonikidze died had
been and perhaps still are kept secret helps explain the disappearance of all three signatories of the medical bulletin. Dr. L.
Levin was accused of poisoning Maxim Gorky and executed with
seventeen other defendants in the Bukharin-Rykov trial; the
other two signatories—Health Commissar Kaminski and Dr.
Khodorovsky—were ousted from their posts in 1937 and disappeared. There remain, however, witnesses who must know the
real cause of Ordzhonikidze's death. These witnesses are Khrushchev and Bulganin: they were members of the official committee
which arranged the funeral of the dead Politburo member. Stalin
who, according to Khrushchev, forced Ordzhonikidze to commit
suicide, must have had complete confidence in Khrushchev and
Bulganin who, as members of the funeral committee, were in
a position to know the real cause of Ordzhonikidze's death.

In his speech at the funeral, Khrushchev, who was one of the
three speakers—the others were Molotov and Beria—used the
occasion to blast the "bourgeois dogs" who "furiously hate
the Party for its faithfulness to the working class and for its
mercilessness to its enemies," and blamed the Trotskyites for
Ordzhonikidze's death.

"It was they," Khrushchev sorrowfully exclaimed, "who struck
a blow to thy noble heart. Piatakov—the spy, the wrecker, the
enemy of the working people, the base Trotskyite—is caught red-

handed, caught and condemned, crushed like a reptile by the working class, but it was his counterrevolutionary work which hastened the death of our dear Sergo.

"Let us, Comrades, rally closer around our Leninist-Stalinist Party, around our great *vozhd*, Comrade Stalin, and with all passion of hatred of the enemy let us finish off these damned monsters, betrayers and traitors."[4]

The old Bolshevik Georgi L. Piatakov was one of the six most capable men in the Party mentioned in Lenin's testament and one of the thirteen defendants "tried" and executed six weeks before Ordzhonikidze's death. Thus in 1937, Khrushchev accused the old Leninist, Piatakov, executed as Stalin's enemy, of being responsible for the death of Ordzhonikidze; in 1956, Khrushchev, wearing the toga of a faithful Leninist, accused Stalin of being responsible for the death of Ordzhonikidze! In 1937, Khrushchev exploited Ordzhonikidze's death as a weapon against Stalin's enemies, asking the Muscovites to "finish them off" and to rally around the living *vozhd*, while in 1956, he used the same event as a tool against the dead *vozhd* and threw stones into the grave of Beria. In both cases he delivered a monologue; graves are silent.

Whatever the cause of Ordzhonikidze's death, his disappearance, like the deaths of Kirov, Gorky, and Kuibyshev, cleared from Stalin's path another opponent of his policy of "mass repressions." That Ordzhonikidze died five days before the plenary session of the Central Committee began its work is not accidental. The timing was very convenient for Stalin and Yezhov. Khrushchev's 1956 speech makes it clear that they planned to convince the members of the Central Committee of the necessity of enhancing the scope of the Purge and of accelerating its pace. It has always been known that the expulsion of Bukharin and Rykov from the Party and their being turned over to the NKVD was a major point of discussion. It has also been known that Stalin delivered the report "Deficiencies of Party Work and Methods for the Liquidation of the Trotskyites and of Other Two-faced Men," a report which, to use Khrushchev's words, "contained an attempt at theoretical justification of the mass terror policy under the pretext that, as we march forward toward socialism, class war must allegedly sharpen."[5] What is new is Khrushchev's disclosure that Yezhov also delivered a report entitled "Lessons Flowing from the Harmful Activity, Diversion, and Espionage of the Japanese-German Trotskyite Agents," and that the resolution passed on that report contained the following passage:

"The plenary session of the Central Committee of the All-Union Communist Party [Bolshevik] considers that all facts revealed during the investigation into the matter of an anti-Soviet Trotskyite center and its followers in the provinces show that the People's Commissariat of Internal Affairs [NKVD] *has fallen behind by at least four years** in an attempt to unmask these most inexorable enemies of the people."[6]

This resolution was a green light for the NKVD to catch up

---

* Piotr N. Pospelov, an alternate member of the Party Presidium, and in 1937 a member of the Party Control Commission and deputy chief of the Propaganda and Agitation Division of the Central Committee, in an article, "The Bolshevik Party in the Struggle Against the Enemies of Socialism" (*Pravda*, November 7, 1937), pointed out that a "number of Right-wing Trotskyite groups were exposed *a few years ago*," but the Party "did not succeed in reaching the real roots of these groups," and that "this was done later, in 1936-37." Pospelov identified one of these groups as the Riutin group. In 1956, Khrushchev accused Stalin of having forced Yezhov's nomination to the post of People's Commissar of Internal Affairs (NKVD), on the grounds that the OGPU, the predecessor of the NKVD, and its chief, Genrikh G. Yagoda, had "definitely" failed in unmasking the Trotskyite-Zinovievite bloc. "The OGPU is four years behind in this matter," Stalin cabled to Molotov and Kaganovich and other Politburo members from his vacation villa in Sochi. ("Secret speech of Khrushchev Concerning the Cult of the Individual" quoted from *The Anti-Stalin Campaign and International Communism* [New York: Columbia University Press, 1956], p. 26.) The fact that Pospelov mentioned Riutin throws some light on the whole matter. The Riutin affair came up at the end of 1932, i.e., exactly four years before Yezhov's appointment. According to the well-informed "Old Bolshevik" whose testimony is extensively quoted elsewhere in this book, Riutin produced at that time a 200-page program, fifty pages of which contained a severe criticism of Stalin. This program fell into the hands of the OGPU, but, since Riutin was an old Party leader, the affair was taken up in the Politburo. Stalin demanded the death penalty for Riutin. "I can no longer recall," wrote the Old Bolshevik, "the actual division of opinion of the Politburo when this question was being considered. I only know that Kirov spoke with particular force against recourse to the death penalty. Moreover, he succeeded in winning the Politburo over to his view." The confrontation of Khrushchev's statements, Pospelov's article and the Old Bolshevik's testimony confirm that at least four Politburo members—Kirov, Ordzhonikidze, Kuibyshev, and Kosior voted against Stalin. Three of them—Kirov, Ordzhonikidze, and Kosior—died a violent death, while the case of Kuibyshev still remains a mystery. The above facts also show why Stalin was interested in the removal of these men.

with the neglected work. It seems that Yezhov's demand for more power touched off a heated discussion, as this plenary session of the Central Committee lasted eleven days—the longest session in the Stalin era. On the other hand, in his 1956 report Khrushchev said that many members of the Central Committee "actually questioned the rightness of the established course regarding mass repressions," and that Pavel P. Postyshev most ably expressed these doubts:

I have philosophized [Postyshev said] that the severe years of fighting have passed; Party members who have lost their backbones have broken down or have joined the camp of the enemy; healthy elements have fought for the Party. These were the years of industrialization and collectivization. I never thought it possible that after this severe era had passed, Karpov* and people like him would find themselves in the camp of the enemy. And now, according to the testimony, it appears that Karpov was recruited in 1934 by the Trotskyites. I personally do not believe that in 1934 an honest Party member who had marched the long road of unrelenting fight against enemies, for the Party and for socialism, would now be in the camp of the enemies. I do not believe . . . I cannot imagine how it would be possible to travel with the Party during these difficult years and then, in 1934, join the Trotskyites. It is an odd thing . . ."[7]

Postyshev, with a spark of honesty in his heart, expressed the doubts of millions of thinking people all over the world. He spoke in the name of tens of thousands of innocent people who already had lost their lives or were turned into living corpses by Yezhov's investigators, and he spoke in the name of those who lived in constant fear of a nocturnal raid. Postyshev even dared to retort to Stalin. When Stalin expressed his dissatisfaction with Postyshev and asked him, "What are you actually?" Postyshev answered clearly, "I am a Bolshevik, Comrade Stalin, a Bolshevik."[8]

---

* Karpov was a worker in the Ukrainian Central Committee whom Postyshev knew well.

Reporting Postyshev's answer to Stalin's question, Khrushchev remarked that Postyshev's reply had at first been considered a lack of respect for Stalin; later it was considered a harmful act and consequently resulted in Postyshev's annihilation. Postyshev was not alone in challenging Stalin and Yezhov. As Khrushchev said, there were many members who dared to question the justification for the bloody purge. According to Khrushchev, of the 139 full-fledged and alternate members of the Central Committee elected to that body at the Seventeenth Party Congress in February, 1934, ninety-eight persons or 70 per cent, were arrested and shot in 1937 and 1938.[9] There can be no doubt that many of these victims, still alive at the time when the February-March plenary session took place, either openly joined Postyshev in his desperate fight against the intensification of Stalin's terrorist measures, or tacitly supported him. In his concluding speech Stalin himself pointed out that there were seven points of "our organizational and political practice on which a full understanding has not been yet reached." There is indirect evidence that one of those who opposed Stalin and Yezhov was Stanislav V. Kosior, then First Secretary of the Ukrainian Party, who was arrested in 1938 and liquidated in 1940. In January of that year Stalin assigned Khrushchev to take Kosior's place. Twenty-eight years later, Khrushchev rehabilitated Kosior by returning him to the status of "comrade," and "eminent Party worker." In his 1956 de-Stalinization speech, Khrushchev tried to avoid a full explanation of his personal behavior and that of his colleagues from the Party Presidium at the time Postyshev attempted to oppose the annihilation of innocent people. But he could not entirely avoid the question of responsibility. He said: "Some comrades may ask us: 'Where were the members of the Politburo of the Central Committee? Why did they not assert themselves in time against the cult of the individual?' "[10] The best answer Khrushchev could find was that "the members of the Politburo viewed these matters in a different way at different times," namely, "during the first years," after Lenin's death, when Stalin "actively fought for Leninism against the enemies of Leninist theory" (that is, 1924-27), the "members of the Politburo" who survived Stalin wholeheartedly supported him; they also supported Stalin when he "started on a large scale the work of socialist industrialization of the country, agricultural collectivization, and the cultural revolution" (that is, in 1927-34); but later, when Stalin, "abusing his power more and more, began to fight eminent Party and government leaders and to use terroristic methods against honest people," [11] such as Kosior, Postyshev, and others, it had become impossible to oppose Stalin, because "Attempts at opposing groundless suspicions and charges resulted in the opponent falling victim to the oppression. This characterized the fall of Comrade Postyshev";[12] because "When Stalin believed in anyone or anything, then no one could say anything which was contrary to his opinion, anyone who dared express opposition would have met the same fate as Kaminski";[13] * because "When Stalin said that one or another should be arrested, it was necessary to accept on faith that he was an 'enemy of the people.' " [14] "It is clear," Khrushchev concluded, "that such conditions put every member of the Politburo in a difficult situation."[15] † In giving his reasons for Stalin's unopposed terror, Khrushchev mentioned only the helpless position of the "members of the Politburo." Thus, he implied that in the period under discussion (1937-38) he himself and Bulganin were less responsible since at the time they had not been members of that supreme Party body. Only four post-Stalin rulers—Kaganovich, Molotov, Voroshilov, and Mikoyan—belonged to the Politburo in 1937, at the time the historical February-March plenary session of the Central Committee took place, while Khrushchev joined that body in 1939, and Bulganin in 1946. It is noteworthy that in "mourning" Postyshev's annihilation, Khrushchev said in the same breath:

"In the situation which then prevailed I talked often with Nikolai Aleksandrovich Bulganin; once when we two were travel-

* Kaminski, People's Commisar of Public Health, was executed in 1937.

† When Khrushchev made these statements (February, 1956), Malenkov, Kaganovich, and Molotov belonged to the Kremlin's ruling circle. After the June, 1957, purge, their record was revised. The 1959 version of the *History of the CPSU* says that "it was not accidental" that they opposed Party measures toward the liquidation of the consequences of the cult of [Stalin's] personality. They did so "because they were involved in the mistakes caused by that cult" (*Istoria Kommunisticheskoi Partii Sovetskogo Soyuza* [Moscow. 1959], p. 654).

ing in a car, he said: 'It has happened sometimes that a man goes to Stalin on his invitation as a friend. And when he sits with Stalin, he does not know where he will be sent next, home or jail.' "[16]

Thus Khrushchev and Bulganin allegedly questioned Stalin's honesty and were in accord about his treacherous nature. This heart-to-heart conversation had allegedly taken place around 1937. At that time ultimate "vigilance" was the order of the day, and such a discussion of the *vozhd's* bad character must be regarded as entirely impossible, especially if carried on among Party officials, who were Yezhov's primary target. Khrushchev pointed out that he and Bulganin discussed the delicate issue "in a car," and not, let us say, in their apartments where walls might have ears. No doubt Khrushchev introduced this detail to make the story more believable. In reporting it, Khrushchev meant to single out himself and Bulganin from those other members of the 1956 Party Presidium who in 1937 had belonged to the Politburo, and also to impress the delegates of the Twentieth Party Congress with the "fact" that he had been in constant danger of becoming a victim of Stalin's suspicious character. Such an allegation is in direct contradiction of Khrushchev's record.

In 1934, at the Seventeenth Party Congress, Khrushchev was elected to the Central Committee. He must have attended the plenary session of that Committee in February-March, 1937, and heard Postyshev's daring remarks. What was Khrushchev's attitude toward these remarks? Did he support Postyshev and others in opposing Stalin and Yezhov and their policy of bloodletting, or did he wholeheartedly and unconditionally assist Stalin and Yezhov in overcoming the opposition? Was he searching his soul in the face of the moving sword of terror or did he placate Stalin's suspicions with showers of praise and assurances of unlimited faithfulness? These questions are answered by the fact that Khrushchev survived Stalin.

A totalitarian state has always put before politically minded people the alternative: either subservience or political, and in most cases, physical death. People with unswerving faith in principles, both political and moral, had to make way for sycophants. Some observers of Soviet history have conveyed the wrong impression that, using the most refined means of torture and brainwashing, the totalitarian regime has *always* succeeded in forcing its victims to give up their beliefs and converting them into soulless robots "cured" by Big Brother. No statistics are available with regard to the number of people who died because they refused to be "cured," but they numbered in the thousands. In 1956, Khrushchev agreed to readmit some of his former comrades into the canon of Communist saints, but, if they were to return to earthly life, they would undoubtedly express their disdain for those who assisted Stalin and Yezhov in pushing them to their graves.

III

On the Winding Road to Power

11

"Climbing Over Corpses"

Khrushchev's climb to power was an almost uninterrupted process from his arrival in Moscow in 1929. It was not easy for a postrevolutionary newcomer with no ideological and a poor educational background to gain a high position among old Bolsheviks whose revolutionary zeal was born in times of persecution and danger and strengthened by a doctrine whose standard bearers they were believed to be. Under "normal" political conditions Khrushchev would have been unable to make such a swift jump toward the higher Communist hierarchy. But the conditions were abnormal in the sense that intellectuality was not in high demand; the totalitarian dictatorship whose birth coincided with Khrushchev's arrival in the capital needed simple-minded people with overemphasized ambition, strong nerves, without scruples, ready to follow blindly the Party line drawn by Stalin and his closest collaborators and thus to help build the foundation for the rule of a single person. The Great Purge of the 'thirties was the touchstone by which the fitness of the newcomers for the incoming era had been tested. Khrushchev passed that test with distinction. When the year 1937 reached its end, the decision to admit Khrushchev to the highest Party body, the Politburo, was about to be made. But this was also the time when the bloody Purge reached its climax.

Nikolai Yezhov, the diminutive, long-eared maniac with the shrieking voice, still enjoyed unlimited authority to extort confessions from innocent people. The places of detention were

filled with men and women whose bodies ached from tortures
and whose minds approached the brink of insanity. Fear and
anguish stifled friendship and sympathy. The persistent, threatening appeals for vigilance, in which Khrushchev excelled, had
brought results. To avoid accusations of "faint-heartedness" and
"rotten liberalism," frightened men and women produced false
reports charging others with spying, wrecking, and counterrevolutionary acts. In one district in Kiev one man wrote sixty-
nine,[1] another over one hundred false reports;[2] in Odessa a man
fabricated 230 reports,[3] and in Poltava province one Communist
accused the entire membership of the Party organization to
which he belonged of being "enemies of the people." [4]

Yezhov was the hero of the day. On December 20, 1937, on
the occasion of the twentieth anniversary of the Cheka, the
Bolshoi Theatre was crowded with Stalin's supporters, and
Anastas Mikoyan, one of the present rulers, paid tribute to
Comrade Yezhov as a "talented, faithful pupil of Stalin, [a man
who] is beloved by the Soviet people, [and who] has achieved
the greatest victory in the history of the Party, a victory we
will never forget." Khrushchev, Kaganovich, Voroshilov, and
Molotov presided over this meeting and applauded warmly
when Mikoyan cried out: "Learn the Stalinist style of work
from Comrade Yezhov, as he learned it from Comrade Stalin." [5]
The same day, *Pravda* editorially greeted Yezhov with a "Long
live the faithful son of the people, the Stalinist People's Commissar, Nikolai Ivanovich Yezhov!" and carried news to the
effect that eight old Bolsheviks, among them Avel S. Yenukidze,
had been sentenced to death as "traitors to the Motherland." * [6]

---

* The fate of Avel S. Yenukidze is typical of how Stalin treated his old
"friends" who were witnesses to the minor role he had played in Transcaucasia in the early years of his political life. Yenukidze was two years
older than Stalin. He was one of the pioneers of the Baku Social Democratic organization and of the famous Baku underground printing plant.
After the Revolution of 1917, he had for seventeen years been secretary
of the Executive Committee of the Soviets of the R.S.F.S.R. and U.S.S.R.
An old friend of Stalin's, Yenukidze was chosen in 1929 to be one of the
four editors of an anthology on Stalin. In his memoirs, however, Yenukidze
made the mistake of omitting mention of Stalin as the founder of the Baku
organization and the printing plant. On January 16, 1935, in an article
published in *Pravda*, Yenukidze himself revised his biography in the *Large
Soviet Encyclopedia* to the effect that it was not he, Yenukidze, who played

It was around this time that Stalin chose Khrushchev to become his vicar in the Ukraine.

Attacking Beria, Khrushchev said in his February, 1956 speech:

"It has now been established that the villain had climbed up the government ladder over an untold number of corpses." [7]

This was certainly so. Beria's Chekist record in Transcaucasia probably surpassed many other records of the kind as far as brutality was concerned. This was the main reason for his advancement. But reading Khrushchev's statement one cannot help remembering that Khrushchev's appointment to the Ukraine in January, 1938, which really launched him on his career, was closely related to the annihilation of Pavel P. Postyshev and Stanislav V. Kosior, Politburo members and First and Second Secretaries of the Ukrainian Communist Party. In view of this relation, a brief look at the circumstances under which they were purged is required.

Postyshev's daring behavior at the February-March plenary session of the Central Committee in 1937, described in some detail in the preceding chapter, is all the more remarkable because he was aware of the fact that he was approaching his end; at the Thirteenth Ukrainian Party Congress (May-June, 1937), one of Postyshev's former "friends," a member of the

---

a role in the foundation of the organization but a group of other Georgian revolutionaries, including Stalin. It seems that Yenukidze did not realize how far Stalin wanted to go in falsifying his own biography. The fact that he was only mentioned in Yenukidze's recantation did not satisfy Stalin, since the role ascribed him was still too insignificant. Six weeks later, on March 3, 1935, Yenukidze was relieved from his post in Moscow "because of his promotion to the post of Chairman of the Transcaucasian Soviet Federative Socialist Republic." At that time Beria was Stalin's vicar in that Republic, and Yenukidze's "promotion" within Beria's domain—a "promotion" which never materialized—was a shrewd maneuver, since Beria was preparing "materials" denouncing Yenukidze for his playing down of Stalin's role in the history of the Transcaucasian Bolshevik movement. The next act in Yenukidze's tragedy took place at the plenary session of the Party Central Committee in June, 1935, when Yenukidze, a Party member since 1898, and member of the Central Committee, was expelled from the Party for his attempts to help relatives of NKVD victims. In his speech of June 10, 1935, Khrushchev informed the Moscow Party activists that "Yenukidze, having lost all qualities of a Bolshevik, wanted to play 'the good-hearted uncle' with regard to the enemies of our Party." (*Pravda*, June 13, 1935.)

Kiev Province Party Committee, M. S. Vasilenko, had revealed
Postyshev's resentment at the criticism which the All-Union
Party Central Committee in Moscow had leveled against "mistakes" of the Kiev Party organization on January 13, 1937.[8] This
was why Kaganovich was immediately dispatched to Kiev to
straighten out the situation. A plenary session of the Kiev Province
Party Committee was urgently convoked for January 17 with
the participation of Kaganovich in his capacity of Secretary of
the Party Central Committee. At this session, Postyshev was
relieved from his post of First Secretary of the Kiev Committee
"because of the impossibility of combining" this position with
that of the Second Secretary of the Ukrainian Central Committee.[9] The actual reason for Postyshev's dismissal was, of
course, not the duality of offices held by him. From 1930 to
1935, Kaganovich himself simultaneously controlled three Party
offices in Moscow, and Khrushchev repeated this performance
in Kiev in 1938, when he managed to carry the burden of first
secretaryship in the Central, Kiev Province, and Kiev City Party
Committees.

Postyshev was to be reduced, but his popularity among the
Party workers in Kiev and the Ukraine was the reason for
camouflaging the first blow Stalin dealt him through Kaganovich.
The second indirect attack at Postychev came at the beginning of
February when the name of Karpov, Postyshev's protégé, appeared in the Ukrainian press with the epithets "enemy of the
Party, loathsome Trotskyite."[10] For more than two weeks after
that about sixty prominent Kiev Party workers in political, educational, economic, and other fields, including a large number of
people who had worked under Postyshev, were labeled as enemies of the people, Trotskyites, and the like. On March 17,
twelve days after the plenary session in Moscow, Postyshev was
officially relieved of his post of Second Secretary of the Ukrainian
Party Central Committee "in connection with his transfer to
another job."[11] The other job was the secretaryship in the
Kuibyshev Province Party Committee. On January 20, 1938,
Postyshev was expelled from the Politburo, to which he had belonged as an alternate member for four years, and Khrushchev
was nominated to that position instead. Although the official
announcement still called Postyshev "comrade," there can be no

doubt that he already was under arrest, since his name entirely disappeared from the Soviet press after November 17, 1937.

The same issue of the Kiev *Visti* which reported Postyshev's dismissal from his post in the Ukrainian Party Central Committee (March 18, 1937) and editorially accused him of "political blindness" devoted half a page to Khrushchev's report on the results of the February-March plenary session which he had delivered two days earlier in Moscow. His speech was prominently displayed on page two, while the report on the same subject made by the Ukrainian leaders was not carried. Two days later, in an editorial, *Visti* repeated a motto from Khrushchev's speech. This was certainly not accidental: It seems that as early as March, 1937, Khrushchev was considered a man of influence in Kiev. It had not taken long before Khrushchev, who left Kiev in 1929 as a low-echelon worker, returned there as a ruler.

Following Postyshev's dismissal and arrest, Kosior still remained Party boss in the Ukraine, but his position was considerably weakened. On January 18, 1938, the newspapers announced that Kosior had been appointed deputy chairman of the Soviet Control Commission. This was not a favorable appointment; it was Stalin's kiss of death. Three months later, probably around the end of April, Kosior was arrested.* The investigating judge, Rodos, testified in February, 1956: "I was told that Kosior and Chubar† were people's enemies and for this reason, I, as an investigative judge, had to make them confess."[12] It was Khrushchev who informed the Twentieth Party Congress about Rodos' shocking testimony, but it was also Khrushchev who, in June, 1938, addressing the Fourteenth Ukrainian Party Congress in Kiev, said:

> The enemies of the people who sat in the leadership of the Central Committee of the Communist Party [Bolshevik] of the Ukraine and in the [Kiev] Provincial Party Committee knew very well that the stronger the Party organization, the more dangerous it is to the enemies of the working

* According to Khrushchev, another Politburo member, Robert I. Eikhe, was arrested on April 29, 1938. It is probable that Kosior was arrested at the same time, since his name was last mentioned in the Soviet press on that day.

† V. Y. Chubar, Politburo member, was arrested in the summer of 1938.

class and, first of all, to the Polish landlords and the German
barons. And therefore they—the Polish agents, the Pilsudchiks*—did everything in order to weaken the Bolshevik
discipline, to corrupt the Party organization." [13]

It is evident that in his diatribe against the "enemies of the
people who sat in the leadership of the Ukrainian Central Committee and in the Kiev obkom," Khrushchev had in mind Kosior
and Postyshev. The epithets, "the Polish agents, the Pilsudchiks,"
were, in all probability, reserved for Kosior, who was of Polish
origin.

At the same time that Khrushchev assailed Kosior, Rodos
"made him confess," and it was not long afterward that Khrushchev filled the vacancy of full-fledged member in the Politburo
vacated by Kosior's removal.

There are several reasons why such leading old Bolsheviks as
Postyshev and Kosior had to make way for the intellectual low-
brow, Khrushchev. One of the reasons was their intellectual
superiority and more independent thinking—a quality for which
there is no place in a totalitarian dictatorship. Another reason
was, as stated above, that in spite of their brutality, Postyshev
and Kosior, like Kirov and Ordzhonikidze, possessed a spark of
honesty in their hearts; it seems that they showed insufficient
readiness to go along in putting the label of "enemy of the
people" on just anybody at the whim of a Yezhov or even a
Stalin. Finally, the last but not least reason for their downfall was
their popularity among the Ukrainian Party workers and, in the
case of Postyshev, among the younger generation (Pioneers and
Komsomol). Stalin could not permit Kosior, Postyshev, and others
to be called "*vozhds* of the Ukrainian people," which had been the
case on several occasions.[14] In Stalin's time, this planet could
have only one *vozhd*. That Postyshev's fall was in part caused
by the violation of this rule is evident from a statement made by
one of his former "friends," N. N. Popov, who recanted but was
nevertheless liquidated. Popov said: "One of the reasons why
Comrade Postyshev became so quickly susceptible to intoxica-

---

* Joseph Pilsudski (1867-1935), the leader of Polish Socialist Party at
the end of the nineteenth and beginning of the twentieth centuries, became
virtual dictator of Poland after World War I.

tion with success was the noise which our press made around
his name."[15] S. A. Kudryavtsev, who succeeded Postyshev as
First Secretary of the Kiev Party Committee and who was purged
and liquidated after Khrushchev took over, made it more precise
by pointing out that the former leaders of the Committee had
"spent a great deal of energy . . . to build up their personal
authority."[16]

Khrushchev was aware of the danger of self-promotion, and
thus at the first appropriate occasion "promoted" Stalin instead
to the status of "*vozhd* of the Ukrainian people." This was done in
a resolution passed at the Fourteenth Ukrainian Party Congress.[17]
Furthermore, Khrushchev demonstrated his modesty by allowing
himself to be called only "glorious son of the proletarian
Donbas,"[18] "best son of our people."[19] These appellations, however, were used less frequently than those describing Khrushchev's closeness to Stalin: "faithful pupil of Stalin,"[20] "friend and
comrade-in-arms of I. V. Stalin,"[21] "Stalin's closest pupil and
comrade-in-arms,"[22] "Stalinist leader of the Ukrainian Bolsheviks,"[23] "closest companion-in-arms of the great Stalin, militant
leader of the Ukrainian Bolsheviks."[24]

"Modesty" was not the only advantage Khrushchev had over
his predecessors. Another more important advantage was his
greater ruthlessness and readiness in exposing and liquidating
the "enemies of the people." Actually the purge in the Ukraine
had not been greatly hampered by Postyshev and Kosior. As
everywhere else, Yezhov's terror machine worked well enough
in the Ukraine even before Khrushchev's arrival, but Stalin and
Yezhov were perfectionists, and the slightest obstruction capable
of slowing down the speed or impairing the smooth functioning
of the machine was not tolerated by them. They expected Khrushchev to do a better job than his predecessors. In a speech before
the Fourteenth Party Congress, Demyan S. Korotchenko, at the
time Chairman of the Ukrainian Council of People's Commissars
and at present alternate Party Presidium member, stated that
Khrushchev, "the best son of our [Ukrainian] people, the excellent Bolshevik, the Doniets miner," was sent by Stalin to the
Ukraine "to deal the final blow at all this Trotskyite, Bukharinite,
and bourgeois-nationalist gang in the Ukraine."[25]

While First Secretary of the Moscow Party Committee, Khrush-

chev probably possessed only limited authority in carrying out
the Great Purge, since Moscow was also the seat of the central
Party and government machines. The situation was different
in the republics and regions (*krais*) where the organs of the
NKVD worked in close contact with the top Party men, provided
that they enjoyed full confidence of the *vozhd*. There the local
NKVD chiefs did not undertake any important measures without
the approval of the First Party Secretaries.

The purge of top local Party officials was carried out by
Khrushchev with remarkable speed. S. A. Kudryavtsev, who had
become First Secretary of the Kiev Province Party Committee
after Postyshev's dismissal in January, 1937, and Politburo member
of the Ukrainian Party in June of the same year, was purged at
the end of that year and arrested as an "enemy of the people."
On April 17, 1938, Khrushchev purged Kudryavtsev's successor
and member of the Ukrainian Central Committee, D. M. Yev-
tushenko, and took over his position. The same procedure was
repeated with regard to the Kiev City Party Committee, of which
Khrushchev also became First Secretary. With the helping hand
of Mikhail Alekseevich Burmistenko,* whom Moscow had dispatched to the Ukraine together with Khrushchev to become
Second Secretary of the Ukrainian Central Committee. Khrushchev, appearing in many cases in person, purged practically all
top Party and government officials in the Ukrainian provinces.

Khrushchev's assignment called not only for full cooperation
with Yezhov's henchmen in the Ukraine but also for initiative in

---

* Born in 1902, Mikhail A. Burmistenko entered the Party in 1919. The
same year, at the age of seventeen, he became a Chekist and as such held
"responsible jobs" until 1922 in the Tambov and Penza regions, actively
participating in the suppression of "counterrevolutionary kulak rebellions."
(*Visti*, January 28, 1938.) From 1923 to 1926, Burmistenko worked as a
political worker in the Red Army. In 1929, he graduated from the Com-
munist Institute of Journalism (KIZh). From 1932 through 1935, he was
Party secretary in the Kalmuk Autonomous S.S.R. From January, 1936, to
January, 1938, he worked as instructor and then as deputy chief of the
Division of Leading Party Organs (ORPO) under Georgi M. Malenkov.
The ORPO was an instrumental part of the Great Purge machine, and
Burmistenko's appointment to the Ukraine as Second Secretary of the
Ukrainian Central Committee, was therefore, indicative. Burmistenko was
killed in World War II in 1941 (*Vazhneishie Operatsii Velikoi Otechestven-
noy Voiny*, 1941-45 [Moscow, 1950], p. 72).

exposing the "enemies of the people." In May, 1938, in a letter of consent to "run" for the Supreme Soviet, Khrushchev wrote: "I pledge to spare no efforts in seizing and annihilating all agents of fascism, the Trotskyites, Bukharinites, and all these despicable bourgeois nationalists on our free Ukrainian soil."[26]

Only a few months after his arrival it became clear that Stalin had not made a mistake when he selected Khrushchev for the job. The Ukrainian press and prominent Communist speakers soon described the situation on the Purge front in the following manner:

"The merciless uprooting of the enemies of the people—the Trotskyites, Bukharinites, bourgeois nationalists, and all other spying filth—began only after the Central Committee of the All-Union Communist Party (B) sent the unswerving Bolshevik and Stalinist, Nikita Sergeyevich Khrushchev, to the Ukraine to lead the Central Committee of the Ukrainian Communist Party (B)."[27]

This flattering statement in an editorial in *Bilshovik Ukrainy* was seconded by leading Communists such as A. S. Shcherbakov, at the time First Secretary of the Stalino Province Committee, who said:

I subscribe to the opinion of the comrades that a really merciless crushing of the enemies of the people in the Ukraine began after the Central Committee of the All-Union Communist Party (B) had dispatched Comrade Nikita Sergeyevich Khrushchev to lead the Ukrainian Bolsheviks.

Now the toiling people of the Ukraine can be assured that the crushing of the agents of the Polish landowners, the German fascists will be carried out to the end, that the enemies of the people, every one of them, will be completely annihilated."[28]

The most interesting statement of this kind was, however, made by the "master of ceremonies" himself, the chief of the NKVD in the Ukraine, A. I. Uspensky. At an election meeting in Proskurov he introduced himself in the following manner:

I consider myself a pupil of Nikolai Ivanovich Yezhov. Comrade Yezhov teaches us to fight the enemies of the people, to clean up our country, our Motherland from the enemies. I pledge to follow Comrade Yezhov, the militant leader of the NKVD, in every respect. [This pledge materialized: Uspensky disappeared at the end of 1938 as did his beloved teacher.]

And only after the faithful Stalinist, Nikita Sergeyevich Khrushchev, arrived in the Ukraine did the smashing of the enemies of the people begin in earnest. [He concluded his speech with a personal note:]

Nikita Sergeyevich Khrushchev asked me to transmit to you his regards and to ask you to prepare yourselves in a Bolshevik manner for the collection of a rich Stalinist harvest. . . .[29]

The exact number of the top Party and government officials arrested and executed in the Ukraine is not known, but since these officials belonged to the Ukrainian Party's Central Committee, a comparison of the composition of this body before and after Khrushchev's arrival in the Ukraine may serve as a yardstick by which Khrushchev's ruthlessness can be measured. The last Central Committee of the Ukrainian Communist Party, elected before Khrushchev's arrival, consisted of 117 members with voting rights and forty-nine candidates or alternate members. These 166 men had been elected at the Thirteenth Ukrainian Party Congress on June 3, 1937,[30] when the Great Purge approached its peak. Postyshev and many of his friends and followers were already purged, and this was also reflected in the fact that only 31 per cent of the members of the outgoing Central Committee elected at the Twelfth Congress in January, 1934,[31] reappeared on the new list. On June 19, 1938, five months after Khrushchev took over, at the Fourteenth Party Congress, a new Central Committee was elected, to which only three men from the 1937 Committee,[32] or less than 3 per cent, were re-elected. The Fifteenth Party Congress took place in 1940, when the Great Purge was over, but, in spite of this fact, 53 per cent of the members of the preceding Central Committee were not re-elected to the new Committee.[33]

In his secret report of February 25, 1956, Khrushchev disclosed that "of the 139 members and candidates of the [All-Union] Party's Central Committee who were elected at the Seventeenth Congress [in 1934], ninety-eight persons, i.e., 70 per cent, were arrested and shot." [34] On the other hand, it can be established that twenty-three members and candidates, or 16.5 per cent of the same Committee were re-elected to the Central Committee at the Eighteenth Party Congress in 1939.[35] A comparison of the composition of the Ukrainian Party Central Committee elected in 1934 at the Twelfth Congress with that of the one elected in 1938 at the Fourteenth Congress shows that not a single member of the 1934 Committee was re-elected and, as stated above, 97 per cent of the Central Committee members were removed in 1937-38.

"The only reason why 70 per cent of the [All-Union] Central Committee and candidates elected at the Seventeenth Party Congress [in 1934] were branded as 'enemies of the Party and the people' was that honest Communists were slandered, accusations against them were fabricated, and revolutionary legality was gravely undermined." [36]

Such was Khrushchev's explanation of the massacre of the members of the All-Union Party Central Committee which took place in 1937-38. Putting on the mask of indignation, Khrushchev further revealed that of the 1,966 delegates with either voting or advisory rights, 1,108 persons had been arrested on charges of antirevolutionary crimes—decidedly more than a majority.

"This very fact," said Khrushchev, "shows how absurd, wild, and contrary to common sense were the charges of counter-revolutionary crimes made, as we now see, against a majority of the participants at the Seventeenth Party Congress." [37] The subordinate clause, "as we now see," was obviously inserted to suggest to his comparatively young audience who hardly knew the particulars about the Great Purge, that at that time he, Khrushchev, was not aware of the fact that over 56 per cent of the delegates to the Seventeenth Congress (which he also attended as a delegate, at which he was presiding officer, and which elected him to the Central Committee) were arrested on trumped-up charges of treason. Khrushchev did not spare kind words for

these victims: they "were active participants in the building of
our Socialist state"; many of them "suffered and fought for Party
interests during the prerevolutionary years in the conspiracy and
at the Civil War fronts"; and "they fought their enemies valiantly
and often nervelessly looked into the face of death." And then
with underlined naiveté Khrushchev asked: "How then can we
believe that such people could prove to be 'two-faced' and had
joined the camp of the enemies of socialism. . . ?" [38]

It was "the abuse of power by Stalin" which was responsible
for these crimes, Khrushchev asserted. But who was responsible
for the far wider swing of the terror sword in the Ukraine that
cut down more than 70 per cent of the Ukrainian Party Central
Committee in one year? Had Khrushchev not been the highest
Party authority in the Ukraine who decided the fate of these
members? And was not Khrushchev—the ruler over 40 million
Ukrainian inhabitants for more than a decade—also responsible
for the liquidation of tens of thousands of non-Party people who
died for no good reason during and after the Great Purge?

Khrushchev himself was proud of the first results of his purging
activities in the Ukraine, but he would not cease brandishing the
sword until he heard the last gasp of the last "enemy." On May 26,
1938, in a public speech before a crowd described as "100,000
people," Khrushchev boasted that "this year was a distinctive year
as far as crushing of the enemies of the people is concerned";
the Polish and German fascists have good reason to "bemoan the
death of their agents," while "the peoples of the Soviet Union
rejoice that they have uprooted this foul, abominable, treacherous
gang, the loathsome Trotskyite-Bukharinite bandits, that they
have eradicated and exterminated them under the leadership
of our great Stalin, under the leadership of our Nikolai Ivanovich
Yezhov." At the same time Khrushchev threatened with complete
annihilation "all kinds of bourgeois nationalists" who survived.[39]

On June 5, 1938, in his first major speech delivered at the
Fourth Kiev Party Conference, Khrushchev asked the Party
workers not to relax their vigilance:

"We got rid of a considerable number of enemies. But as
[Party] workers of the Ukraine, and particularly of the Kiev
province, we should not be conceited. We must not relax, for the
enemies will never, under any circumstances, cease carrying out

their subversive work against our state. Comrades, we have annihilated quite a few enemies, but not all of them. That is why we
should be vigilant. *We should not be lulled either by applause,
or by approval, or by unanimous votes.* We should always keep
in mind Comrade Stalin's word that as long as the capitalist
encirclement exists, spies and diversionists will be sent to our
country. We should carefully ponder these words of Comrade
Stalin." [40] One might think that in speaking of the "enemies"
Khrushchev actually referred to regular agents of foreign intelligence services. But he really referred to others:

"The Yakirs,* the Balitskis,† the Liubchenkos,‡ the Zaton-

---

* Yona Emmanuilovich Yakir was born into a Jewish family in Kishinev
(formerly Bessarabia, now the capital of the Moldavian S.S.R.) in 1896.
He joined the revolutionary movement while still a high-school student. At
the time of the February revolution in 1917, he belonged to a group of
active Bolsheviks, and during the October upheaval distinguished himself
in organizing Red detachments. A veteran of the Civil War, Yakir swiftly
climbed the military ladder and became Commander of the Kiev Military
District in 1925. He was a member of the Ukrainian Party Politburo and
alternate member of the Central Committee of the All-Union Party (*Bolshaya Sovetskaya Entsiklopedia* [1st ed.; Moscow, 1931], LXV, 447). In
June, 1937, he was "tried" and executed for alleged conspiracy with the
Nazis. At present he is posthumously rehabilitated.

† Vsevolod Apollonovich Balitsky was born into a Ukrainian family in
Verkhnedneprovsk (Ukraine) in 1892. He became active in the revolutionary movement in 1913 as a student in Moscow and joined the Bolshevik
Party in 1915. After the October Revolution he became Deputy Chief of
the All-Ukrainian Cheka. In 1931, he was appointed Deputy Chairman of
the OGPU (predecessor of the NKVD) of the U.S.S.R. In 1933, he was
dispatched, together with Postyshev, back to the Ukraine and appointed
Chairman of the Ukrainian OGPU and Commander-in-Chief of the frontier
and internal security troops of the Ukraine. In 1934, he became chief of
the Ukrainian NKVD. "The name of Comrade Balitsky," wrote *Pravda* on
November 27, 1933, "is highly popular in the Ukraine. He enjoys sincere
love on the part of the wide Party masses and among the workers and collective farmers" (*Bolshaya Sovetskaya Entsiklopedia* [1st ed.; Moscow,
1926], IV, 496, and *Pravda*, November 27, 1933). In 1937 he was arrested
and executed.

‡ Panas Petrovich Liubchenko, born in 1897 in the Kiev region into a
poor peasant family, joined the Bolshevik Party in 1918. After 1920, Liubchenko occupied responsible positions in the Ukrainian Party and Government. At the end of 1927, he was elected Secretary of the Ukrainian Party
Central Committee and at the Seventeenth All-Union Party Congress, alternate member of the All-Union Central Committee. On January 28, 1934,
Liubchenko was appointed Chairman of the Council of People's Commissars of the Ukrainian Republic (*Visti VTsVK*, April 29, 1934). He committed suicide in 1937.

skys,* and the other riffraff wanted to let in the German fascists, the landowners and bourgeois, and make the Ukrainian
workers and peasants slaves of fascism, and the Ukraine a colony
of the Polish-German fascists."[41] The absurdity of this statement
is evident from the background of the "Yakirs, Balitskis, Liubchenkos, and Zatonskys." These men, as shown in the footnotes,
had been active in the revolutionary movement long before
Khrushchev joined it, and rendered great service to the Bolshevik
cause.

These statements by Khrushchev referring to the Great Purge
show that he was not merely following the general Party line.
Excerpts from some of Khrushchev's speeches, quoted elsewhere
in this study, also distinguish him from other leading Communists
as a more forceful inspirer and promoter of the bloody Purge,
the need for which he later denied in his secret speech of 1956.
There was hardly a speech that he delivered in the Ukraine
which did not contain the same violent threats to annihilate the
"people's enemies" as did his Moscow harangues. The Ukranian
speeches of 1938-40 differ, however, from the Moscow orations,
in firmness of tone and selection of targets. As Stalin's vicar over
40 million people, Khrushchev spoke with greater authority and
self-confidence. As for the targets, an additional enemy was
added: the so-called bourgeois nationalists. The Great Purge
reached this category of enemies at the end of the summer of
1937. In August, *Pravda* began the campaign, and all Soviet
republics, one by one, suddenly discovered that they were seats
of "bourgeois nationalists."

It was to be expected that the Ukraine, "the western outpost

---

* Vladimir Petrovich Zatonsky was born in 1888, and joined the
revolutionary movement in 1905. He was arrested several times while a
student at Kiev University. After graduation he became a teacher of physics
at the Polytechnical Institute. He joined the Bolshevik Party in 1917. After
the October Revolution, Zatonsky occupied prominent positions in the Red
Army during the Civil War, and in 1921 participated in the suppression of
the Kronstadt rebellion, for which participation he was awarded the Order
of the Red Banner. After 1923, Zatonsky held several posts in the Ukrainian
government, primarily the post of Commissar of Education. Zatonsky was
a member of the Ukrainian Politburo and a candidate member of the All-
Union Party Central Committee (*Bolshaya Sovetskaya Entsiklopedia* [1st
ed.; Moscow, 1933], XXVI, 392-393). He was arrested in 1937 and disappeared. At present he is posthumously rehabilitated.

of the Soviet Union," bordering on Poland and Rumania and threatened by Hitlerite Germany, was selected to "expose" a greater number of "spies and traitors" than any other non-Russian republic. This explains why the "bloody touch" in Khrushchev's speeches delivered in the Ukraine became more accentuated. A resolution of the Moscow Party organization proposed by Khrushchev in May, 1937, read:

"The Moscow Party Conference assures the Central Committee of the Party and our *vozhd,* teacher, and friend, Comrade Stalin, that there has not been and will not be mercy for the spies, diversionists, and terrorists who raise their hand against the lives of the toilers of the Soviet Union; that we will annihilate the spies and the diversionists also in the future and will not let the enemies of the U.S.S.R. live; and that for every drop of workers' blood the enemies of the U.S.S.R. will pay with *poods* of blood of spies and diversionists." This part of the resolution was considered so well phrased that *Pravda* quoted it in an editorial.[42] One year later, in a speech delivered at the Fourteenth Ukrainian Party Congress, Khrushchev reworked his Moscow mottoes in the following way:

> Our cause is a holy cause. And he whose hand trembles, who stops half-way, whose knees shake before annihilating ten, a hundred enemies, exposes the Revolution to danger.
>
> It is necessary to fight the enemies without mercy. Let us erase from the surface of the earth everybody who plans to attack the workers and peasants. We warn that for every drop of honest workers' blood we will shed a bucketful of the enemy's black blood.[43]

In the Communist dictatorship purges of dissenters have been "substantiated," almost without exception, by alleged connections of the defendants with foreign intelligence services. It was with treason to the country that the best pupils of Lenin were charged at the great trials of the 'thirties. Much later alleged treason was also chosen as the most appropriate charge to finish off Beria. Treason and espionage were also high on the list of particulars in charges against "bourgeois nationalists."

Hitler's aspirations included the Ukraine, and there can be no doubt that some agents were actually dispatched to that part of

the Soviet Union. However, tight passport controls, close supervision of the borders, and travel restrictions made spying in the
Soviet Union incomparably more difficult than in free countries.
In addition, there were no common borders between the Soviet
Union and Germany at that time, and small neighboring Poland,
herself threatened by Hitler, certainly had no aggressive designs
against her mighty neighbor to the East. Thus there cannot have
been many spies in the Soviet Union. Fully aware of the absurdity of the espionage and treason charges against old Party
members whose elimination was desirable for other purposes,
Stalin and his associates used the natural aversion of the people
against spies to cover up the real reasons for the Great Purge.

When Khrushchev became Party boss in the Ukraine, he
charged into the fray as a prosecutor of "traitors" and "spies" to
an almost incredible extent. His speeches delivered in the late
'thirties were so violent that, reading them, one might wonder
whether the hard-headed, intelligent Khrushchev did not lose
control over his ability to reason and become a victim of a mania.
However, his 1956 secret speech shows that he knew what he was
doing; of particular interest is the passage concerning the loyalty
of those military men who were arrested and tortured as traitors,
but who miraculously survived and later rendered invaluable
services in the defense of their country:

> As you know, before the war we had excellent military
> cadres which were unquestionably loyal to the Party and to
> the Motherland. Suffice it to say that those of them who
> managed to survive despite severe tortures to which they
> were subjected in the prisons, from the first war days have
> shown themselves real patriots and have fought heroically
> for the glory of the Fatherland. . . . Many such commanders,
> however, perished in camps and jails, and the Army saw
> them no more.[44]

Khrushchev also explained that many prominent Red Army
officers perished because "for several years officers of all ranks
and even soldiers in the Party and Komsomol cells were taught
to 'unmask' their superiors as hidden enemies."[45] Khrushchev
failed to mention who the teachers were. The preceding chapters
contain conclusive evidence that Khrushchev was one of the most

—in all probability, *the* most—persistent teacher of extreme "vigilance." In Moscow he had hardly a chance to teach "vigilance" in the Party and Komsomol cells of the Army. With his transfer to the Ukraine he became a member of the Military Council of the Kiev Military District, representing the highest Party authority. In this capacity he taught and helped to unmask the "hidden enemies" among the military; in June, 1938, only four months after Khrushchev's arrival in the Ukraine, Marshal Semyon K. Timoshenko, at the time Commander of the Kiev Military District and at present Commander of the Belorussian Military District, stated: "I must say that the Military Council, with the enormous support of Comrade Nikita Sergeyevich Khrushchev, has already achieved a lot in the field of strengthening the defensive might of socialist Ukraine."[46] In the years of the *Yezhovshchina*, "strengthening of the defensive might" meant, first of all, liquidation of the "hidden enemies."

It seems scarcely necessary to adduce more evidence, although there is much of it to prove Khrushchev's substantial and active part in the Great Purge. What Yezhov lacked in eloquence was more than compensated for by Khrushchev. No Communist leader, dead or alive, showed greater verbal zeal in turning this Purge into the greatest blood bath ever conducted by any group of men against their own comrades.

12

The History of a Cult

In a recent article entitled, "The Lessons of Stendhal," Ilya Ehrenburg recalled Stendhal's words that "it is not the personality of the tyrant that counts, but the essence of the tyranny. The tyrant may be clever or stupid, good or evil; in both cases, he is omnipotent and powerless; he is frightened by conspiracies, he is flattered, he is deceived; the prisons fill, the pusillanimous hypocrites whisper, and the silence, that almost stops the heart from beating, stiffens."[1] That a Soviet writer, a Stalin Prize winner, recalled in 1957 these powerful words of the last century's famous French writer is perhaps characteristic of the state of mind of many Soviet men of literature to whom the death of the tyrant meant a breath of fresh air and a sunbeam capable of restoring the warmth of their hearts which tyranny had attempted to drain, debase, and chill for more than three decades.

Such feelings might have been harbored by a Soviet writer, but not by a Communist leader who succeeded the dictator and had helped to establish his tyranny. In his secret report to the Twentieth Party Congress in 1956, Khrushchev presented an entirely different view from that implied in Ehrenburg's article. To Khrushchev it was not the tyranny but the personality of the tyrant that counted. Khrushchev went out of his way to prove that it was not the system that had created tyranny, but that it was Stalin's evil nature and the cult of his personality that should be blamed for the monstrous state of affairs so eloquently described by Stendhal and recalled by Ehrenburg with such timeliness.

156

According to Khrushchev, the "cult of the individual acquired such monstrous size chiefly because Stalin himself, using all conceivable methods, supported the glorification of his own person." [2] Before 1934, Stalin "still reckoned with the opinion of the collective," but after the Seventeenth Party Congress in 1934, "Stalin had so elevated himself above the Party and above the nation that he ceased to consider either the Central Committee or the Party," [3] and this was the reason for the murder of tens of thousands of innocent men and women from 1936 to 1938.

Khrushchev did not explain how it was possible that a leader who for some time had honored the views of the "collective," suddenly began to elevate himself above the Party and the nation. Why did not the "collective" stop this development in its early stages and thus prevent a barbarous tyranny? Had not the "collective" been warned of such a danger? If Khrushchev wanted to give an honest answer to these questions he would be forced to admit that the "collective" could not possibly have prevented Stalin from establishing his personal rule, for the simple reason that it was the "collective" itself which elevated Stalin. And this elevation began much earlier than 1934, as Khrushchev claimed.

At the Fourteenth Party Congress in December, 1925, clear warnings were already sounded against Stalin's arbitrariness and dangerous ambitions. Mikhail M. Lashevich, a veteran of the Revolution and the Bolshevik movement whom Lenin had planned to appoint Commander-in-Chief of the Red Army, openly stated then that collective leadership had ceased to exist after Lenin's death. [4] The old Bolshevik Grigori Ya. Sokolnikov, arguing against Stalin's constant quest for more power, said: "If Comrade Stalin wants the same esteem as Lenin, let him earn it." [5] Sokolnikov called upon the Congress to "return" to Lenin's rules of directing Party affairs and to re-establish "freedom of opinion in the Politburo." [6] He was shouted down. In spite of numerous recantations and capitulations he was executed in 1937. Furthermre, Khrushchev could hardly have failed to hear the most prophetic warning by Kamenev, executed one year earlier than Sokolnikov: "We are against creating the theory of a *vozhd*. We are against creating a *vozhd*." [7] Kamenev also expressed his conviction that Stalin was unable to "fulfill the role of a unifier of the Bolshevik staff."[8] The last remark threw the house into an uproar. Shouts of "We want Stalin! Long live Stalin!" ended with an ovation on behalf of the future *vozhd*. Thus, as early as 1925, the groundwork for Stalin's personal dictatorship was laid, and Stalin's heirs cannot escape responsibility for participating in this work.

In December, 1927, Khrushchev and others who were delegates to the Fifteenth Party Congress witnessed how "delegations," one after another, mounted the rostrum to greet Stalin with a "Long live" and heartily applauded when a "workers' representative" of a sugar refinery in the Kiev region, Comrade Korolkov, presented the Congress with a bas-relief portrait in sugar of "our iron, unswerving General Secretary, Comrade Stalin."[9]

The tumultuous celebration of Stalin's fiftieth birthday in December, 1929, was a further step in promoting the "cult of the individual." It was a deliberate political act organized not by Stalin himself, but by his well-wishers and promoters, with some of the present ruling circle among them.

In fact, Anastas I. Mikoyan accompanied his congratulations with a complaint that Stalin's life was still not known to the "wide circles of the working class." He added: "One should think that Comrade Stalin's fiftieth birthday will serve as an inspiration for us so that we, meeting the rightful demand of the masses, begin finally to work on his biography and make it available to the Party and to all working people in our country." [10] What Mikoyan had in mind, of course, was a falsified glorification of Stalin's life that would impress the "wide masses." Ten years later, in December, 1939, on the occasion of Stalin's sixtieth birthday, Mikoyan urged again the "creation" of a "scientific biography" of the dictator.[11]

Were not Mikoyan's urgent proposals made with the intention of elevating Stalin's personality to the extreme heights which was finally done in his *Short Biography*, a work that, according to Khrushchev, "is an expression of the most absolute flattery, an example of making a man into a godhead, of transforming him into an infallible sage, 'the greatest leader,' 'sublime strategist of all times and nations' "? [12] What Khrushchev did not tell his audience was the fact that Stalin's self-elevation was the result of years of fawning, subservience, and "the most absolute flattery," which Stalin's companions had initiated while he was alive. As shown above, the sycophancy began as early as 1925, and in the 'thirties the leaders of the Moscow Party organization, Khrushchev and Kaganovich, were the "most absolute" flatterers. In the early 'thirties the expression *vozhd* was not yet popular, but in Moscow it was intensively propagated. At the Moscow Party Conference in January, 1932, only Khrushchev and Kaganovich used this term. Khrushchev, who was elected secretary of the Moscow Party organization at this conference, finished his speech as follows:

"The Moscow Bolsheviks rallied around the Leninist Central Committee as never before and around the *vozhd* of our Party, Comrade Stalin, are cheerfully and confidently marching toward new victories in the battles for socialism, for the world proletarian revolution." [13]

Gradually, Khrushchev and Kaganovich, in the name of the "Moscow Bolsheviks," elevated Stalin to the "Great *vozhd* of the battle-hardened Leninist Party and the multitudes, our Stalin" and "our teacher and leader, our *vozhd*." [14] In June, 1933, in an address to Stalin (beginning with the 'thirties such addresses became frequently a device of expressing admiration and adoration for the dictator), "our teacher and our *vozhd*" was additionally honored as "the greatest strategist of Bolshevism" and "our beloved friend, Comrade Stalin." This address was adopted at the Moscow Province Party Conference, with Khrushchev in the chair.[15] It took no more than six months for a plenary session of the Moscow organization, guided by Kaganovich and Khrushchev, to pass an address in which Stalin and Lenin were called "*vozhds* of genius." [16] This was premature flattery, since at the end of January, 1934, a *Pravda* editorial had used the term only with regard to Marx, Engels, and Lenin, for whom "the proletariat found a most worthy successor—the great Stalin, the titan of revolutionary thought and actions." Stalin also was called "*vozhd* of the Party, the iron brigadier of the international revolution, the great architect of the first socialist revolution in the world," [17] but not yet a genius. Thus Stalin's promotion to genius was initiated by Khrushchev and Kaganovich, no doubt primarily by the former because shortly after this promotion, at the Seven-

teenth Party Congress in 1934, it was Khrushchev, and Khrushchev alone, who called Stalin "*vozhd* of genius." [18] Other speakers
also used the adjective *genialnyi** but not in this combination.
Beria, for instance, spoke of the "brilliant clarity" with which
Stalin defined the roads of "our movement toward a classless
society";[19] Bulganin and Kaganovich praised Stalin's report as
"brilliant," while Voroshilov applied this adjective to Lenin
alone. Only Mikoyan and Khrushchev attached it not only to
Stalin's deeds but also to his personality; Mikoyan called him
"strategist of genius," and Khrushchev expressed his adoration
for Stalin with the appellation "genius." It is interesting to note
that Kirov, the Leningrad boss who was killed ten months after
the Congress, was far behind Khrushchev; the highest praise
Kirov had in store for Stalin was "the greatest strategist of
socialist construction." [20] It is also noteworthy that Ordzhonikidze,
whose death in 1937 remains a mystery, could not find in his
vocabulary even these flattering words and concentrated on
Lenin as the object of his praises. The fate of another old
Bolshevik was sealed because his flatteries did not contain
enough superlatives. Avel S. Yenukidze, executed in December,
1937, once said to Serebryakov, a leader of the Left Opposition:
"What more does he [Stalin] want? I am doing everything he
has asked me to do, but it is not enough for him. He wants me
to admit that he is a genius." [21]

At the end of October, 1936, addressing Stalin, the "Moscow
Bolsheviks," of whom Khrushchev was the leader, made a further contribution to Stalin's cult by praising him as "the genius
of humanity." [22] In November, 1936, at the Fourth Congress of
the Moscow Province Soviets, Khrushchev told "the greatest
vozhd of all toiling people" that "ardent love and limitless faithfulness" fill the heart of every Soviet citizen.[23] A few days later,
in a *Pravda* article, Khrushchev informed the genius that the
"working people of the capital are happy and proud to live and
work in the same city as the beloved *vozhd* of the peoples." [24]
At the Eighth All-Union Congress of the Soviets, Khrushchev
insisted that the Soviet Constitution, which was to be adopted

---

* If referred to a man, the Russian adjective *genialnyi* is translated as
of genius; if referred to actions or works, it is translated as *brilliant.*

by the Congress, be called the Stalinist Constitution, because "it was written from beginning to end by Comrade Stalin himself." [25] This was another flattery made up by Khrushchev to please the dictator. Had it been true, other speakers would have also expostulated this great achievement of the *vozhd*, but this was not the case. Rather, Stanislav V. Kosior, whom Khrushchev had succeeded in the Ukraine, merely claimed that the Constitution was "created under Comrade Stalin's direct guidance," while Molotov, at the time Chairman of the People's Commissars, and Zhdanov, the Leningrad Party boss, did not mention Stalin's personal merits in drafting the Constitution at all.* It was in the same speech that Khrushchev coined the expression "Stalinism":

"Our Constitution," Khrushchev said, "is the Marxism-Leninism-*Stalinism* that has conquered one sixth of the globe. We do not doubt that Marxism-Leninism-*Stalinism* will conquer the entire globe. . . . We adopt our Constitution and we celebrate the victory of Marxism-Leninism-*Stalinism* which is not only our victory but also that of the working people throughout the world." [26]

Today the term Stalinism is banned in the land of the Soviets: "Actually, 'Stalinism' as a special teaching or social system has never existed; [Stalinism was] invented by the imperialist propaganda with the purpose of fighting against Marxism-Leninism and the world Communist movement and, in particular, for the purpose of the revision of the principles of proletarian internationalism," one reads in the Communist press nowadays.[27]

The elevation of Stalin was closely interwoven with the Great Purge of 1936-38, and Khrushchev showed himself a master in exploiting this interconnection for the purpose of strengthening Stalin's rule and the cult of his personality.

In August, 1936, during the Kamenev-Zinoviev trial, Khrush-

---

* Today Soviet historians are urged to prove that the Constitution was not written by Stalin "from beginning to end," but rather drafted by a Constitutional Commission elected at the session of the U.S.S.R. Central Executive Committee in February, 1935. "The documents of the Constitutional Commission," says a Soviet historical journal, "convincingly show that the draft of the U.S.S.R. Constitution was prepared collectively . . . by a group of leading [Party and government] workers" (*Istoricheskii Arkhiv* [*Historical Archives*], No. 2, 1959, p. 200).

chev, in his capacity as Moscow's Party boss, inspired his "activists" to address Stalin in the following fashion:

> They [the defendants] pulled the strings of this bloody plot and directed a blow at the heart of the Revolution, at thee, our own Stalin, and at thy closest disciples. Damned fascist degenerates! They lifted their hands against one whose name millions of toilers pronounce every day, every hour, with pride and limitless love. . . . Miserable pygmies! They lifted their hands against the greatest of all men . . . our close friend, our wise *vozhd*, Comrade Stalin! The victorious struggle of our Party for socialism is indissolubly bound to thy name. . . . Thou, Comrade Stalin, hast raised the great banner of Marxism-Leninism high over the entire world and carried it forward. We assure thee, Comrade Stalin, that the Moscow Bolshevik organization—the faithful supporter of the Stalinist Central Committee—will increase the Stalinist vigilance still more, will extirpate the Trotskyite-Zinovievite remnants, and close the ranks of the Party and non-Party Bolsheviks even more around the Stalinist Central Committee and the great Stalin." [28]

Khrushchev's speech with which he tried to whip up a public meeting of 200,000 in Moscow in January, 1937, during the Piatakov-Radek trial was in a similar vein:

> These murderers aimed at the heart and brain of our Party. They have lifted their villainous hands against Comrade Stalin.
> By lifting their hands against Comrade Stalin they lifted them against all of us, against the working class, against the toiling people! By lifting their hands against Comrade Stalin they lifted them against the teaching of Marx, Engels, and Lenin.
> By lifting their hands against Comrade Stalin they lifted them against all the best that humanity possesses. For Stalin is hope; he is expectation; he is the beacon that guides all progressive mankind. Stalin is our banner! Stalin is our will! Stalin is our victory! [29]

In November and December of 1937, the bloody Purge was raging all over the country. This particular period when, to use Khrushchev's 1956 formulation, "a situation was created where one could not express one's own will,"[30] was considered the most appropriate time for the "election campaign" to the Supreme Soviet. How close Khrushchev was to Stalin in general is a matter of speculation, but apparently at that time the personal relationship between the *vozhd* and his companion-in-arms was fairly close. On December 11, 1937, at an election meeting in one of Moscow's districts, where Stalin "ran" for the Supreme Soviet, he opened his speech with the following remark:

"Comrades, to tell you the truth, I had no intention of speaking. But our respected Nikita Sergeyevich dragged me here by force to the meeting: 'Make a good speech,' he said."[31]

In this "election" campaign all prominent Communist leaders delivered speeches in praise of Stalin. There were, however, various degrees of sycophancy. While one group among Stalin's heirs showed some restraint, another group excelled in subservience. To the first group belonged Molotov, Malenkov, and Voroshilov; to the second group belonged Khrushchev, Beria, Kaganovich, and Mikoyan. Again, as at the Seventeenth Party Congress in 1934, Khrushchev and Mikoyan alone used the adjective *genialnyi* with reference to the person of Stalin and not only to some of his qualities: while Kaganovich praised Stalin as a "genius of political intellect,"[32] Khrushchev and Mikoyan assessed Stalin's person as a whole as that of a genius.[33]

Beria on this occasion praised Stalin's "brilliant wisdom and foresight";[34] on another, he called him the "greatest genius of humanity."[35] It would be a mistake, however, to believe that Beria was the winner in this bootlicking contest, or to take seriously Khrushchev's assertion (made in his 1956 secret speech) that besides such terms as "the greatest leader" and "supreme strategist of all times and nations"—phrases used in Stalin's *Short Biography*—"no other words could be found with which to lift Stalin up to the heavens."[36] On several occasions between 1938 and 1952, Khrushchev showed much greater inventiveness in this respect than the authors of Stalin's biography. This can be seen from the following samples: "genius of humanity,"[37] "our great genius, our beloved Stalin,"[38] "the greatest genius of humanity, teacher, and *vozhd* who leads us toward Communism, our very own Stalin,"[39] "our great leader of the peoples, our friend and father, the greatest man of our epoch,"[40] "our great *vozhd* and teacher, and commander-in-chief of genius," "military genius,"[41] "great Marshal of the Victory."[42]

In his secret speech of February, 1956, Khrushchev ridiculed Stalin's military ability,[43] saying that he "planned operations on a globe,"[44] and interferred with military operations, causing "our Army serious damage."[45] This is not the place to assess or defend Stalin's military abilities, but this deliberate downgrading of Stalin as a strategist sheds light on the character of Khrushchev who had called Stalin a "military genius" many a time.

Khrushchev distinguished himself not only as an outstanding panegyrist, but also as a talented promoter of the cult of Stalin's personality. He tried to instill the cult into Party and non-Party audiences, he urged them to become Stalin's "loyal shield-bearers"—a term he contemptuously used in 1956 with regard to Stalin's private secretary, Poskrebyshev—and also to fill their hearts with love for the "genius" and with hatred for his enemies.[46] Nor did he forget the young. In a *Pravda* article Khrushchev gave a sample of how love for Stalin should be instilled in children.

"I had the opportunity," Khrushchev wrote, "to see many children in parks. When they were asked: 'Children, whose idea was it to create these parks?' they immediately answered: 'Stalin's, Stalin's.' And their answer is correct."[47] While in the Ukraine, Khrushchev inspired the "people" to address Stalin with greetings on every suitable occasion. Kiev housewives for instance, were induced to make Stalin happy with an address full of extreme flatteries:

"The Soviet people," the housewives wrote, "pronounce the word 'Stalin' with affectionate warmth, with cordial sincerity! The eyes of our children burn with joy when they say: 'Stalin, you are our pride, you are our hope, you are our beautiful today, you are our still more beautiful future.'"[48]

As time went on, the fawning became more intense, and in 1944, Khrushchev encouraged thirteen prominent Ukrainian writers to write a poem entitled "To the Great Stalin From the

Ukrainian People"[49] under which 9,316,973 signatures were "collected." In this lengthy poem one reads:

> Today and forever, oh, Stalin, be praised
> For the light that the plants and the fields do emit!
> Thou art the heart of the people, the truth and the faith!
> We're thankful to Thee for the sun Thou hast lit!

The poem did not omit the boss of the Ukrainian people, Nikita Khrushchev, to whom two quatrains were devoted:

> Kiev is free, will remain so for ages,
> Our land, our Mother, salutes it with cheer,
> Khrushchev and Vatutin,* brave and courageous,
> Lead forward the armies who fight without fear.

> We're united and solid, and no one will dare,
> To touch our young land which is clean as first love,
> As fresh and as young with his silver-gray hair,
> Is Stalin's companion, Nikita Khrushchev.

This poem was written in 1944. Five years later, a luxurious leatherbound book was published in Kiev entitled "To the Great Stalin,"[50] in which one reads the following verses:

> We are the great foundation
> That is the summit's base,
> On the ancient Kiev elevation
> I see Khrushchev's fine face.

> And if my eyes look higher,
> I see our Lenin, the foreseer,
> The truth and power that inspire,
> And Stalin's glorious name I hear.

There can hardly be any doubt that these verses were published with Khrushchev's approval and that, having cleared them, he

---

* General N. F. Vatutin, Commander of the First Ukrainian Front, died in 1944.

must have been confident that the mention of his own name along with that of the dictator would not disturb the latter, since Khrushchev is placed by the poet on a low Kiev hill, while the *vozhd* is sitting high in the sky.

A careful examination of speeches and writings by Stalin's principal survivors, including the executed Lavrenti P. Beria, with the purpose of assessing the degree of their sycophancy, places Khrushchev and Beria at the top of this list, followed by Mikoyan, Kaganovich, Bulganin, Malenkov, and Molotov. It is noteworthy that the last three, purged by Khrushchev as incorrigible Stalinists in 1957 and 1958, are at the bottom of the list.

What were the motives for creating the Stalinist cult? Khrushchev's claim that the glorification of Stalin stemmed only from fear is certainly untrue as far as the postrevolutionary newcomers, such as Khrushchev himself, are concerned. It is true that fear of annihilation motivated Kamenev and Zinoviev when at the Seventeenth Party Congress (1934) they filled their recantations with sickening flatteries of Stalin. It is also true that feelings of insecurity caused many old Bolsheviks, who considered themselves potential victims of Stalin's brutality, to use flattery as a means of diverting the bloody sword from their heads. But such hard-boiled Stalinist "old timers" as Kaganovich, Molotov, Voroshilov, and Mikoyan, or the rising stars—Malenkov, Bulganin, Khrushchev, and Beria—who in the second half of the 'twenties and in the 'thirties had appeared on the political scene as faithful promoters of Stalin's personal rule—had nothing to fear. This is why Molotov and even the much younger Malenkov could afford to devote their intellectual abilities to serious discussions of pending problems in articles and speeches and show moderation in praising their leader.

Khrushchev did not belong to this group of Stalinist intellectuals. Politically, he grew up as simply an agitator and propagandist, and for the sake of his advancement he was forced to look for other means to make himself appreciated. This becomes obvious from a comparison of the few superficial writings by Khrushchev with Malenkov's serious and interesting contributions to Party magazines. Stalin esteemed Malenkov's intellectual abilities highly, and because of this, Malenkov could spare some space in his writings and time in his speeches for serious discussions, rather than for excessive flatteries. For Khrushchev, however, subservience was the most important tool in paving his way to the top. It is possible, of course, that in the 'thirties, when the cult of Stalin's personality was in its initial stage, the somewhat simple-minded Khrushchev actually felt deep love and devotion for the *vozhd*. On the other hand, this feeling could hardly have remained intact after Khrushchev, due to his advancement, gained insight into the real state of affairs behind the Kremlin walls. It was at this stage that subservience must have replaced whatever genuine admiration there was before. It would, of course, be an underestimation of Stalin to believe that subservience alone was sufficient to gain prestige and authority in the Party and government machines. But Khrushchev could offer Stalin, in addition to limitless subservience, his experience in propaganda and agitation, immense energy, mobility and practical common sense. These features, although far from being unique, made Khrushchev valuable. Above all, he was effective. In the promotion of the idea of Stalin's greatness he certainly was more useful than Malenkov and other Stalinist intellectuals.

The de-canonization of Stalin began almost immediately after his death. His name was gradually blacked out in Soviet publications and, instead, articles criticizing the "cult of personality" began to appear. Until Khrushchev's de-Stalinization speech in 1956, this gradual downgrading was not consistently implemented. Observers of Soviet affairs were greatly surprised that in December, 1955, Communist newspapers and magazines within the Communist bloc remembered Stalin's seventy-sixth birthday, after their resounding silence on his seventy-fifth. It is now established that this inconsistency was the result of a struggle within the Party Presidium on the question of whether and how the personality cult should be dismissed.*

This writer learned from a completely reliable source that, at

* The decision of the June, 1957, plenum to expel (from the Central Committee) Malenkov, Molotov, and Kaganovich reveals that they "put up a stubborn resistance to the measures which the Central Committee and our entire Party were carrying out to do away with the consequences of the personality cult."

the July, 1955, plenary session of the Party Central Committee, Molotov vigorously cautioned against an all-out attack against the "great continuer of Lenin's work," since such an attack might initiate a chain reaction the result of which would have been a gradual disintegration of the Communist fortress erected with so much difficulty under Lenin's and Stalin's guidance. In his reply to Molotov, Khrushchev said: "Viacheslav Mikhailovich, don't be afraid, we would not hurt the old man [*my starika v obidu nie dadim*]." This probably is why the Party ordered a commemoration of Stalin's birthday in 1955. If this assumption is correct, then Khrushchev's indictment of the late dictator in February, 1956, must have been the result of a last-minute decision adopted against the wishes of Molotov, Kaganovich, and Malenkov.

The "old man" has been a major object in the strife among his satraps since the day of his departure. The saying "Death pays all debts" is in general less applicable to rulers than to ordinary people. This is especially true in totalitarian states where the supreme leader can under no circumstances be an object of criticism while he is alive. Khrushchev has not yet reached the status of a full-scale totalitarian dictator, but every statement he has made since the 1957 purge has already been described as "extremely remarkable," "inspiring and deep," and he himself has been immortalized in stone[51] and in paintings which, as far as contents and pose are concerned, remind one of the typical paintings of Lenin.[52] The present Khrushchev-worship has not yet reached the proportions of the Stalin-worship, but there are visible trends going in the same direction. In the chapters to follow these trends will be discussed in more detail.

13

Russifier in Disguise

Whether a Ukrainian or a Russian, Nikita Khrushchev will go down in history as one of the most rigorous Russifiers in the land he many times referred to as "our Ukraine." He was sent to the Ukraine in January, 1938, when the Purge had reached its peak. It was his task to expedite it, and this he did with the utmost energy and ruthlessness. In the Ukraine and other non-Russian republics the Purge was directed not only against the general, "cosmopolitan" type of "enemies of the people," but also against the native intelligentsia which was accused of national deviation, "bourgeois" nationalism, and conspiracy with the potential enemy. Regarding the Ukraine these accusations were more accentuated than in other republics, mainly because of its geographical position. The Kremlin was aware of the probability that in case of war with Germany this geographical position might be a great danger to the Soviet Union. The Kremlin, therefore, decided to launch an all-out attack against everybody and everything that might help crystallize the existing popular discontent into a strong national movement which, under war conditions, might become disastrous. To carry out this preventive attack was Khrushchev's second major task. The scope and significance of Khrushchev's activity in that field will become clearer after a brief review of the previous Soviet policy in the Ukraine.

Comprising approximately only 3 per cent of the territory of the U.S.S.R. but inhabited by 20 per cent of the Soviet population, the Ukraine belongs strategically and economically

169

to the most vital regions of the Soviet empire. The great hopes
for independence which the Ukrainians had cherished when
the Czarist regime crumbled in March, 1917, did not materialize.
The Ukrainian national problem was not solved, and this unhappy place on the globe has seen more bloodshed and tears
than any other part of the "land of socialism." Perhaps the most
dramatic illustration of the misfortunes that befell the Ukraine
is the fact that as late as April, 1956, the Ukrainian population
was below the 1940 level, while other Soviet republics showed
an average increase of 7.3 per cent.[1]

A few highlights from the history of the Bolshevization and Sovietization of the Ukraine will be sufficient to place Khrushchev's
activity there in the proper perspective.

The Seventh Conference of the Bolshevik Party in April, 1917,
formulated its nationality policy in unmistakably clear terms:

"The right of all nations forming part of Russia," one reads in
the resolution adopted at this Conference, "to freely secede and
form independent states shall be recognized. To negate this right
or to fail to take measures guaranteeing its practical realization
is equivalent to supporting a policy of seizure and annexation."[2]
Pronounced before the Bolsheviks came to power, this principle
was violated as soon as they enthroned themselves in the Kremlin.
An armed attempt was made to incorporate the Baltic nations
and Poland into the Soviet State, and by 1921, all Transcaucasia
including Georgia, whose independent status the Kremlin had
recognized in the Soviet-Georgian Treaty of May 7, 1920, had been
seized by the Red Army. The attempt of the Ukrainian Central
Rada—a governing body born in the chaotic days of the 1917
democratic revolution—to oppose Moscow's domination, was
frustrated by Lenin's ultimatum of December 16, 1917, and the
subsequent seizure of Ukrainian territory by armed force. After
that, for three years, the Ukraine was the scene of German
occupation, under which the moderate Rada was dissolved and
the rule of Hetman Skoropadsky established. The Ukraine then
became the scene of the most bloody Civil War in history,
ending in the reoccupation of the area by the Red Army.

After the Civil War the Bolshevik rulers in the Ukraine,
consisting mostly of Moscow emissaries of non-Ukrainian nationality, were preoccupied with mopping-up operations against

all anti-Bolshevik political and trade union groups. Ukrainian cultural and educational institutions created under the democratic Ukrainian Central Rada were liquidated. As a result the Ukrainian population, particularly in the countryside, found great similarity between the Russian Communists and the Czarist gendarmes. Carried away by the vision of a Communist Utopia, the Bolsheviks disregarded the national aspirations of the Ukrainians and antagonized them to such an extent that the Party was later forced to make some concessions in the form of so-called Ukrainization.

In the summer of 1923, a series of decrees and ukases confirmed the equality of the Ukrainian language with the Russian, and promised the Ukrainization of the Party and state machines in order to move them nearer to the Ukrainian masses. The number of schools with Ukrainian as the language of instruction increased considerably and the volume of printed matter in that language rose steadily. Ukrainization was further encouraged at the end of the 'twenties and in the early 'thirties when the industrialization and collectivization drives brought the surplus population from the villages, overwhelmingly Ukrainian, to the large cities and newly constructed industrial centers. To deal with these masses the Ukrainian language became an indispensable tool. But the principal aim of the Ukrainization was to bring the Ukrainian population, primarily the peasants, under Communist influence. In this the Kremlin did not succeed: nowhere in the Soviet Union was the resistance against collectivization more determined than in the Ukrainian villages. The real aim of the Kremlin's Ukrainization policy was so transparent that the opposition against Moscow's rule affected many leading Communists of Ukrainian origin, among them Mykola Khvylovyi, Oleksandr Shumskyi, and Mykola Skrypnyk. Staunch Communists, they nevertheless opposed Kremlin domination. All three longed for more independence from Moscow, and in that respect they were promoters of the same ideas which sprang up within the Communist orbit after World War II. Titoism and Gomulkaism have their roots in Khvylovism and Shumskyism.

Khvylovyi, a Ukrainian writer, did not question the merits of Leninism; what he questioned was the supremacy of Russian literature and art. He called for the development of an original

Ukrainian proletarian literature and art free from slavish imitations along the Russian pattern. Khvylovyi believed that Ukrainian literature must lean upon the great European civilization created by Goethe, Darwin, Byron, Newton, Marx, et al.[3] In 1928, Khvylovyi repented in a most undignified manner, begging for forgiveness from those against whom he had carried on his heated struggle for several years. His subsequent behavior, however, proves that his confessions were forced upon him.

On May 13, 1933, Khvylovyi invited some of his friends and read to them his last work, written in full conformity with the Party line. Having fiinished the reading, he went to an adjoining room, tore up the piece he had just read and shot himself. The next day, in the announcement of his death, the Ukrainian newspaper Visti described him as a weakling ("he lacked revolutionary strength").

Another deviationist, Oleksandr Shumskyi, occupied a prominent place in the Ukrainian Communist Party and Government as a member of the Central Committee and its Politburo and People's Commissar of Education. Shumskyi's deviation was more dangerous to the Kremlin since it aimed at the ouster of the non-Ukrainians (most important, Lazar M. Kaganovich, who at the time was Secretary General of the Ukrainian Party) from the leading Party and government posts in the Ukraine. According to a letter Stalin wrote to Kaganovich, Shumskyi had a two-hour conversation with him during which he complained that the "Ukrainization is progressing too slowly . . . it is considered an imposed obligation which is being carried out with reluctance and great procrastination," and that, therefore, the Ukrainization movement should be headed by people "who are or want to be acquainted" with Ukrainian culture.[4] The Shumskyi deviation had repercussions beyond the border of the Soviet Union, as his view had been supported by and caused the split of the Communist Party of the Western Ukraine which was part of the Polish Communist Party. This was a blow to the line the Kremlin had worked out for the Comintern which, a few years before the Shumskyi affair, had ordered the Communist Parties of Poland, Rumania, and Czechoslovakia to propagate the idea of joining all Ukrainian lands to the Soviet Ukraine. Between 1928 and 1930, Shumskyi repented three times.

However, in 1933, he was arrested, and his fate remains unknown.

Mykola O. Skrypnyk was one of the most colorful personalities among the Ukrainian Communist leaders. Born in 1872 into the family of a railroad employee, he became a Marxist in 1897 and joined the revolutionary movement in 1900 while a student at the St. Petersburg Technological Institute. He was sentenced six times to exile by the Czarist regime, and managed to escape five times. Between arrests he worked as an agitator, propagandist and editor in the underground. After the Revolution, Skrypnyk played an important role in the Ukrainian Communist Party, of which he was one of the founders, and in the Government which he headed in 1918. In 1927, he was elected Chairman of the Council of Nationalities of the U.S.S.R. His last position, to which he was appointed on February 28, 1933, was chief of the State Planning Committee of the Ukraine. On July 7 of the same year he shot himself in his office. The next day the Soviet newspapers described the suicide as an "act of cowardice," and Skrypnyk himself as an "unworthy member of the Central Committee." [5] Four months later, Kosior and Postyshev charged their dead colleague with "lack of vigilance" and "nationalist degeneration." In 1938, a few months after Khrushchev took over the Ukrainian Party, the monthly *Bilshovik Ukrainy* editorially attacked in turn the former Party leadership, that is, Kosior and Postyshev, for having "overlooked the formation of a new nationalist nest headed by the enemy M. O. Skrypnyk." [6] How false these accusations were is evident from the fact that all three men—Skrypnyk, Postyshev, and Kosior—have since been rehabilitated.[*]

Khvylovyi's and Skrypnyk's suicides and Shumskyi's disappearance become clear if one takes into consideration that all three events took place in 1933, after the Kremlin had ordered a new purge of the Party ranks to be "organized in a manner which would secure an iron discipline and cleanse the Party

---

[*] Kosior and Postyshev were honored as "comrades" by Khrushchev himself in his February, 1956, secret speech. Skrypnyk's name reappeared in 1957 in the Soviet press (*Kommunist Ukrainy,* No. 6, 1957, p. 65), and his reminiscenses about Lenin are scheduled to be published (*Novye Knigi,* No. 15, 1957, p. 24).

of all unreliable, unstable, and careerist [*primazavshikhsia*] elements."[7] One of the purposes of this purge was to expel from the Party those who expressed doubts concerning the wisdom of the coercive collectivization which brought death and terrible suffering to millions of Ukrainian peasants, with its man-made famine, executions, and mass deportations to the Far North. All these measures were ruthlessly carried out by Moscow's emissaries who were mostly of non-Ukrainian origin, and this circumstance stirred up anti-Russian feelings. Even Skrypnyk, who accepted Moscow's guidance in exchange for an "honest" Ukrainization policy, became convinced that this policy was only a means to strengthen the Great Russian rule in the Ukraine. Khvylovyi and Skrypnyk shot themselves not because of "cowardice" or "lack of revolutionary strength"; it was the call of the "great duty," to use Khvylovyi's phrase, that forced them to make their fateful decisions. The alternative was silent disappearance forever or forced self-incrimination. The shots they fired were loud signals of protest, heroic acts of passive resistance which under the circumstances was the only form of opposition left to fearless and tireless revolutionaries of the Skrypnyk type. The shots marked the beginning of a new era in the Kremlin's national policy in the Ukraine.

In 1923, the Twelfth Congress of the Russian Communist Party had regarded Great Russian chauvinism, in both Party and Soviet organs, as the major deviation from the Bolshevik national policy. "To talk of the superiority of Russian culture and to advance the thesis that the victory of the superior Russian culture over the cultures of more backward peoples (Ukrainian, Azerbaidzhanian, Uzbek, Kirghiz, etc.) is inevitable, is nothing but an attempt to perpetuate the domination of the Great Russian nationality," reads a resolution passed by this Congress. "Thus," continued the resolution, "the first immediate task of our Party is to wage determined warfare against the remnants of Great Russian chauvinism."[8] Local nationalism was then considered a "peculiar form of defense against Great Russian chauvinism" and consequently treated as a minor danger. Such was the official line until the end of 1933. Then local nationalism, called "bourgeois nationalism," was officially declared to be the greatest danger while Great Russian chauvinism was played down and the term itself gradually disappeared from the Soviet vocabulary.*

The national problem was declared solved once and for all, and facts proving the opposite were branded either as propaganda tricks of the imperialists or as acts instigated by them for the purpose of undermining the harmonious and indissoluble unity of all non-Russian nationalities with the "elder brother," the Russian people.

Soviet patriotism was pronounced the only legitimate feeling of devotion to one's native soil, and Soviet "socialist" culture was pictured as the only permissible composite of material, social, and intellectual achievements—as a culture that had outgrown national limits. As for the national cultures of the non-Russian nationalities, they were allowed to be national only in form but not in content. For content the non-Russian peoples had to look to Moscow, the seat of the "elder brother." Thus began the era of Russification.

In the Ukraine, Kosior and Postyshev had been in charge of carrying out the new line. They had faithfully fulfilled their duty. Nevertheless, whatever the main reason for their fall and subsequent violent deaths, they were also held responsible for "overlooking" the "bourgeois-nationalist" danger. Then, with the appointment of Khrushchev in January, 1938, Stalin finally found an unswerving, energetic, and enthusiastic executive, known for his supersensitive vigilance, speedy decisions, and swift actions.

What Khrushchev had in store for the Ukrainian people was clearly expressed in *Bilshovik Ukrainy*, organ of the Party's Central Committee, a few months after his arrival in Kiev. "The fascist degenerates . . . introduced compulsory Ukrainization," the magazine wrote. This "crime" was, of course, nothing but the previous official policy in the Ukraine. Now, when in the eyes of the Kremlin Russification had become a political necessity, those who had followed that former policy were, in typical Bolshevik manner, branded "fascist degenerates." The list of particulars against them started with "expurgation from the

---

* The 1956 *Soviet Political Dictionary* carries on page 76 an item, "Great Power Chauvinism," defined as the "aggressive policy of the bourgeoisie of the ruling nations aimed at the enslavement of other nations and deprivation of their sovereignty."

Ukrainian language of Russian-sounding words," and ended with "Polonization of the Ukrainian speech."

"The bourgeois nationalists—these abominable Polish and German fascists—" the magazine continued, "knew perfectly well how the Russian language, the Russian culture, and the teaching of Lenin and Stalin influence the minds of the Ukrainian people. This is the reason why they [the bourgeois nationalists] so furiously drove out the Russian language from the schools. Miserable attempts!" [9]

With Khrushchev's arrival in the Ukraine, the Russification drive came into full swing. In his first major speech delivered in Kiev in May, 1938, Khrushchev charged the "Fascist-Polish-German gangs" with having done "everything to detach the Ukraine from the Great Soviet Union, from the heart of our Motherland—Moscow. This will never happen," Khrushchev continued, "because the Ukrainian workers and peasants are knit together with the Russian workers and peasants by one thought, by one will—the Stalinist will." [10] In June, 1938, in his report to the Fourteenth Ukrainian Party Congress, Khrushchev attacked the "enemies" for the "suppression of the Russian language in the Ukraine," and informed the delegates that "all peoples now study Russian," because the Russian workers had raised the banner of rebellion and shown to the world "how the enemy must be crushed and freedom conquered." There was, however, one more reason why the Russian language was to be studied. The Bolsheviks, Khrushchev said, had studied German in order to read Marx in the original version, and, since Lenin and Stalin had "further developed" the Marx-Engels teaching in Russian, the study of Russian had become a necessity. Having established these "axioms," Khrushchev assailed the "enemies" who "by every means have detached the culture of the Ukrainian people from the Russian culture." [11]

In July, 1938, at the First Session of the Ukrainian Supreme Soviet, Aleksandr S. Shcherbakov, secretary of the Doniets Province Party Committee, revealed that "the leader of the Ukrainian Bolsheviks, N. S. Khrushchev, is busy every day with questions of public education," and that these questions are "permanently" on the agenda of the Ukrainian Politburo.[12] The results of these labors were drastic changes in school programs, in the vocabulary

and spelling of the Ukrainian language, in Ukrainian historiography, and in other fields of Ukrainian culture. The entire
might of the terroristic apparatus was put to work to eradicate
the remnants of the "enemies of the people," who "sitting in
the People's Commissariat of Education and the [local] departments of public education, had encroached upon the indissoluble friendship of the peoples of the whole U.S.S.R. and
dreamed of detaching the Ukrainian culture from the culture of
the great fraternal Russian people."[13] The author of this quotation, a teacher of the Russian language, bitterly complained
that "in the secondary schools, teaching of the Russian language
used to begin in the third grade and be carried on without a
system, the theory of the language not being coordinated with
the practice of the living language," and that "only in the fifth
grade was the Russian language systematically taught."[14]

With Khrushchev's arrival in the Ukraine, the school programs
were changed in such a way that the school hours devoted to
the teaching of Russian increased tremendously. While, in 1937,
240 hours had been allotted to Russian in Ukrainian-language
elementary schools, by 1939 this allotment increased to 390
hours in urban and 429 hours in rural schools.[15] The scope of
Russification of non-Russian schools can be judged by the fact
that of 171,000 teachers in the Ukraine, 20,000 were scheduled
to take "courses for the improvement of their qualifications as
instructors of the Russian language,"[16] and such courses were
organized in all Ukrainian provinces, for which purpose five
million rubles were appropriated.[17]

Parallel with the Russification of the schools began the "purification of the Ukrainian language from bourgeois-nationalist riffraff."[18] In July, 1938, the Ukrainian press reported that a new
Russo-Ukrainian dictionary was to be published soon; that a
special commission of "linguists" had been created to "engage
in searching for and collecting new words," and that more than
20,000 such words had been created and would be in the new
dictionary.[19] In their eagerness to please Khrushchev these
"linguists" went so far that two years later, at the Fifteenth
Ukrainian Party Congress, Aleksandr E. Korneichuk, a well-
known Ukrainian writer, faithful to Moscow, had to admit the
harm which had been inflicted on the language. In the same

speech, however, Korneichuk praised the "wonderful words" by
which the Party "has enriched our language" such as *Stakhanovets*
(Stakhănovite), *brigadir, Piatisotnitsa* (an "advanced" *kolkhoz*
woman who is able to collect 500 centners of sugar beets from
one hectare) and the like, and disdainfully rejected genuine
Ukrainian words such as *postoli* (bast shoes) and *ochkur* (a rope
used to hold up trousers),[20] probably because these words reminded one of the less happy aspects of the Ukrainian peasants.

Before Khrushchev's arrival in the Ukraine the Rumanian-
speaking Moldavian population had used the Latin alphabet for
the written language. At the beginning of June, 1938, the Presidium of the Central Executive Committee of the Moldavian
Autonomous S.S.R. (which at the time was part of the Ukraine)
announced the introduction of the Russian alphabet, because
"the Latin alphabet is incomprehensible to the toilers of Mol-
davia." Beginning June 6, 1938, the Moldavian paper *Moldovia
Sotsialiste* appeared in Russian transcription.

Ukrainian historiography was the last but not the least target
of Khrushchev's Russification activity. The "enemies of the people"
were charged with "having done everything to prevent the great
Ukrainian people from knowing their true history" by "con-
cealing the historical fraternal ties between the Ukrainian and
the Russian peoples." "After the organs of the NKVD have
crushed the criminal fascist gang," wrote the official organ of
the Ukrainian Government, "the Institute of History has undertaken to undo the consequences of this sabotage."[21] The statement speaks for itself. The Russification drive was just about
to demolish most of the "conquests" achieved during the "Ukrani-
zation" period, when the Red Army crossed the Soviet-Polish
border on September 17, 1939, to "liberate" the West Ukrainian
and Belorussian "brothers" from the Polish yoke.

Shortly before the invasion of Poland, Khrushchev had attacked
several prominent Ukrainians as "vile spies, monsters, and trash
of humanity"[22] and liquidated all those who worked under them,
mainly because they tried to keep the Ukrainian language free
from Russianisms. After the liquidation of the prominent representatives of the Ukrainian Communist intelligentsia Khrushchev
was now faced with the urgent problem of refurbishing the façade

with Ukrainian national colors in order to appeal to the West Ukrainian intellectuals. As tools he used a few young Ukrainian writers headed by Aleksandr Korneichuk, who climbed to various influential positions by denouncing his elder colleagues as bourgeois nationalists and traitors. Korneichuk was the first Ukrainian writer to arrive in Lvov, immediately after the city had been seized, together with Khrushchev and the commander of the invading forces, Timoshenko. There, according to *Sovetskaya Ukraina*, Korneichuk became the object of a "real pilgrimage." Among the pilgrims were some Ukrainian writers and the Polish writer Wanda Wasilewska, whose pilgrimage to Korneichuk ended with a love affair and marriage. When in June, 1940, the Red Army "again extended the frontiers of socialism" by invading Bessarabia, Korneichuk "was again the plenipotentiary representative of the Soviet Ukrainian culture in the liberated lands of North Bukovina," added *Sovetskaya Ukraina*.[23]

This description of Korneichuk's role shows Khrushchev's tactics of winning new native cadres by exhibiting a young Soviet writer of Ukrainian origin who had achieved not only fame in the Soviet Union but also material prosperity—things of which a Ukrainian writer in former Poland could not have dreamed. Khrushchev applied to the newly acquired areas the same strategy the Kremlin had used in the Soviet Ukraine: he tried to attract the native intelligentsia by a deceptive policy of "Ukrainization," selecting corruptible elements upon whom he could rely to carry out Bolshevization and eventually Russification policies. Translated into terms of educational policy, this strategy meant first to create Ukrainian-language schools in which the Russian language would be only one of the subjects, and not the basic language; the second stage was to create Russian-language schools in far greater numbers than required by the small percentage of Russians in these areas, and also to introduce Russian textbooks in the Ukrainian-language schools. This was the first step in the direction of Russification of the educational system in the "liberated" areas. Further steps would have followed if the German invasion had not interrupted Khrushchev's efforts to assimilate the booty, so easily seized with Hitler's approval.

Khrushchev's role as Sovietizer and Russifier of the Ukraine

was perhaps best of all formulated by one of his adjutants—
Central Committee Secretary K. Z. Litvin, who at the time was
in charge of agitation and propaganda:

> Comrade Khrushchev [wrote Litvin in 1945] works un-
> tiringly to drive into the minds of the widest masses of
> the Ukrainian people [the idea] that the Ukraine could
> have achieved all its historical victories as an inseparable
> component of the U.S.S.R.; that the best and sole insurance
> for the prosperity of the Ukraine, for its freedom and
> independence lies in the might of the U.S.S.R.; that for all
> its great achievements the Ukrainian people are indebted
> to the aid [they have received] from the fraternal Soviet
> peoples, to the strength of the Soviet socialist system, to
> the leadership of the Bolshevik Party, and to the great
> Stalin.[24]

14

The Postwar Juggling with Nationality Policy

After World War II, the principle of equality of nationalities inhabiting the Soviet Union—a principle grossly violated but still officially recognized in the past—was plainly thrown overboard. In promoting this new key in Soviet nationality policy Khrushchev outran Stalin himself. In a speech delivered on March 1, 1944, before the Sixth Session of the Ukrainian Supreme Soviet, Khrushchev singled out the "elder brother—the great Russian people" from among all the peoples of the Soviet Union who "contributed to the liberation of the Ukraine." [1] With this statement Khrushchev had anticipated to some extent Stalin's toast of May 24, 1945, in which he praised the Russian people as "the most outstanding nation of all nations forming the Soviet Union," a nation possessing "a clear mind, a staunch character, and patience." [2] In January, 1947, without referring to Stalin's toast, Khrushchev expressed his "cordial thanks to the Russian people for their selfless service to the entire Soviet people, for their clear mind, staunchness, patience, and fraternal aid." [3]

After 1945, subservience to the "Russian people" became an obligatory ingredient in every public speech made by leading non-Russian Communists. The idea of Great Russian supremacy, decidedly repudiated by Lenin, was now being enforced by all means, including falsification of the history of non-Russian peoples. All prior textbooks and essays on the history of these nations, in which their joining the Russian empire had been described as a result of Czarist imperialism, were scrapped and the authors purged and punished. New textbooks were ordered and even they had to be rewritten and edited, because at first the mission of the Russian people as "liberator" of non-Russian nations had not been sufficiently stressed. Outbursts against "bourgeois nationalist" tendencies in literature and art, in linguistics and history, and in all other cultural fields raged in every non-Russian republic, with the Ukraine high on the list.

The attack against leading Ukrainian writers and historians began in June, 1946, with a smashing criticism of the *Outline of the History of Ukrainian Literature*, published in 1945.[4] Six weeks later, at a plenary session of the Ukrainian Party's Central Committee, Khrushchev himself admitted that his Party machine had "underestimated the particular importance of ideological work and ideological-political education of cadres in the fields of science, literature and art, and not organized large-scale criticism of the bourgeois ideology in the press." Therefore, Khrushchev continued, "ideological errors, distortions and attempts at reviving bourgeois nationalist concepts have found their way into some books and magazines, and into speeches of some Ukrainian historians and writers." Then Khrushchev attacked the Institute of Linguistics and Literature and the Institute of History for tolerating "bourgeois nationalist views on history and culture" in the *Outline of the History of Ukrainian Literature* and in the first volume of the *History of the Ukraine*. Khrushchev paid special attention to those Ukrainian writers who had shown a tendency to "keep away from the most serious problems of the present and to idealize the past" and had been partisans of the idea that "writers have a right to commit ideological mistakes, i. e., a right to deviate from our Soviet ideology, a right to become free from criticism." [5]

Following Khrushchev's speech the Central Committee passed a special resolution blaming the Presidium of the Union of Soviet Writers in the Ukraine, and in particular its chairman Maksym Rylskyi, for "not having undertaken in time any measures to condemn in the press and at writers' meetings tendencies alien to Soviet literature." [6] A few days after Khrushchev's speech and the Party decision had been published, Maksym Rylskyi was criticized for supporting the view of some writers that men of letters should have "a right to commit ideological mistakes." Rylskyi was also accused of lack of vigilance, complacency, and a conciliatory attitude toward "hostile manifestations in literature." [7] According to a recent Ukrainian broadcast, Rylskyi was "purged and twice imprisoned" during the Stalin period.[8] It is in the light of this attack on Rylskyi, inspired in 1946 by Khrushchev, that one should view Khrushchev's statement of 1957 concerning this very same writer in *Kommunist*, the Party's central ideological organ. Khrushchev said:

> I had great difficulty in fending off smashing criticism of such a deserving writer as Maksym Rylskyi for his poem, "Mother," which is filled with deep patriotic feelings. The main pretext for unsubstantiated accusations against Rylskyi and attacks on him was that in his poem eulogizing the Soviet Ukraine, Stalin's name was not mentioned. Comrade Kaganovich, who kowtowed to Stalin and sponsored anything to inflate the cult of Stalin's personality, pictured Maksym Rylskyi as a Ukrainian bourgeois nationalist. He [Kaganovich] played on Stalin's weak points without taking into consideration the grave consequences which these unsubstantiated accusations against the honored Ukrainian writer and patriot Maksym Rylskyi could have had for Ukrainian literature, and not only for Ukrainian literature." [9]

There can be no doubt that Kaganovich, while he had been First Secretary of the Ukrainian Party in 1947, actually assailed Rylskyi, but Khrushchev, at the time Chairman of the Ukrainian Council of Ministers, certainly did not go out of his way to "fend off smashing criticism" of the writer. In fact, Rylskyi did not escape "smashing criticism" at all; in September, 1947, he was expelled from the post of Chairman of the Union of Soviet Writers in the Ukraine and the editorial board of the magazine *Vytchizna*. Even one year after Kaganovich had been recalled to Moscow and Khrushchev had again become the Party boss in the Ukraine, his protégé Aleksandr Korneichuk, who had replaced Rylskyi as Chairman of the Writers' Union, attacked Rylskyi's past "blunders." [10] It can hardly be assumed that Korneichuk, a member of the Ukrainian Central Committee and therefore a subordinate of Khrushchev's, would have been permitted to make such humiliating remarks had Khrushchev really been Rylskyi's defender. It can be assumed that Rylskyi expected Khrushchev's protection, if only as a reward for his readiness to immortalize Nikita Khrushchev in his poems. To mention only a few: in the poem "We Met Him" (1942) Rylskyi pictured Khrushchev as "quiet and glowing as strong as fire," sang of his "silver-gray youthfulness" and anticipated the joyful reunion with the leader after the liberation of the homeland: "We'll shake the firm hand of Nikita Khrushchev in the name of the people we so cherish and love." [11] In another poem, "The Ukraine is Being Liberated" (1944), Rylskyi again foresees the moment when Khrushchev will "meet us with a tender smile"; [12] in a third poem, "Return," the poet speaks about his son's pride in the man who is restoring the ravaged city of Kiev—Khrushchev—"the brother and friend of Moscow and Leningrad." [13] It is interesting to note that Rylskyi is now bringing up to date his poetry. In the last mentioned poem, for instance, published in 1950, when Stalin was still alive, Rylskyi sings of "Nikita Khrushchev, Stalin's companion," [14] while in its edition of 1954, when the disgraced tyrant was lying in the mausoleum, Nikita Khrushchev was turned into "our glorious Leninist." [15]

The assault on Ukrainian writers was only a partial reflection of the Kremlin's policy change in 1946 aimed at tightening the screws in all fields of cultural life that had been loosened somewhat in the war years in order to gain the wholehearted support from all strata of Soviet intelligentsia, and even the Church, in the war effort. While the Ukraine was occupied by the Germans, Rylskyi, and other Ukrainian men of letters, art, and science were evacuated to the Urals and given assignments to compose ardent patriotic addresses to their people urging them to resist the invaders. But then they were sometimes carried away to days of the past when their homeland's aspirations had not yet been extinguished by the Bolshevik Revolution. Rylskyi's poem "Mother," which Khrushchev now claims to have defended, and other poems for which Rylskyi was criticized in 1946-47, were published in the war years and did not provoke any criticism at that time; on the contrary, in 1943 Rylskyi was awarded the Stalin Prize and in 1945 the Order of Lenin. As soon as the war ended, however, these works were considered dangerous, because, as Khrushchev said in 1946, they showed a tendency to idealize the past and, whoever among the non-Russian writers has feelings for the old times is, by Soviet definition, bound to become a bourgeois nationalist striving to "detach" the non-Russian peoples from "the great Russian nation."

In June, 1953, after Stalin's death, the Russification policy in the Western Ukrainian provinces underwent a reversal. On June 13, the Kremlin disclosed that Leonid G. Melnikov, at the time First Secretary of the Ukrainian Party, had been ousted from that position for "having permitted distortions in the Leninist-Stalinist national policy." The charges against Melnikov were a frontal attack against the Stalin Russification policy. They were also an indictment of Khrushchev who in the course of his twelve-year rule in the Ukraine had vigorously put this policy into practice. Melnikov had worked under Khrushchev in 1939-40 and from 1944 to 1949,* and carried out the Kremlin's Russification policy as efficiently as his boss. In his bid for power, Beria, himself a non-Russian, tried to rally around himself the non-Russian nations, and he used the Russification issue as a pretext to press for the removal of Malenkov's partisans, such as Melnikov.*

Melnikov subsequently re-emerged and rose again. A few weeks after Beria's fall, Melnikov was appointed Soviet Ambassador to Rumania;[17] in April, 1955 (after Malenkov's demotion from premiership), he was recalled to Moscow and appointed Minister of Construction of Coal Industry Enterprises; and in June, 1957, he was identified as Chairman of the Planning Committee and First Deputy of the Council of Ministers of the Kazakh S.S.R. Thus Khrushchev moved a notorious Russifier of the Ukraine to a Moslem republic to replace a prominent local leader.

---

* The Ukrainian press, controlled by Melnikov, attempted to continue building up Malenkov's personality even after the Moscow *Pravda*, probably under Beria's pressure, virtually ceased quoting Malenkov or any other member of the "collective leadership." From March 11 to March 31, 1953, *Pravda Ukrainy* carried thirty-seven quotations from Malenkov's speeches, while the Moscow *Pravda* had only one quotation, and this was in an article by Melnikov. In May, 1953, Melnikov's attempts at aggrandizing Malenkov's personality were stopped, and a series of personnel changes indicated Beria's growing influence in the Ukraine.

Another case in point is the re-emergence of Semyon D. Ignatiev, a former Minister of State Security (MGB), who had been appointed to that post at the end of 1951 as a replacement of Viktor S. Abakumov, who was executed in December, 1954. Ignatiev was in charge of the so-called "doctors' plot," in which several doctors, mostly Jews, were accused of intentionally applying improper methods of medical treatment to high Soviet officials.

In his secret speech at the Twentieth Party Congress Khrushchev blamed Stalin for "setting up this shameful 'case.'" "We felt," Khrushchev said, "that the case of the arrested doctors was questionable. We knew some of those people personally because they had once treated us."[18] Khrushchev, at that time one of the secretaries of the Central Committee and First Secretary of the Moscow Party organization, granted himself general absolution for not having intervened in favor of the victims of Stalin's brutality because "there was no possibility of trying to verify facts by contacting those who had made the confessions of guilt."[19] But did Khrushchev give the benefit of the doubt to those whom he had known personally as efficient and honest doctors and who had treated him and probably his family? Evidently not. The day the Tass announcement on the doctors' plot was published, *Moskovskaya Pravda*, the organ of the Moscow Party organization of which Khrushchev was the boss, treated the doctors as if they were already convicted "criminals and foul murderers," and this in spite of the fact that the announcement stated that the investigation was not yet completed.[20] The doctors' plot was started in June, 1952. This was exactly the period when Beria's position in the Politburo was at its lowest.

Beria's downgrading does not, of course, indicate that he took a definite stand against Stalin in the doctors' case, but it does indicate that the case was initiated against his advice and conducted without his guidance. This was the reason why Ignatiev became Beria's target immediately after Stalin's death. On March 7, 1953, Ignatiev lost his position in the Ministry of State Security and was shifted to the Party apparatus, where Khrushchev was consolidating his position. However, this attempt to save Ignatiev from Beria's onslaught failed: not even a month passed before Ignatiev was accused of "political blind-ness" [21] in connection with the doctors' case which, according to *Pravda's* later admission, "kindled feelings of national animosity." [22] With Beria's downfall, Ignatiev was appointed First Secretary of the Bashkir Autonomous Republic. Thus, under the Khrushchev regime, another Moslem republic came under the rule of a Great-Russian whose career had not exactly mirrored sympathy for other nationalities and races.

In speeches, particularly those delivered abroad, Khrushchev goes out of his way to emphasize that in the Soviet Union the nationality problem has been solved once and for all and that full equality of all nations reigns. Racial discrimination and the supremacy of the numerically preponderant Great Russian nation have been declared incompatible with Communist ideology. However, in his de-Stalinization speech, Khrushchev admitted that in 1943 and 1944 quite a few Soviet national republics had been liquidated and that "whole nations together with all Communists and Komsomols," including "women, children, and old people," underwent mass deportations "from their native places." Khrushchev mentioned four Moslem nationalities—the Karachai, the Ingushs, the Chechens, and the Balkars—and the Buddhist nationality of the Kalmucks. "The Ukrainians," he added, "avoided meeting this fate because there were too many of them, and there was no place to which to deport them."

Such total deportations are possible only in totalitarian states. The twentieth century witnessed another example of such indiscriminate large-scale actions, which, incidentally, also included "all Communists and Komsomols." These were the mass deportations undertaken by Adolf Hitler. According to Khrushchev, Stalin, and Stalin alone, was responsible for the mass deportations in the Soviet Union. Khrushchev's sincerity in blaming Stalin is questionable, particularly in view of a remark he made in an interview with Canadian Communists in August, 1957, to the effect that he, Khrushchev, "agreed with Stalin that the Crimea . . . should not be turned into a Jewish colonization center, because in case of war it would be turned into a base for attacking the U.S.S.R." [23] Thus Khrushchev makes a distinction between nationalities who are by nature faithful to the principle of "Soviet patriotism" and those with an allegedly natural inclination to treason. But this was also Stalin's reasoning when he ordered the mass deportations in 1943 and 1944.

To support the claim that the Soviet nationality policy has been a complete success Khrushchev resorts to figures and percentages showing the economic development in the once-underdeveloped areas inhabited by non-Russian nationalities. These statistics are impressive, but they tell only the story of a successful exploitation of available resources initiated, performed, and controlled by Moscow. This is not synonymous with happy, flourishing ethnic cultures, or with increasing national autonomy. Moscow's influence and control can be demonstrated by the fact that between 1926 to 1959, percentages of native populations in the Central Asian republics diminished considerably, while those of the Great Russian population increased. In the Turkmen S.S.R., the percentage of the Turkmens fell from 72 per cent in 1926 to 60.9 per cent in 1959; in the Tadzhik S.S.R., during the same period, the corresponding percentages of the Tadzhiks fell from 68.5 to 53.1; in the Kirghiz S.S.R., the Kirghizs became a minority in 1959—representing only 40.5 per cent of the population, as against 66.6 per cent in 1926; and in the Kazakh S.S.R., the Kazakhs were gradually outnumbered to a greater extent than the Kirghizs and, in 1959, constituted only 30 per cent of the population, as compared to 57.1 per cent in 1926. During the same period (1926-59), the percentages of the Great Russian population rose: in Turkmenistan from 7.5 to 17.3 per cent; in Tadzhikistan from a fraction of 1 per cent to 13.3 per cent; in Kirghizia from 11.7 to 30.2 per cent; and in Kazakhstan from 19.7 to 42 per cent.

As for the unfortunate nationalities mentioned by Khrushchev in his 1956 speech, the extent of their mishandling in 1943 and 1944 can be measured by a comparison of their numbers in 1939 and 1959 with those of the Great Russians during the same period: Between 1939 and 1959, the total of the Great Russian population increased by 14.1 per cent. Only that of the Ingushs showed a similar increase, while the number of Chechens rose only by 2.9 per cent; that of the Balkars decreased by 0.2 per cent; and the number of the Kalmucks decreased by 44.5 per cent.[24] In 1937, the *Large Soviet Encyclopedia* wrote: "National oppression and exploitation, combined with the extremely low economic and cultural level, resulted in a systematic dying out of the Kalmucks in the pre-Revolutionary period. From 1897 to 1917, the population dropped 15.3 per cent." This enormous decline of the Kalmucks population during the two decades from 1897 to 1917 under the Czarist regime was almost trebled during the two decades (1939-59) under the Soviet regime, while the Great Russian population showed an increase of more than 14 per cent.

Now all these nationalities have been "rehabilitated." But the question arises: Has Khrushchev relinquished Stalin's discriminatory policy? Khrushchev himself partially answered this question in the statement made in 1957 before the Canadian Communist delegation. But to answer this question fully it is necessary to determine whether Khrushchev has departed from the Stalinist practice of limiting, or even forbidding, national minorities in their quest to preserve and develop their cultural heritages and spiritual life in accordance with their religious beliefs and customs. Unfortunately, in this respect no changes are apparent. The natural desire of any nationality to "idealize the past" is still considered "bourgeois nationalism" and religious ceremonies and customs are treated as capitalist survivals which must be eradicated. As in the past, all religions have remained targets for rigorous and intensified Communist campaigns. But the national minorities have always considered an attack on their religions as an attacks on their traditional way of life. Freedom of worship formally continues to exist, but the regime does not refrain from resorting to the most slanderous means of undermining and destroying religious communities of ethnic minorities.

In the 1957 interview with the Canadian Communists, Khrushchev elaborated on the "bad features" of the Jews and noted that "Wherever a Jew settles, the first thing he does is build a synagogue."[25] There is clear evidence that such an attitude has encouraged Khrushchev's local Party subordinates to play havoc with the religious practices of this minority.

On December 9, 1959, the Kirovograd regional radio service carried a broadcast in which the religious leaders of the local Jewish community were attacked in the most violent language:

Sermons of Rabbi Ayzik Spektor hardly differ from the woeful theory of the uniqueness of the Aryan race and its destiny to rule over the peoples of the entire world. . . . Thus praying, they call for the killing of all those who deny the Pentateuch—the Jewish prayer book. . . . With their tentacles, the Jewish bourgeois nationalists, with the help of Judaism, try to reach our Soviet garden. But they will never succeed.

On August 9, 1960, *Kommunist*, the organ of the Buynaksk City Party Committee carried a similar attack. Buynaksk has a population of about 30,000, predominantly Kumyks, a people of Turkish stock. *Kommunist* editorially accused the local Jews —a minority of the city's population— of stressing the superiority of their religion over Islam and informed its Moslem readers that, for purification purposes, the Jews have to drink human blood of people belonging to other faiths.

In Czarist Russia, the canard about the Jews' need of human or animal blood for ritual purposes was circulated in 1881 in the very city of Kirovograd (then Elisavetgrad) from which the radio waves carried the above-mentioned broadcast in 1960.

It would seem that now, in the Khrushchev era, a situation prevails that makes possible the revival of a calumny which dates back to the darkest days of medieval obscurantism. Of greater significance, however, is the fact that insinuations of this kind are printed in publications controlled by the Communist Party without public repudiation, since all avenues of free public opinion are blocked by the totalitarian regime. Even in Czarist Russia such avenues were open, and prominent figures like Tolstoi, Gorky, Chekhov, and Korolenko made ample use of them, raising their influential voices against this "kindling of feelings of national animosity."

These samples of Soviet propaganda, tolerated and perhaps even inspired from above, clearly indicate that the nationality policy in the Khrushchev era has not deviated from the Stalinist pattern.

15

"Liberator of the Oppressed Brothers"

On September 17, 1939, the Red Army invaded the eastern provinces of Poland in accordance with the Hitler-Stalin agreement. A special "Ukrainian Front" was set up under the command of Semyon K. Timoshenko, at the time Commander of the Kiev Special Military District (KOVO). Khrushchev, as a member of the Military Council of KOVO, automatically became a member of the Military Council of the Ukrainian Front. In an appeal signed by Timoshenko and Khrushchev, the Red Army troops were told that they marched into the Western Ukraine "not as conquerors but as liberators of our Ukrainian and Belorussian brothers . . . from the rule of the landlords and capitalists." ("Fascists" were no longer mentioned, since "liberation" was made possible because of an agreement with the Nazis.) At the same time the troops were encouraged to "erase from the surface of the earth everybody who obstructs the fulfillment of this great historical cause of emancipation of our brothers." [1]

In his capacity as Military Council member, Khrushchev, at that time already a member of the All-Union Politburo, exercised only part of the authority he had been invested with by the Kremlin. It was also his responsibility to take all appropriate measures for a speedy political assimilation of the former Polish territory. In addition to military force, Khrushchev had at his disposal the propaganda machine of the Ukrainian Party and the secret police under Ivan Aleksandrovich Serov, who became head of the Committee of State Security in March, 1954, and was dismissed from that post in December, 1958.

Khrushchev used all three levers of dictatorship to the fullest extent. He personally took part in the dismemberment of Poland. He was not sitting in Kiev in his office awaiting reports from his subordinates and flashing back orders; he was on the move all the time during and after the occupation of Polish territory. He moved along with the troops, visited the occupied areas to acquaint himself with the political frame of mind of the population and with economic problems, selected people from among the native Ukrainian intelligentsia who would agree to the idea of a "reunited" Ukraine under Moscow's boot, and acted as a propagandist and agitator in "heart-to-heart" conversations, delivering speeches before selected audiences and at large public meetings.

Khrushchev's movements in the occupied area, as far as they have been recorded in the Soviet press, give an idea of the enormous role he played in the operation "Liberation." On September 17, the day the Red Army units crossed the Soviet-Polish border, Khrushchev, following the tanks, showed up in the city of Podvolochisk and the town of Kamenka, where he was "enthusiastically" met by the "jubilant" population and "had a talk" with the inhabitants about almost everything.[2] On September 18, together with Timoshenko, he visited the seized cities of Tarnopol, Trembovl, and Skalat.[3] From there he rushed to the outskirts of Lvov to "participate" in the seizure of that city. On September 22, he entered Lvov. On September 26, Khrushchev visited Drogobych and Borislav. On his way to Drogobych he talked with farmers of the village Gaivezne, district of Dragomysh, where the peasants, "full of emotion, told him how joyfully they received the Red Army." In Drogobych Khrushchev inspected the oil-refining plant and assembled its workers to discuss the measures necessary to resume the work of the plant as soon as possible. In Borislav he acquainted himself with the oil-extracting installations and then left for Lvov.[4] On September 29, Khrushchev visited Peremyshl (Przemyśl), where he was "surrounded by the population asking him a great number of questions," to which he gave "detailed answers." Here he also talked to the "provisional administration" and gave them instructions concerning the work of the municipal enterprises.[5]

Khrushchev's participation in the invasion and in the subsequent military occupation of the newly acquired territory has been highly praised by one of the "heroes" of this operation, F. I. Golikov. In May, 1940, at the Fifteenth Ukrainian Party Congress, Golikov emphasized "the concrete and active part" Khrushchev had taken "in the liberation of the West Ukrainian toilers." Golikov based his assertion on "several personal encounters [with Khrushchev] in those days of fighting beyond the Zbruch, on the way to Tarnopol, and directly at the approaches of Lvov." Golikov described Khrushchev's role in seizing Lvov in the following terms:

> I would like to reveal to you one of the incidents connected with the seizure of Lvov, and, on the basis of this incident, to stress the particular significance of Comrade Khrushchev's participation in it. The army operated on the outskirts of Lvov. The main preparations for the seizure of this big city had already been completed, and our units waited only for the signal to attack it with a large number of tanks and artillery. At this point, however, two new circumstances occurred. The main question was which means should be used for the seizure of the city, since, as a result of measures we had undertaken, it seemed certain that we could force the Polish command to give up the city and its garrison of over 20,000 without a battle. At this particular moment Nikita Sergeyevich Khrushchev, together with the Military Council member Comrade Borisov arrived at the command post. I believe that it is easy to understand the great significance of the support we received in the form of participation and advice at this decisive moment.[6]

This rather vague account does not discuss the measures taken by the Soviet command to force submission on the part of the Poles, nor does it mention the nature of Khrushchev's participation and advice, but it can be assumed that the role he played in the seizure of Lvov was concerned rather with political subversion than with military operations.

According to Golikov, "for the last seven months" (October, 1939, to May, 1940), Khrushchev also took an active part in "raising the preparedness" of the Red Army forces in the West Ukraine, in "studying the terrain, the border, and in sealing it off." [7]

The military invasion was accompanied by a large-scale political and "cultural" offensive. Hundreds of leading Party and government workers followed the Red Army's footsteps to organize local organs of Soviet dictatorship and to "prepare" the forthcoming elections to the so-called People's Assembly which was to take a unanimous decision to join the Soviet Ukraine. Simultaneously Soviet "cultural workers" of Ukrainian origin—writers, artists, dancers, singers, dramatic troops, film operators—were sent to the seized regions to impress the "liberated" Ukrainians with the achievements of the "Ukrainian socialist culture." [8] To support this drive the occupied areas were flooded with propaganda material. Tons of newspapers were delivered every day by air. In less than one week, 800,000 portraits of Soviet Communist leaders, 300,000 posters and slogans, 2 million brochures, 1.5 million leaflets, [9] and 100,000 records with fifty-six titles in Ukrainian, [10] were rushed to the scene. However, while the records were playing and the dancers and singers were entertaining politically inexperienced West Ukrainians, NKVD men, headed by Ivan Aleksandrovich Serov, were mopping up thousands of open and potential anti-Communists —members of Ukrainian national parties and organizations, of the Polish Socialist Party (PPS), the Jewish Labor Association "Bund," the Zionists, and even members of the Polish Communist Party which the Comintern had dissolved on Stalin's orders in the summer of 1938.

The fate of the Polish Communist Party deserves to be described in some detail, because Khrushchev was personally involved in this delicate matter. At the same time the Soviet troops were ready to move into Poland, a special Committee on National Minorities had been set up in the Ukrainian Party Central Committee. In view of the complicated nature of the matters which the Committee had to deal with in the area under occupation, no major decision could have been taken without consulting the First Secretary of the Party, Khrushchev. It was the Polish section of this Committee that received Khrushchev's order not to consider as Party comrades the Polish Communists who had fled *en masse* from Nazi-occupied territory to the Soviet-occupied zone, hoping to find refuge and work. According to the order, each case was to be treated individually. The well-informed source—a former leading Polish Communist—who furnished this information put it this way: "A membership card in the Polish Communist Party meant death or, in the best case, investigation." This attitude toward comrades in the faith was not surprising in view of the Comintern decision of 1938 to dissolve the Polish Communist Party, which allegedly had turned into a Party of "traitors and spies" and whose entire top leadership had been liquidated under Yezhov. For the bloody Purge of 1937-38 was aimed not only at prominent Soviet Communists such as Kamenev, Zinoviev, Bukharin, Rykov, and others, but also at the leaders of foreign Communist Parties. The fate of the leadership of the Polish Communist Party was terrible indeed. In 1937-38 its leading officials were called to Moscow, allegedly for the purpose of discussing important ideological matters. Instead, they were thrown into jail. Some died while under "investigation," others were shot or disappeared in the gears of Yezhov's terror machine.

The scope of the Purge can be seen from the fact that only one member of the Polish Central Committee, Franciszek Fiedler, escaped the fate of his colleagues, for the simple reason that he lived in France. Two years after Stalin's death the liquidated leaders were rehabilitated in the Polish press [11] and in February, 1956, the Comintern resolution which had provided the basis for the dissolution of the Party was rescinded. Allegations in the Polish daily *Trybuna Ludu* [12] that Beria was to blame for the liquidation of the Polish Communist leaders are unfounded, since Beria succeeded Yezhov only in December, 1938, after the massacre had been virtually completed. Beria, however, can be blamed for the purges and deportations in the "liberated" areas which began at the end of 1939. Here, Beria's terror apparatus was put into full operation and worked hand in hand with Khrushchev's Party machine.

The brutality with which the Polish Communists were treated is exemplified by the case of a Mrs. X, whose name is known to this writer but cannot be divulged at the present time. Mrs. X had been an old Bolshevik, as had her husband who was executed by the NKVD without trial. They knew Lenin well personally. Mrs. X taught in the Academy of the Comintern and in the Institute of Red Professors in Moscow, and some high-placed Communists had been her pupils. In September, 1939, Mrs. X fled from the Nazi-occupied part of Poland, where she had carried on underground Communist activities before World War II, to Lvov, which was occupied at the time by the Red Army. There she reported to the Lvov Communist Party Committee, an outfit which had moved in with the Soviet tanks and was closely supervised and guided by Khrushchev himself. She was arrested without explanation. In the Lvov jail a young NKVD man interrogated her, and, as she had nothing to confess, assailed her in the most violent manner. Three weeks later, an NKVD man, accompanied by a representative of Khrushchev's Party Committee, entered the prison cell and declared that she had been tried *in absentia* and sentenced to ten years in a "corrective labor camp" for the assistance she allegedly had rendered to the Polish "fascist" government. She was placed in a Siberian concentration camp where she served for five and a half years in the company of prostitutes and various criminals. She was still in the camp when a new Polish Communist Party headed by some of her former pupils was formed. She was freed in 1945 by virtue of the agreement signed by the Kremlin and the Polish government-in-exile in London.

Khrushchev's participation in the case of Mrs. X is beyond any doubt, because she was so well known that a decision about her fate could not have been made without his knowledge and approval. The case of Mrs. X had a tragicomic epilogue. In 1954, the son of Mrs. X, who at the time was studying engineering in Moscow, was called to the MVD and officially informed that his father had been posthumously rehabilitated and that his reputation as an honest and honorable Leninist had been restored. Then the MVD representative presented his condolences to the son and handed him an envelope as a compensation for the great loss that he and his family had suffered because of Beria's criminal activity. The envelope contained a check for 700 rubles, not even the equivalent of an average month's earnings of a Soviet worker.

Khrushchev and Serov practiced even greater ruthlessness toward members of other political parties and organizations and toward suspected anti-Communists. There are numerous accounts about the brutal behavior of the Soviet invaders toward the remnants of the defeated Polish Army, particularly officers, who, driven by the Germans to the East, fell into the hands of the Red Army and the NKVD. The mopping-up operations were also directed against Polish, Jewish, and Ukrainian socialists, clergymen, shop-owners, small businessmen (the wealthier ones had already left the country), and all those who, in Communist terminology, belonged to the bourgeois class. In short, the "liberated" areas underwent the same process of Bolshevization and Sovietization as had the "mother country." The only difference was that the pace had been accelerated, and that the experience gained by the "organs of the proletarian dictatorship" in the course of two decades enabled them to achieve greater perfection in a shorter time.

The Soviet press celebrated the "liberation of the oppressed brothers" and, of course, publicized as little as possible the bloody purge which raged in the Soviet-occupied zone of Poland. But even the microscopic dose of information that has been published, especially the statements in editorials and speeches, reveals the spirit of the new masters. A few days after the invasion had been completed, the Ukrainian magazine *Bilshovik Ukrainy* carried an editorial saying that "the toilers of West Ukraine will not forget even for one minute that the struggle against the ferocious enemy is not yet finished," and that they remember the appeal Khrushchev made at the meeting of the toilers in Lvov concerning the "revolutionary vigilance and the merciless struggle against the enemies of the people." Then the editorial continued: "With the support of the Soviet people [*sic*] the people of the West Ukraine will annihilate the wicked nests of the masked enemies of the people—the bourgeois nationalists, the officer gangs, and other hostile nests, and clean its soil from the foul rotters." [13] Another Soviet source asserted that the "toilers of the liberated region are convinced that all sorts of parties—the UNDO,* the PPS, and the like—were and are nothing but faithful dogs of the landowners and capitalists." [14] The Soviet singer Patorzinsky, in his capacity as deputy to the Ukrainian Supreme Soviet, said two months after the Soviet invasion:

"The Red Army fighters brought to the Western Ukraine on their sharp steel bayonets death for the enemies of the people." [15] Another deputy to the Supreme Soviet, Piotr I. Franko, confirmed the salutary effect of the Soviet bayonets by saying that "with the aid of the valiant Red Army, the people of the Ukraine caught the Polish *pans* [landowners] and their grovelers—the Petlurovites, the UNDO-ists, the Endeks,† the Zionists, and the other riffraff—by their throats and threw them out beyond the borders of the Ukraine." [16]

This frank statement speaks for itself: it implies all elements of Soviet terror, including deportation. This deputy also expressed his joy and happiness that the "Soviet Ukrainian people, led by the wise instructions of Comrade Stalin, guided daily by the Central Committee of the Communist Party [Bolshevik] of the Ukraine and Comrade N. S. Khrushchev, rapidly caught the spies and diversionists and annihilated them like poisonous snakes, like mad dogs." [17] ‡

The above statements were made in November, 1939, two months after the Soviet forces had invaded Poland. The first wave of terror did not, however, wash out all opposition, in spite of the fact that in the "election" to the People's Assembly on October 22, 1939, 92.83 per cent of the total number of electors participated and 90.93 per cent allegedly voted for the sole candidates nominated by Khrushchev's Party machine. [18] In January, 1940, the Kiev Komsomol paper complained that "the enemy is still alive," and cited a case where "nationalist thugs from 'Prosvita' § had tried to hold back rural youths from joining

* Ukrainian National Democratic Organization.

† Polish National Democratic Party.

‡ In May, 1940, at the Fifteenth Ukrainian Party Congress, Khrushchev received a similar compliment from Ivan A. Serov, NKVD chief of the Ukraine, who praised Khrushchev's help in "unmasking, crushing, and eradicating all enemies and spies of foreign intelligence services." (*Visti*, May 20, 1940).

§ Traditional Ukrainian Cultural and Educational Community Center.

the Komsomol." But the "scheme of the enemy failed," as the Komsomol organization was informed about these "detestable attempts of 'Prosvita.'"[19] (One can imagine what happened to the young men from this organization.) The conclusion the paper drew from this incident was that "we have to insure the complete and final crushing of the enemy who hinders the strengthening of the dictatorship of the proletariat in the Western provinces."[20]

In 1939-40, three elections were held in the West Ukrainian provinces: in October, 1939, the so-called People's Assembly was elected which took a "unanimous" decision to join the Soviet Union; in March, 1940, there were elections to the Supreme Soviets of the Ukrainian S.S.R. and U.S.S.R., and in December, 1940, elections to the local Soviets.

The first electoral campaign in the West Ukrainian provinces was of short duration; the "liberation" had begun on September 17, 1939; Lvov was seized on September 22, and as early as October 10, the newspapers carried the decision of the Military Council of the Ukrainian Front, signed by Khrushchev, Timoshenko, and two other members of the Council, approving the composition of a committee charged with the organization of the elections to the People's Assembly scheduled for October 22.[21] This election campaign was perhaps the shortest in history. As the People's Assembly had only one item on the agenda—the joining of the Soviet Union—the desire to get this formality accomplished as fast as possible explains Moscow's haste. Khrushchev's opinion on whether the necessary preparations could be made in such a short time was certainly sought and taken into account. This is probably the reason why he personally conducted this election campaign on the scene. On October 9, in Lvov, he attended a conference of the "provisional administrative organs" to discuss with them "in detail the Statute of the Elections and to outline the measures which would ensure all conditions necessary for the citizens of the West Ukraine freely to express their will [*sic!*]."

"Comrade Khrushchev," the communiqué continued, "explained in detail to the participants of the conference the tasks of the organizational and agitational-propagandistic preparation of the election . . ."[22] On October 11, also in Lvov, Khrushchev spoke at a public meeting.[23] On October 17, again in Lvov, he participated in an election meeting followed by a concert.[24] On election day Khrushchev visited several electoral districts in the city and province of Stanislav and "talked to electors about the election." He also used this occasion to acquaint himself "with the changes which had occurred in the life of the people after liberation . . . and with the activity of the local Workers' Red Guard," and to "give advice to the officials of the provisional administration concerning their future work."[25] All this was, of course, a small part of his tight electioneering schedule in those strained days.

The second electoral campaign (to the Supreme Soviets) lasted two months, from January 24 to March 24, 1940, and the third campaign (to the local Soviets), from October 15 to December 15, 1940. The longer duration of the campaign periods suggests that the resistance to the new regime, particularly on the part of the peasants who were strongly opposed to Khrushchev's collectivization drive, was growing. More time was needed to "persuade" the "liberated" population of the advantages of "socialism."

The results of the elections would have been most gratifying to any political party in democratic non-Communist countries: the number of voters for the Party ticket exceeded 90 per cent in the first election, and approached 100 per cent in the last two elections. No party in the history of mankind (with the possible exception of fascist states) ever chalked up such victories. But from Khrushchev's point of view the results of the first election could have been even better. The results of the first election had, of course, been a success, but in comparison with the election results scored in the "mother country," where the 100 per cent mark is reached but by a fraction of 1 per cent, they seemed still meager. The results of the second election had been more encouraging; the number of voters increased by over 6 per cent, and that of the supporters of the Party ticket by over 7 per cent.[26] At the Fifteenth Ukrainian Party Congress Khrushchev boasted of these results:

"As a result of our work there was a vote which showed the strength of our Party and the solidarity of our people with the Bolshevik Party."[27] He must have been even more satisfied with the results of the third election, at which 99.26 per cent rushed to the polls and 98.07 to 98.93 per cent of them joyfully cast their "ayes" for the Bolshevik Party.[28] Their anxiety to vote for the party of Lenin and Stalin was so great that many voters "could not sleep all night," the papers reported.

It is. however, interesting to note that the elections to the local Soviets—which the Stalinist (now called "Soviet") Constitution defines as the "Local Organs of Government Power"— were held on December 15, 1940, fifteen months after the Red Army had "liberated" the West Ukrainian provinces, while the elections to the "Supreme Organs of Government Power," the Supreme Soviets, had been held much earlier. Why this delay? Why could the elections not have been held, for instance, on December 24, 1939, when the citizens of eight Soviet republics, including the Soviet Ukraine, had enjoyed the right to demonstrate their solidarity with the Party by electing the "local organs of the government power"? Why had Khrushchev deprived the "liberated" West Ukrainians of the privilege their Eastern brothers were given on that day? The only logical answer to these questions is that for fifteen months the "liberators" hesitated to consult the "liberated," and that Khrushchev was unable to find the necessary number of sufficiently faithful candidates from among the 8 million inhabitants of the seized region to fill the 79,010 seats in the local Soviets.[29] This was a far more difficult task than the nomination of the 113 deputies to the All-Union and Ukrainian Supreme Soviets elected in March, 1940, had been. Despite Khrushchev's extraordinary efforts, his Party apparatus needed more than one year to create local Soviet cadres in the Western Ukraine. Not all the cadres, of course, were of local origin; a substantial number were imported from the "mother country."

Cries for vigilance and mercilessness to the "enemies" had been especially loud prior to the elections, which would justify the assumption that the terror waves reached their crests around this particular time. This, of course, does not mean that Khrushchev and his NKVD chief, Serov, were putting the terror machine into high gear before the elections with the purpose of ensuring their favorable outcome. Rather, the elections themselves were used as an occasion to expose those whose sympathy for the new regime was doubtful. This was done in two stages: during the electoral campaign and at the polling places. In the first stage thousands of agitators were in touch with the electors and thus learned what their thinking was on political and economic matters; at the second stage, information was collected from observation of the voters' behavior at the polls.

In election periods Soviet propagandists and agitators fulfill a triple function: first, they canvass for the candidates to be elected; second, they popularize the Communist ideology, stressing its connection with the tasks which the Party and government expect to see fulfilled (increase of productivity, fulfillment and overfulfillment of the industrial and agricultural plans, and the like); and, third, they act as feelers, as emissaries sent out to determine the degree of dissatisfaction of the population with the regime. In general, this has been true for decades in the entire Soviet Union, but with respect to the territories newly acquired in 1939 and 1940, the third function was perhaps the most important. In the "liberated" areas the electoral campaigns fulfilled also a police function designed to collect the names of people who had expressed oppositionist views during the campaigns. The effectiveness of this method depends on the experience of the people. In the "mother country" they learned the trick a long time ago and behave accordingly: they listen, but do not talk. In the newly conquered regions, the population, and especially the farmers, lacked this experience, and many of them fell into the net. And the net was a finely meshed one: on the average there was one agitator for each sixteen or seventeen electors in the city and for each forty-five or fifty electors in the rural districts.[30]

Having under their supervision relatively small numbers of electors, the agitators were able to check the names of those who did not show up at the frequent small-scale meetings set up for them and, what is more important, to notice unfriendly remarks made during these meetings. This material was then turned over to the NKVD, where the names of the "enemies" were divided into three categories: the exposed enemy who should be dealt with immediately; the suspected enemy who, in case of a purge campaign, should be rounded up; and the dubious potential enemy who should remain under observation. The first category was considered hopeless, but the last two categories were not brushed away altogether, as there was still hope of "straightening them out" by means of propaganda and agitation. In this connection, Khrushchev's view on "work with the masses" is of interest. In June, 1935, he instructed the Moscow Party activists on how a Party agitator should approach the masses. First of all, Khrushchev drew a sharp line between a citizen who can be turned into a supporter of the regime and a "class enemy":

> There is no need to waste time on the class enemy, it does not pay trying to persuade him, you cannot break him by our agitation; to him one ought to apply other measures, measures prescribed by our class law. But one should treat patiently our working men and women who require intense work on our part.[31]

Khrushchev criticized Party agitators who dismiss as hopeless the "taciturnists"—those who prefer to keep silent at meetings or to evade them. He pointed out that vigilance also means "enveloping" every citizen with Communist agitation.

> If people stay away from our meetings [Khrushchev said], if workers who belong to the Party do not talk with them, other agitators will approach them and agitate against us, educate them against us, and all our words about vigilance will remain empty sounds.
>
> But if we envelop each and every worker with our political work, we will unmask the class enemy who is worming his way into our enterprises.[32]

Such was the approach of Khrushchev's agitators five years later in the "liberated" areas during the electoral campaigns which were used to expose those whom the Soviet bayonets and tanks had not convinced of the superiority of the regime that had produced them.

There is no way of knowing the number of people arrested, executed and deported from the "liberated" areas in 1939 and 1940, but it certainly runs to the tens of thousands. And the three elections held there in these years certainly yielded most of the names on the lists composed in the offices of the NKVD.

The "liberation" of the West Ukrainians and Belorussians from the "Polish yoke" was a disguised imperialistic act, and Khrushchev performed the Kremlin's assignment in the best Communist tradition. But a few years later he made territorial claims upon Poland which exceeded considerably those made at any time during and after the war by the Kremlin. In a public speech he claimed genuine Polish territories which Stalin himself was prepared to leave in Polish hands.

In March, 1944, when the Soviet armies were approaching the borders of Polish territory, the future of the Polish-Soviet frontier was still unsettled. Discussions behind the scene had been going on since the end of 1941. At that time Stalin had intimated to the Premier of the Polish government-in-exile, Władysław Sikorski, that he was willing to return some of the Polish territory the Soviet Union had seized with Hitler's approval in September, 1939, including the industrial center of Lvov.[33] It is debatable whether at that time Stalin was ready to sign a boundary settlement which would have been more favorable to the Poles than what they signed in 1945, and whether, if signed, it would have been honored three years later, when Soviet tanks rolled on Polish roads. The fact remains, however, that while Stalin's divisions were hard-pressed by the Germans, the Polish government-in-exile, backed by its Allies, was in a "position of strength" vis-à-vis the Kremlin.

After the debacle which the Germans suffered at Stalingrad the situation changed radically. On January 11, 1944, the Kremlin announced that the future Polish-Soviet frontier "could approximately follow the so-called Curzon Line, which was adopted in 1919 by the Supreme Council of Allied Powers. . . ."[34] Thus the line drawn by the "imperialists" in 1919 became acceptable to Stalin in 1944, because it ran about 150 to 200 miles to the west of the border established in the Polish-Soviet Peace Treaty of Riga in 1921. Cutting off a big chunk of Polish territory, the Curzon Line did not, however, penetrate as deeply into Poland as the Stalin-Hitler Line of 1939. This "generosity" on the part of the Kremlin was a political move to strengthen the position of the so-called Polish People's Council (Krajowa Rada Narodowa), a pro-Soviet outfit headed by the Communist leader Bolesław Bierut, who was to become President of Poland. The Soviet declaration made it clear that the "Soviet Government does not consider the frontiers of 1939 [drawn in agreement with Hitler] to be unchangeable [and that] the borders can be corrected in favor of Poland in such a way that regions in which the Polish population predominates would be ceded to Poland."[35]

Although Khrushchev was aware of the Kremlin's decision to make territorial concessions to the future Polish Government, whose "friendliness" to the Soviet Union was, however, Moscow's *conditio sine qua non* for the existence of a Polish state, he officially disagreed with the Moscow declaration, or, to be more precise, was allowed to express his own opinion on the border issue between Poland and the Soviet Ukraine.

On March 1, 1944, less than two months after the announcement of the Soviet declaration on Polish-Soviet relations, Khrushchev delivered in Kiev his first major postwar report before the Sixth Session of the Ukrainian Supreme Soviet.[36] Speaking as Chairman of the Ukrainian Council of People's Commissars, Khrushchev devoted a part of his report to the question of the "reunification of the great Ukrainian people." He intimated that in September, 1939, this question had not been solved to his full satisfaction, and that the Ukrainian people must insist on the "completion" of the reunification. He complained that "now, when one can already see the end of the rout of the German-fascist armies, our misguided neighbors encroach upon the rights, the legitimate rights of the Ukrainian people." He explained that the "misguided neighbors sit in London restaurants and dream of extending the Polish borders beyond the Dnieper to the Black Sea." This was, of course, a deliberate misrepresentation of the position taken by The Polish government-in-exile, and Khrushchev was aware of it. But whom could he have accused of "encroaching upon the legitimate rights of the Ukrainian people"? Had he been frank, he would have had to attack the Moscow declaration, for it promised to correct the injustices inflicted on the Poles in 1939, and to return to them some of the territory which Khrushchev considered to be legitimate Ukrainian soil. That Khrushchev was really thinking of the Moscow "concessions" is evident from the following passage in his speech which drew "stormy and prolonged applause" from the audience:

"The Ukrainian people," Khrushchev said, "will not permit those primordial Ukrainian lands, which were joined in a United Ukrainian Soviet state in accordance with the will of the population of the Western provinces of the Ukraine, to be detached [again] from the Soviet Ukraine."

It was true that these western provinces were claimed by the Polish government in London, but it was also true that, in spite of Khrushchev's claims, the Kremlin was ready to return bits of these territories, which were inhabited predominantly by a Polish population, to a future pro-Soviet Polish government. Furthermore, Khrushchev was disturbed not only about the fate of the Western provinces which he had helped to seize in September, 1939; he dreamt of a complete "reunification" of the Ukraine. He said:

> The Ukrainian people will strive for the completion of the great historical reunification of their Ukrainian lands into a united Ukrainian state. The Ukrainian people will strive for the inclusion of the primordial Ukrainian lands such as the Chełm region, Hrubieszóv, Zamość, Tomaszów, and Jarosław into the Ukrainian Soviet state.

All these areas are known as primordial Polish territory. Neither the Curzon Line of 1919 nor the Hitler-Stalin Line of 1939 included them in Soviet territory. The demands put forward by Khrushchev provoked an angry reply from the so-called Union of Polish Patriots in the U.S.S.R., a pro-Soviet organization of Polish Communists in the Soviet Union, which had been permitted to organize a Polish division to fight in the ranks of the Soviet Army. In April, 1944, *Wolna Polska (Free Poland)*, the organ of this group, rejected as improper Khrushchev's claims of Polish areas west of the Curzon Line. "In our decision to stand on the Curzon Line," *Wolna Polska* concluded, "we count on the support of Soviet public opinion." [37] The pro-Communist *Krajowa Rada Narodowa* which, according to the *Large Soviet Encyclopedia*, "encompassed all democratic forces of the anti-imperialist, antifascist underground," took a similarly negative attitude toward Khrushchev's demands, and instead "shared the views [expressed] in the declaration of the Soviet Government of January 11, 1944, on the restoration of Poland . . . through the establishment of a Polish-Soviet frontier along the so-called Curzon Line." [38]

Thus Khrushchev's imperialistic aspirations with regard to

Poland put on guard not only the Polish government-in-exile in London, but also the Polish pro-Soviet organizations which the Kremlin looked upon as the core of a future pro-Soviet Polish government. Khrushchev's appeal to Stalin to include indisputably Polish territory into the Soviet Ukraine failed, but apparently the late dictator did not resent Khrushchev's imperialist deviation, as one month later Khrushchev was awarded an additional Order of Lenin on the occasion of his fiftieth birthday.[39]

16

The Military Adventures of a Civilian General

All the feats which Khrushchev achieved during the three and a half years of his rule in the Ukraine—the fulfillment and over-fulfillment of industrial and agricultural plans, the purge of all classes of "enemies of the people," the strengthening of Party and NKVD control over all aspects of life, the "liberation of the oppressed Slavic brothers," and their Russification—were erased by the German invasion in June, 1941. After less than four months of fighting, the Ukrainian capital fell, and the avalanche of the German armed forces overran the entire Ukraine. In the early stages of the German invasion, most of those who had not been evacuated or had refused to go willingly accepted the change, and in many instances met the German "liberators" with flowers, and with bread and salt—the old Russian and Ukrainian custom of meeting dear guests. This was perhaps the most striking manifestation of hatred against the Communist way of life that had been imposed upon the peoples of the Soviet Union for almost a quarter of a century.

Soon, however, the unfortunate population realized that their joy had been premature, and that the fascist variety of totalitarian dictatorship was perhaps even worse, because, in addition to having the ordinary features, its philosophy was based on the supremacy of the German race over all other races, including the Slav race. Khrushchev and the high-ranking Party and government bureaucrats had fled, leaving behind small underground cells designed to become the cores of partisan detachments whose task it was to harass the enemy's rear.

Khrushchev's wartime role has been presented differently in each of the six official biographical accounts of his life published after World War II. The number of words devoted to his war record in the Soviet encyclopedias made available between 1947 and 1957 gradually increased from fifteen, in 1947, to eighty-one, in 1957.[1] The 1947 and 1948 versions mentioned only that Khrushchev was a member of the Military Council at the front; the 1955 version elaborates that he was a member of the Military Council of the Kiev Special Military District and that he occupied a similar position at four fronts (Southwestern group, Stalingrad, Southern, and First Ukrainian fronts); the subsequent versions (1956 and 1957) add for the first time that "simultaneously with his work at the fronts," Khrushchev "carried on large-scale work" in organizing the guerrilla activity (partisan movement) in the Ukraine, and the 1957 account also stresses his "active participation in the defense of Stalingrad and in preparing the defeat of the German-fascist forces at Stalingrad."

Even with the recent additions, Khrushchev's wartime record, as shown in Soviet political dictionaries and Soviet encyclopedias, is not too impressive if compared with that of political leaders such as Bulganin or Voroshilov. When the Soviet-German War broke out, a State Defense Committee (GKO) was created with Stalin as its chairman, Molotov as its deputy chairman, and Voroshilov, Malenkov, and Beria as its members. In 1944, Mikoyan, Kaganovich, Bulganin, and Voznesensky were added to the membership of that organ of supreme leadership which "united in its hands the entire military, political, and economic leadership of the country."[2] Thus Khrushchev did not belong to the core of state power during the war. But with his rise to the top of Soviet leadership, the role he actually played in achieving national victory has been greatly enhanced. This has been done through expunging from the record the names of those who had been defeated in the struggle for power and through embellishing the record of the victor. The first operation —falsification by omission—had been systematically applied during the Stalin era and continues to be a normal procedure after his death. After the liquidation of Voznesensky, his name was

eliminated from the list of the GKO members;* the same happened to Beria's name after he had been liquidated in 1953. In
1959, after four of the six living members of that body—Molotov,
Malenkov, Kaganovich, and Bulganin—had been purged by
Khrushchev during his rise to power, the full membership of
the GKO was no longer listed either in the *History of the CPSU,*
or in articles and books dealing with the history of World
War II published after the Purge. Instead they only report that
the GKO was headed by Stalin.[3]

In 1951, a Soviet official source listed names of fourteen
"closest companions-in-arms of Stalin in organizing the struggle
and the victories of the Soviet Army and the Soviet people in
the Great Fatherland War."[4] In this list, the names of Stalin's
lieutenants were placed according to their political standing, and
Khrushchev was ranked eleventh. In 1953, the same source
compiled a list of eleven "eminent political figures" whom "the
Party dispatched for leading work in the Armed Forces and
placed at the head of vital spheres of Soviet national economy."[5]
In this list, Khrushchev's name appeared in third place, the
first two being occupied by Malenkov and Molotov. In 1957,
almost immediately after the purge of the Malenkov-Molotov-
Kaganovich "anti-Party" group, the same source again published
a list of eleven "eminent Party workers" who "directly carried
out political, military, and economic leadership of the country
[and] headed the Armed Forces."[6] In this list the purged
leaders were eliminated, and Stalin's name, hitherto placed
separately and above those of his companions-in-arms, was listed
among the lesser figures, together with Khrushchev, Mikoyan,
and others. Finally, the 1959 version of the *History of the CPSU*[7]
established three lists: one for the "eminent Party figures who
were dispatched for leading work in the Army"; another for
those who "headed the most important spheres of the national
economy and ensured the Red Army with all necessary supplies";
and a third for "experienced Party workers" who became members of Military Councils of fronts and armies. Khrushchev, who,
in accordance with his official war record, should have been

* Three years after Stalin's death, Voznesensky's name reappeared as a
member of the GKO (*Vazhneyshiye operatsii Velikoi Otechestvennoi voiny*
[Moscow, 1956], p. 23).

placed in the third category, is listed, together with Voroshilov and three dead high Soviet officials (Zhdanov, Manuilsky, and Shcherbakov), in the first group. Mikoyan, Andreyev, Shvernik, and the late Voznesensky compose the second group, while Bulganin, Brezhnev, Suslov, and others form the third group. Malenkov, Molotov, and Kaganovich are, of course, not mentioned. The elevation of Khrushchev to the highest category of wartime leaders and the omission of the names of purged political figures who played a far greater role in World War II than he did is one of the most evident falsifications of Soviet history.

The latest official versions of Khrushchev's biography stress his "active" role in the defense of Stalingrad and in the defeat suffered there by the German army. But an analysis of the numerous books and articles about the Stalingrad battle and the role Soviet political and military leaders played in it shows that Soviet World War II historians are still undecided how to reconcile the hard facts with the changes they are required to make so that Khrushchev's role is enhanced and embellished.

During the Stalin era the task of Soviet historians was easy to fulfill: all military operations were initiated, prepared, and fulfilled by orders of Stalin, and only Malenkov was allowed to figure in the description of the Stalingrad battle as Stalin's special envoy. In a survey of World War II, the *Large Soviet Encyclopedia* reported in 1951 that Malenkov visited Stalingrad "in order to organize its defense." [8] The Soviet World War II historian B. S. Telpukhovsky, in a book published after Stalin's death entitled *The Great Victory of the Soviet Army at Stalingrad*, stated that at the end of August, 1942, Malenkov, Khrushchev, and General Vasilevsky were present in Stalingrad and "directed the activity of the Commander of the Front and of the [Stalingrad] provincial Party and Soviet organizations." [9]

This was the only mention of Khrushchev's name in the entire book. Malenkov, however, was credited with "carrying out a number of measures in providing [the necessary means] for the military operations at the bend of the Don river, in strengthening the defense of the city." Telpukhovsky also pointed out that it was Malenkov who "suggested doubling the production of tanks and other armaments in the Stalingrad factories." Finally,

Malenkov and Vasilevsky were credited with "bringing into military preparedness the detachments of the people's volunteer corps." [10]

On February 8, 1955, Malenkov was dismissed from his position of Soviet Premier. The next day, a new book, entitled *Outline of the History of the Great Fatherland War,* was ready for the printer. Published by the U.S.S.R. Academy of Sciences and carrying the name of the same Telpukhovsky as "responsible editor," this book omits mentioning Malenkov's name in the description of the happenings in Stalingrad at the end of August, 1942. Instead Khrushchev and Vasilevsky are said to have "taken urgent measures in strengthening the defense of the city." [11] This manipulation clearly reflects the struggle for power between Khrushchev and Malenkov. But the complete dismissal of Malenkov was to come only after his complete fall from power in June, 1957. In a book published by the Soviet Ministry of Defense, which at the time was still under Zhukov's command, the same event is described in the following terms: "In order to render practical aid and leadership in organizing the defense and mobilizing all forces for the repulse of the enemy, G. M. Malenkov, Secretary of the Central Committee of the Communist Party and member of the State Defense Committee, and representatives of the General Headquarters, General of the Army G. K. Zhukov and General A. M. Vasilevsky, were sent to Stalingrad." [12] This paragraph concluded with mention of Khrushchev's assignment as member of the Military Council of the Stalingrad Front. Thus, Khrushchev's role was again minimized, and that of Malenkov restored. This recurrence was of short duration. In a volume of the *Large Soviet Encyclopedia* released for the printer in November, 1957, only a few months after Malenkov's downfall, the event was described in the same terms, but no reference to Malenkov can be found.[13] Also in 1957, the same source credited the organizing of the defense of Stalingrad to Khrushchev alone: "Great work in strengthening the fighting ability of the armed forces and in mobilizing the efforts of the local population to defend Stalingrad was carried out by the member of the Politburo and of the Central Committee of the CPSU (b), N. S. Khrushchev, who was a member of the Military Council of the Stalingrad front." [14]

Marshal Zhukov's downfall in November, 1957, had also contributed to the elevation of Khrushchev's role in the victory at Stalingrad. In 1956, Soviet historians had no doubt that Zhukov "directed all the preparatory work in organizing the crushing of the German-fascist usurpers" at Stalingrad.[15] But in the second half of 1957, when Zhukov's position began to decline, the *Large Soviet Encyclopedia* stated that "in drafting the plan for the Stalingrad counteroffensive operation, an active part was taken by the commander of the Stalingrad front, General A. I. Yeremenko [and] the member of the Military Council, General N. S. Khrushchev," as well as other generals of the neighboring fronts. Having stressed the merits of "General N. S. Khrushchev," the encyclopedia generously admitted that "General G. K. Zhukov played a *certain* part in drafting this plan." (Italics added.) However, in a textbook for teachers released by the R.S.F.S.R. Ministry of Education in December, 1958, Khrushchev's name was omitted, while that of Zhukov can again be found among those who took an active part in drafting the counteroffensive.[16] As in the Malenkov case, the restoration of Zhukov's role did not last long. In 1959, the U.S.S.R. Ministry of Higher Education corrected the "mistake" of its R.S.F.S.R. counterpart. In "Materials for Lectures on the Course in the 'History of the CPSU,'" [17] the 1957 version which attributed to Khrushchev an active part in drafting the counteroffensive plan was restored verbatim, while Marshal Zhukov's name was omitted altogether.

Juggling of historical facts, rude falsification by omission and addition, and misrepresentation of events were methodically used in building up the cult of Lenin's and Stalin's personalities. The same method is being used in the Khrushchev era. The ignoble task of producing "historical essays" of this kind is given to "experienced" Party historians to whom truth is a means to achieve a purpose. But the fabrication and embellishment of a record for a leader who has reached the apex of power is insufficient to make him an object of adoration. In a totalitarian dictatorship the leader must be humanized, popularized as a good-hearted, self-sacrificing beneficent man whose mind is occupied not only with matters of the general welfare of his people and the peoples of the entire world, but also with the daily needs of the man in the street, the frontline soldier, the wounded in battle. This task is being assigned to the writers, poets, historians, and "just plain" people.

The embellishment of Khrushchev as a leader "from the people" and "for the people" began long before he reached his present position. Efforts in that direction were made immediately after the war in the Ukraine, where he was Stalin's vicar, but they were limited to that geographical area. During the "election campaign" in February, 1946, Kiev agitators informed the voters how Khrushchev, together with General N. Vatutin, Commander-in-Chief of the First Ukrainian front, had "directly guided, on Stalin's instructions, the battle for Kiev, and how the Kievites had been happy when Khrushchev showed up on the streets of Kiev on November 6, 1943." [18] It is, of course, difficult to verify the feelings of the Kievites on that day, but it can be assumed that after two years of Nazi occupation they would have expressed their joy at the arrival of a "lesser evil." As for Khrushchev's "direct guidance" of the military operation, much doubt must remain, particularly since the courageous and able General Vatutin died in 1944 and cannot challenge the laurels of the civilian general, Nikita Khrushchev.

During the same campaign a certain Professor Shvets asserted that the "beloved friend and leader, dear Nikita Sergeyevich Khrushchev," was "in the first ranks of the Red Army during the struggle against the German fascist usurpers," [19] and a minor Party official finished his praises of Khrushchev by reading a poem of Maksym Rylskyi composed in 1942, in which the poet described an encounter with the Soviet leader.* At an election meeting in Kiev, allegedly attended by "100,000 toilers," Khrushchev was extolled for "having helped to develop the Doniets Coal Basin, construct the Dneproges, [and] enrich the Ukraine with new plants and factories, with universities and schools, with theaters, clubs, and libraries. . . . There is not a corner in our wide Motherland where Khrushchev is not known. . . . Let us cast our votes for the best son of the Ukrainian people, N. S. Khrushchev," the speaker concluded.[20]

After Stalin's death the exaltation of the Ukraine's "native

* See p. 184.

son" ceased. Stalin's heirs formed a "collective leadership" and closely watched each other lest one of them receive more adoration than the others. This situation lasted until June, 1957, when Khrushchev purged his main rivals for power and thus opened the road to a new cult. His sycophantic aides are already preparing for him the charismatic crown. Although Khrushchev has not yet reached the stage of omnipotence of the late dictator, the logic of dictatorship prevails. Slowly and gradually, sometimes in a subtle manner and sometimes openly, he is being elevated and adorned in reminiscences and in poems.

On February 2, 1958, for instance, *Sovetskaya Rossia*, the organ of the R.S.F.S.R. Bureau of the Party's Central Committee, chaired by Khrushchev, went out of its way to humanize Khrushchev the warrior—an attempt which had its precedents only with regard to Lenin and Stalin. The author, a former colonel, wrote:

The weather was miserable, first snow and then rain. The men had been marching for several hours, overcoming thick mud that was literally gripping their boots as if it had teeth. From across the Volga resounded the heavy and unceasing rumble of cannons that had been incessant for several weeks.

Several cars caught up with the column of Captain Terekhov and stopped. Out of one of the cars stepped the member of the Military Council N. S: Khrushchev and Col. Gen. A. M. Vasilevsky. The fighters quickly huddled around them. A lively conversation ensued. N. S. Khrushchev asked how military and political study was going, how the troops were dressed and how their feet were protected, how feeding was arranged, whether or not the battalion had men who had already been at the front. Soldier Smirnov in a warm voice told Nikita Sergeyevich about his five youngsters, who receive highest marks in school. "And have you gotten a letter from your bride recently?" the member of the Military Council asked of Captain Stogniy. "Yes, today, Comrade Khrushchev," the officer replied. He was embarrassed, everyone was smiling. "Well, there is no need to be shy about it. Love is a good

and noble feeling," said Nikita Sergeyevich. "Russians can
and know how to love. But Russians are also able to hate
those who have broken into our land, who turn our cities
and villages into ashes, and who torture our mothers,
fathers, wives, and children."

In the silence, these angry words sounded like a tocsin
and the blood boiled in the fighters' hearts.

On November 6, 1958, *Pravda* published a poem by the
Ukrainian writer Malyshko. Although Khrushchev's name is not
mentioned in the poem, he can be easily identified. It is a "Song
About the Party," in which two personalities are praised: Lenin
himself and a "Leninite." The reader has no trouble in identifying this "Leninite" as Khrushchev, for the poet makes it clear
that the "Leninite" fought in World War II side by side with
General Vatutin. Here is how the "Leninite" is described:

> I saw a fighting Leninite
> At scorched and burned Poltava site.
> It was in nineteen-forty-three,
> When homes and schools were all debris . . .
> But he arrived and called them all—
> The children, mothers, and the old
> In years and those whose hair
> Turned gray from sheer despair.
> He greeted them with deep respect
> And told them that they should collect
> The seeds they'd need to sow in spring.
> He sent the children back to school
> And urged the mothers: "Try to pull
> Yourselves together and finish crying . . ."
> His smile was warm and pacifying.
> And while the tanks continued rolling
> And father's house was still in flames,
> He visioned how the rip'ning grains
> Would tightly pack the stalks of wheat.
> When he and General Vatutin
> Were planning battles of the day,
> His mind was thinking out the way

Of getting what the schools might need:
The desks, the books, and food to eat.
The years passed by, but in my heart
I'll always keep his deep regard
For all the people in distress.
At scorched and burned Poltava site
I saw a fighting Leninite.

In pamphlets and articles disseminated by Soviet embassies abroad, Khrushchev's kindness toward and paternal care for the front-line soldiers and the wounded during World War II has been particularly stressed. Khrushchev has been described as having been "frequently seen in the front lines, in dugouts, and in the field hospitals visiting among the wounded."

"He was interested in everything: How were the soldiers fed? How were they clothed? How were they supplied with ammunition? . . . That was uppermost in his mind during the war, just as the complaints of the workers and housewives of Moscow and Kiev concerning the poor management of stores had been before the war. And he knew how to reprimand persons who were indifferent to the soldiers' needs," [21] one reads in Khrushchev's biographical sketches published in London and Washington on the eve of his visits there.

It is, of course, not excluded from possibility that Khrushchev occasionally visited a hospital, although exhibitions of warmth and compassion do not fit very well into the materialistic philosophy of Bolshevism, even in times of distress and deep grief. In the war years, Soviet papers and magazines were filled with stories about heroic battles and invulnerable heroes, but not with descriptions of field hospitals or visits to these by high Soviet officials. There is no evidence that Khrushchev showed any particular concern for wounded or fighting soldiers, but one action against a high-ranking officer with a good fighting record, Lieutenant General Kuzma Petrovich Podlas, does not add to Khrushchev's wartime laurels. In his 1956 secret speech at the Twentieth Party Congress, Khrushchev described Podlas as an "excellent commander who perished at the front." [22] He belonged to a group of Soviet officers arrested during the Great Purge who "managed to survive despite severe tortures to which they were subjected in the prisons." [23] When the war broke out, Podlas was released from prison and made commander of the Fifty-seventh Army. General Podlas "perished at the front," but he was not killed by the enemy. Here is the real story:

On May 12, 1942, in the battle of Kharkov, the Soviet armies were ordered to attack, but on May 17 the Germans started a vigorous counteroffensive threatening to encircle and annihilate the attackers. Khrushchev later did not spare words to picture himself as the man who went out of his way to persuade Stalin to withdraw the Soviet troops and prevent the debacle. Khrushchev claimed to have telephoned General Vasilevsky "begging" him to explain to Stalin the situation on a map instead of the globe which Stalin allegedly used for shaping military operations. Not having succeeded in persuading Vasilevsky to intervene, Khrushchev telephoned Stalin himself at his villa, but Stalin refused to talk with Khrushchev and repeated through Malenkov his unchanged order to capture Kharkov at any cost.[24]

In July and August, 1942, some high staff officers of the Fifty-seventh Army commanded by Podlas, captured during the May battle at Kharkov, arrived in the prisoner-of-war camp in Hammelsburg, Germany, and gave a detailed account of the circumstances in which General Podlas died. On May 17, more than a week before the smashing defeat, when a withdrawal of the Soviet troops would still have been possible, Khrushchev, guarded by a platoon of NKVD troops, arrived at the Army headquarters of General Podlas. Podlas reported on the situation, described the strength, the direction, and the aims of the German thrusts, and suggested stopping the Soviet offensive. Khrushchev became enraged and reminded General Podlas of his arrest in 1940. Then, to the best recollection of witnesses, he went on as follows:

> You got away with murder at that time, Comrade General! Keep in mind that this time it would not be so easy for you to slip away. . . . I myself, with my own hands, will blow out your brains! I'll shoot you to death like the lowest dog! I'll finish you off as the lowest scum of the earth! I order you: continue the offensive! Remember this is Stalin's order and also my order! Kharkov must be captured and, today or tomorrow, it will be ours! You are

responsible for the left flank with your head! All your merits will not help you, nor the intercession of various Timoshenkos, Shaposhnikovs, Zhukovs, and other warriors! As you well know, we are shooting scaremongers and cowards and will continue to do so! . . . Keep that in mind, Lieutenant General! Don't forget that you will be responsible for the failure of the operation. . . . Try to better your fate by the strict carrying out of orders you receive, or . . . No, there are no 'ors' . . . I shall not even permit you to carry out the sentence by yourself!"

Those were Khrushchev's words, as witnessed by staff officers who recalled the scene only a few months later. Khrushchev returned with the NKVD guard to the safer rear, and Podlas obeyed the order. Ten days later General Podlas sent his last message to the Military Council of the Front: "There is no more Army. I am carrying out the sentence myself. Podlas." He then shot himself at his command post after the last grenades had been thrown at the approaching Germans. His chief of staff followed his example.[25] It goes without saying that Podlas' stand, as ordered by Khrushchev, also resulted in the death of thousands of soldiers. Fourteen years later, however, Khrushchev claimed that he had prevailed upon Stalin to permit a retreat in order to avoid unnecessary bloodshed.

Khrushchev's role as a member of Military Councils at various fronts was that of a political commissar endowed with extraordinary powers as a Politburo member and Stalin's emissary. These powers included the authority to dispose of "scaremongers and cowards" and extended to all aspects of life behind the fronts. It was for instance Khrushchev's responsibility to see to it that "hundreds of thousands of Stalingradites construct defense belts"[26] around the city, or that "people's volunteer corps be created from among the workers, employees, and collective farms in the Stalingrad province."[27] In 1947, one Lieutenant General I. I. Petrov recalled that "on the battlefields he [Khrushchev] helped us to carry out correctly the Stalinist science to conquer"[28]—a formulation which is in ironic contrast to Khrushchev's downgrading of Stalin's military ability.

It seems that Khrushchev fulfilled all his wartime duties well:

on February 12, 1943,[29] he was made a lieutenant general; on April 10, he was awarded the Order of Suvorov, Second Class;[30] on August 27, he was given the Order of Kutuzov, First Class;[31] and on May 21, 1945, he received the Soviet Union's highest military award—the Order of Suvorov, First Class—and the Order of the Fatherland, First Degree (the first for organizing the partisan movement in the Ukraine, and the second for the "successful fulfillment of grain procurement in 1944").[32]

But despite the fact that Khrushchev received the highest military award for his participation in the guerrilla movement, there is little evidence that he played a prominent role in guiding the warfare behind the enemy's lines. Before 1957, the Soviet people had never been officially informed of his having "carried on large-scale work in organizing the national partisan movement in the Ukraine against the German-fascist usurpers."

In 1951, the *Large Soviet Encyclopedia* reported that the guerrilla warfare was led centrally by I. V. Stalin and K. E. Voroshilov and locally by the underground provincial Party committees and directly controlled by a Central Staff.[33] After Stalin's death and until 1956, Soviet sources elaborated on this set-up as follows: the Central Staff of the Partisan Movement was organized on May 30, 1942, and P. K. Ponomarenko, at the time First Secretary of the Party in Belorussia, was appointed its Chief and as such controlled similar staffs attached to the Front Military Councils.[34] In August, 1942, Voroshilov was appointed Commander-in-Chief of the partisans[35] and in June of the same year a Ukrainian Partisan Staff was organized and T. A. Strokach was made its Chief.[36] These commands, officially reported in Soviet sources before 1956, left little opportunity for Khrushchev to take substantial part in the Ukrainian partisan movement. Unofficially, however, his role in this movement had been mentioned in the exciting stories by partisan leaders S. A. Kovpak, P. P. Vershigora, A. F. Fedorov, and D. I. Bakradze.[37] The later the date of publication of the memoirs, the greater the role credited to Khrushchev.

One of the four local guerrilla leaders wrote in his reminiscences that Khrushchev had suggested at the beginning of July, 1941 "that we immediately begin preparations for a Bolshevik underground movement and organize a partisan detachment in every district in good time." The author expressed his amazement that the Central Committee of the Party "had already [at that time] mapped out the entire organizational scheme of an underground movement." [38] But these preparatory moves, which in most cases did not materialize, cannot be considered "large-scale work in organizing the partisan movement" with which Khrushchev was belatedly credited. On the other hand, all four authors admitted that the Ukrainian Staff of the Partisan Movement was headed by Strokach. In the 1952 edition of his book, Vershigora described Strokach as "a Chekist, border guard, commandant of the border guards on the river Dniester, deputy of the U.S.S.R. Supreme Soviet, and prior to the war Deputy Minister of Internal Affairs (MVD)." [39] Vershigora also praised Strokach's "statesmanship" in having understood the enormous possibilities of guerrilla warfare. All these attributes were omitted in the subsequent editions, and Strokach's authority as Chief of the Ukrainian Partisan Staff was cut down from "guidance" to "management." [40] It seems that these corrections were well planned. However, in 1956, the *Large Soviet Encyclopedia* still reported that the Ukrainian Staff was "headed" by Strokach,[41] but it also pointed out for the first time that the Central Committee of the Ukrainian Party used that Staff as a channel through which it "communicated with the partisan detachments and guided their activity." [42] Though Khrushchev was not yet mentioned by name, the new information implied that it was he who, as First Secretary of the Ukrainian Party, guided the guerrilla activity in the Ukraine. Since 1956, this has been spelled out in Soviet history textbooks for tenth-grade students sponsored by the U.S.S.R. Academy of Sciences as follows: "The Central Committee of the Communist Party of the Ukraine created the Ukrainian Staff of the Partisan Movement which was guided by N. S. Khrushchev." [43] Also in 1956, the Ukrainian historian N. I. Suprunenko asserted that in July and August, 1941, Khrushchev had "conferences with Communists assigned for underground work [behind the front lines], received commanders and commissars of partisan detachments, and personally instructed them." [44] Furthermore, the same source pointed out that around February, 1942, "solid and constant communication had been established between the Ukrainian partisans and the

headquarters of the Southwestern front and personally with
N. S. Khrushchev, so that the partisans could get badly needed
political and military-operational guidance." [45] There is also
ample evidence from other sources that Khrushchev was instrumental in setting up underground Communist cells in larger
cities on the eve of their occupation by the Germans and that he
instructed them to wage a war of annihilation not only against
the foreign enemy but also against Soviet citizens who mistook
the German troops for "liberators" from the Communist regime.
As far as "political and military-operational guidance" is concerned, this refers to the short period when the armies of the
Southwestern front reoccupied some of the lost ground, which
facilitated establishing communication with some partisan detachments in that region. Such communication could not have
been constant for the simple reason that the Ukrainian Partisan
Staff was not yet in operation at that time. The regularity of
Khrushchev's contact with the partisans after February, 1942,
and during the greater part of 1943 must also be questioned, since
the Soviet armies of the front to which Khrushchev was assigned
fell back to the Volga and Stalingrad, and his preoccupations
there were far more important than to "guide" partisans who
operated in the far Ukraine, completely occupied by the Germans. Furthermore, during that period the Central Committee
of the Ukrainian Party and the Ukrainian Partisan Staff had
their seats in Moscow, far away from where Khrushchev had
been active. As a matter of fact, he was even unable to participate in the gathering of local guerrilla leaders including those
from the Ukraine, held in Moscow in the first days of September,
1942. At this meeting Stalin, "together with V. M. Molotov and
K. E. Voroshilov, summed up the results of the first stage of the
partisan movement" and provided military-operational guidance
for the next stage of the warfare behind the front lines. [46]

Thus, the claim that Khrushchev guided the Ukrainian Partisan Staff—a claim which is repeated in all Soviet history textbooks—is largely exaggerated. He can be credited only with
setting up an underground Party apparatus in advance of the
German occupation of the Ukraine and with issuing orders to
finish off ruthlessly all those who actually cooperated or were
suspected of cooperation with the Germans. The war of annihi-

lation on "collaborators" had all the characteristics of a civil war. As a matter of fact, in August, 1944, the more "experienced" partisan detachments were taken over by the Ukrainian NKVD and used for the liquidation of the Ukrainian Insurgent Army (UPA) which hoped to establish an independent Ukraine.

Parallel with Khrushchev's elevation to the status of the sole leader of the Ukrainian partisans, the positions of two *actual* leaders of the partisan movement as a whole—its Commander-in-Chief, K. E. Voroshilov, and the Chief of the Central Staff—have been changed *ex post facto*. It is a matter of record that with the appointment of Ponomarenko in May, 1942, as Chief of the Central Staff of the Partisan Movement, it was his responsibility to plan and coordinate the guerrilla activity everywhere behind the German lines including occupied Ukraine. It is also a matter of fact that Commander-in-Chief Voroshilov occupied a position superior to that of Ponomarenko. Voroshilov's position is still mentioned in some books dealing with World War II. But, in history *textbooks*, these facts have undergone complete distortion since 1956, and nowadays tenth-grade pupils are being taught that "beginning in May, 1942, a Central Staff of the Partisan Movement headed by K. E. Voroshilov was operating." [47] In other words, Soviet writers of history textbooks "relieved" Ponomarenko from his position of Chief of Staff and "demoted" Voroshilov from his position of Commander-in-Chief to Chief of Staff. It remains to be seen whether this pattern of distortion will be followed in future publications by Soviet historians who specialize in World War II.

In any event, Ponomarenko's "demotion" is a completed fact, since after 1955 his name was no longer identified with the position he occupied in the partisan movement. The 1959 version of the *History of the Communist Party* mentions him only among eleven local partisan leaders, some of whom are well known, while others are not known.

Ponomarenko's downfall is of particular interest, because it sheds some light on the struggle for power within the Kremlin. From the end of 1938 until 1948, Ponomarenko was First Secretary of the Belorussian Party, and from 1944 to 1948, he simultaneously occupied the post of Chairman of the Belorussian Council of Ministers. (During the same period, Khrushchev occupied similar positions in the Ukraine: from 1938 to 1944, he was First Secretary of the Ukrainian Party and from 1944 to 1947, he held this job together with that of the head of the Ukrainian Government.) It was only logical that in 1942 Ponomarenko should have been appointed Chief of the Central Staff of the Partisan Movement, since until 1943 the only sizable guerrilla warfare was being conducted in Belorussia. On the other hand, Khrushchev, as First Secretary of the Ukrainian Party, considered himself supreme commander of the underground Party groups which he organized in the Ukraine immediately after the Germans attacked the Soviet Union. With the creation of a Central Staff and with Ponomarenko as its chief, Khrushchev might have lost actual control over his groups, and this might have caused dissension between Khrushchev and Ponomarenko even during the war.

Subsequently Ponomarenko had a spectacular career,* but in May, 1955, i.e., a few months after Malenkov's downgrading, Ponomarenko was reduced to the post of Ambassador to Poland and in 1957 to India, and dropped from membership of the Party Presidium. Now (August, 1960) he is Ambassador to the Netherlands. Such a noiseless drop from membership of the top Party body to ambassadorship has its precedents in the Stalin era of Soviet history; another example was the honorable exile of Molotov in Outer Mongolia after his downfall in 1957.

It is difficult to forecast what more Khrushchev has in store for Ponomarenko, but this is not as important here as the method used for building up Khrushchev's activities in World War II.

Khrushchev's role in World War II has not yet been finally established. Recently a participant of a "Scientific Conference" of Ukrainian historians remarked that despite the fact that over

---

* In 1948, Ponomarenko was recalled from Belorussia to Moscow to become one of the secretaries of the Party's Central Committee. (Here again, Khrushchev's and Ponomarenko's careers show a similarity; Khrushchev was recalled from the Ukraine in 1949, and also was made one of the five secretaries of the Central Committee.) In 1952, Ponomarenko was elected a full-fledged member of the twenty-five-man Party Presidium, which after Stalin's death was reduced to a collegium of ten full members, with Ponomarenko remaining an alternate member of that body. At the same time he was made U.S.S.R. Minister of Culture and remained at this post until February, 1954, when he became First Secretary of the Kazakhstan Party Central Committee.

100 books dealing with World War II had been published in the Ukraine alone, "we are not satisfied with the situation in the sphere of scientific elaboration and clarification of the history of the Ukrainian Communist Party during World War II." [48] Several speakers pointed out the necessity of attracting the attention of Ukrainian historians to the "role of the Central Committee of the Ukrainian Party and its First Secretary, Comrade N. S. Khrushchev, in the organization of the leadership of the partisan movement and the underground struggle." [49] To dramatize Khrushchev's role in the liberation of the Ukraine, the participants of the conference paid a visit to the village "from where General N. F. Vatutin and N. S. Khrushchev directed the military operations which led to the annihilation of the fascist forces in the Kiev region." [50]

Soviet history writers are obedient, and the paper on which they write cannot rebel.

17

The Postwar Ups and Downs

Nikita Khrushchev emerged from the war a Lieutenant General, his chest decorated with several orders and medals, and more self-confident than ever before. But the tasks he faced when he re-entered the Ukrainian capital were unprecedented. Hunger, epidemics, homeless people returning to war-damaged cities and villages, disrupted water and power supplies, and an almost complete standstill of production and distribution —such were the calamities which cried out for immediate remedies. To solve these abnormally difficult problems, Stalin entrusted Khrushchev with the same positions in the Ukraine, as he, Stalin, occupied in Moscow. In February, 1944, Khrushchev became Chairman of the Ukrainian Council of People's Commissars, while retaining his post as First Secretary of the Ukrainian Communist Party. For more than three years he was the supreme Party and government commander of the second largest Soviet republic, and the only Politburo member who ever wielded so much power over more than one fifth of the population of the Soviet Union. Whether this circumstance caused apprehension and jealousy among the other Politburo members is not known, but there are some signs that they were not too enthusiastic about this arrangement. However, it was probably not so much the power which Khrushchev wielded as his growing influence on Stalin that disturbed some of Khrushchev's colleagues in the Politburo.

He did not risk his neck by irritating the dictator with suggestions of far-reaching reforms, as another Politburo member,

226

Nikolai A. Voznesensky, apparently did, and lost his life. He would rather approach Stalin with small practical proposals and back them up with the rich experience he had gained during the long years of practical work "in the field"—something that none of his colleagues could match.

In any event, with the control over the Party and government of the Ukraine concentrated in Khrushchev's hands, his influence kept growing. A former UNRRA representative in the Ukraine reported that Khrushchev needed only a few minutes to get in touch with Stalin from Kiev by telephone and to arrange for an official to meet Stalin personally.[1] In Kiev in 1946, large photographs of Soviet leaders could be seen on many buildings, but often there were only those of Stalin and Khrushchev. The leading art store in Kiev displayed in front windows two busts, one of Stalin, and the other of Khrushchev. There were sculptures and paintings featuring only Stalin and Khrushchev.[2] Significantly, similar pictures of Stalin and Lenin played a symbolic role after the latter's death: several times a year, on appropriate occasions, a Stalin-Lenin photo had been reproduced in all Soviet publications to underline Stalin's closeness to Lenin, and to support the standardized description of Stalin as the "Lenin of today," and "the great continuer of Lenin's cause."

Was the demonstration of Khrushchev's closeness to Stalin a deliberate move on Khrushchev's part in anticipation of a situation in which such pictures might prove useful? Today, of course, the Khrushchev-Stalin pictures cannot be utilized for building up Khrushchev because of Stalin's demotion, but even Khrushchev could not have anticipated this at that time.

Khrushchev's influence on Stalin probably disturbed most those Politburo members who, by virtue of their jobs, had common spheres of activity with Khrushchev. From 1943 to 1945, for instance, Malenkov, at the time only an alternate member of the Politburo, was chairman of a governmental committee on restoring the national economy in the liberated areas—of which the Ukraine was the most important one. It is clear that, in view of his influence in the Kremlin, Khrushchev could overrule Malenkov's instructions, if Khrushchev, for one reason or another, considered them inappropriate. The same was probably true with regard to Andrei A. Andreyev, who was in charge of agricultural policy. Khrushchev's activity in the Ukraine was closely watched by other Politburo members and, whenever an occasion occurred, sharply criticized. However, this was done without mentioning his name, as he was a full-fledged member of the Politburo. For example, in 1946 and 1947, the "Ukrainian leadership" was held responsible for shortcomings in personnel policy and faulty agricultural planning, but Khrushchev's name was not mentioned. It was at that time—shortly after the war —that Khrushchev's career took a sudden downward turn, the first in more than two decades.

This setback was reflected in the decision of the All-Union Party Central Committee of July 26, 1946, concerning the "training, selection, and distribution of leading Party and Soviet personnel in the Ukrainian Party organization." This decision has never been published in spite of the fact that the Ukrainian Party organ, *Pravda Ukrainy*, called it a "most important decision in the life of the Ukrainian Communist Party." [3] Its existence became known from excerpts of Khrushchev's report which he delivered in August at a plenary session of the Ukrainian Central Committee.[4] In this report Khrushchev himself revealed that the All-Union Central Committee in Moscow, in its decision, censured the Ukrainian Central Committee (i.e., Khrushchev) for having underestimated the "significance of the ideological work," for "not paying sufficient attention to the selection and the political and ideological education of the cadres in the field of science, literature, and art," and for neglecting to "organize large-scale criticism of the hostile bourgeois ideology in the press." Such negligence was seen as the reason why "some books, magazines, newspaper articles, and speeches of certain Ukrainian historians and men of literature contain ideological blunders and distortions, attempts to revive bourgeois nationalist concepts."

Thus, the Ukrainian Central Committee, headed by Khrushchev, was accused of mistakes which during the Great Purge had been defined as "political blindness"—a crime for which one of his predecessors, Pavel P. Postyshev, had paid with his life. Khrushchev survived the blow for the simple reason that he had taken certain measures to soften it. In the first place, the July decision which accused the Ukrainian Central Committee of "political blindness" was passed on the basis of a report presented by that Committee, i.e., by Khrushchev himself. In other words, he did not hide the "crimes," but became himself helpful in ferreting them out, leaving perhaps the impression that they had somehow been the result of his having been overburdened with work. Moreover, some seven weeks before the blow fell, he had written, contrary to his custom,* a "serious" article on "Some Problems of Intra-Party Work"[5] in which he discussed questions of political and organizational Party work, selection of cadres, and the role of the press—matters which were to become the subject of the July 26 decision. Thus, Khrushchev tried to anticipate the blow that some high-ranking Party officials in Moscow intended to deal him. He certainly succeeded in his attempt, since the resolution which criticized the Ukrainian Central Committee did not mention his name and he was allowed to remain in both top positions in the Ukraine, that is, in the Party and in the Government.

However, a much more severe attack followed shortly thereafter, in the form of a resolution on agricultural matters adopted at the plenary meeting of the Moscow Central Committee seven months later, in February, 1947. Agriculture in the Ukraine was at that time one of the most vital concerns of the Soviet leaders, for the Ukraine in those days was much more exclusively the breadbasket of the Soviet Union than it is today. The ups and downs of Russia's economic life actually depended upon the yields of the Ukrainian grain, sugar-beet, and corn fields. From the first day of his arrival in the Ukraine in 1938, Khrushchev had paid more attention to agricultural problems than to the Ukrainian coal, steel, and machine-building industries which also contributed considerably to the Soviet national economy. At regular intervals Khrushchev had called conferences of agricultural workers and specialists; made inspection tours during the spring-sowing campaigns and harvesting time; delivered "inspiring" talks and had "heart-to-heart" chats with local agriculturists and collective farmers; suggested "simple" devices such as a "comb," as he himself called a device to raise the stalks beaten down by rain, so that the combine could catch

---

* In the past Khrushchev had written only a few articles on insignificant matters, such as the opening of a Pioneer House or municipal construction.

them,[6] or a beet-cleaning machine,[7] or beet-weevil exterminating machines and devices; had consulted construction engineers and even offered them sketches drawn by his own hand.* In short, he had displayed enormous activity in his attempts to raise agricultural production and, what counted most of all, to deliver

* It is not known whether Khrushchev's technical suggestions were put into operation. In 1938, for instance, Khrushchev suggested the construction of a beet-cleaning machine. In 1940, the Ukrainian press admitted that the first machine was a failure ("It was bulky, had a separate motor and many unnecessary parts.") Khrushchev gave instructions to simplify the machine. Another attempt was also unsuccessful. On November 28, 1940, Khrushchev and other high-ranking officials inspected two new samples, and the results were "quite satisfactory." It seems, however, that Khrushchev was not entirely satisfied with the results, for he "instructed the People's Commissariat of Agriculture to work up a unified draft of a machine, based on both tested constructions," and prescribed that the majority of the parts be made of wood to enable the collective farms to make these machines themselves. (*Visti*, November 29, 1940). Because of the war, the entire project fell apart, but this is of lesser interest than the fact that Khrushchev, formally not a member of the Ukrainian Government, personally issued instructions and orders to government offices on technical questions which formally were of no concern to the Party which he headed.

Khrushchev's manner of handling technical affairs was to some extent discussed earlier in this study, in connection with his role in the construction of the Moscow subway. Khrushchev would first inform himself on how the matter should be handled through consultations with specialists; then, if they disagreed, he would choose the most promising solution, even if less feasible. Once having made up his mind, he would then impose his views on those who disagreed, even on the authors of the proposal, who, under the weight of the arguments presented by his critics, had been ready to revise their initial viewpoint. At a conference of agriculturists in 1941, Khrushchev supported a proposal by Lysenko on a method of exterminating the sugar-beet weevil. The proposal met with considerable criticism on the part of other agriculturists, and Lysenko admitted that "at one time" he had been ready to agree with his critics on a major point, but "the clear and correct indication made by Nikita Sergeyevich" convinced him that his, Lysenko's, critics were wrong. (*Stalinskoye Plemia*, February 13, 1941.) Seven years later, during the "debates" on genetics, Lysenko crushed his opponents with the announcement that his theories had been approved by the Party's Central Committee and Stalin himself. After Stalin's death, Lysenko was openly criticized by many Soviet biologists who disputed his theories and his experiments. It seems that Lysenko has been re-emerging as a significant figure in Soviet biology. In two speeches delivered in March and April 1957, respectively, Khrushchev went out of his way to shield Lysenko from his critics. Referring to Lysenko's new method of fertilizing, Khrushchev said: "If I were asked, 'For which scientist do you vote?' I would say without hesitation, 'For Lysenko,' and I know that he will not let us down, because he will not tackle anything bad. I consider that few scientists understand the soil as well as Lysenko." (*Pravda*, April 1, 1957.)

to the state not only the extraordinary amounts requested by the plans made in Moscow, but even to exceed them. In 1946, however, his attempts had been in vain, since there had been a drought in most of the grain-producing areas, and particularly in the Ukraine, and Khrushchev could not fulfill Moscow's grain requests. With no grain reserve, the bad Ukrainian harvest had a disastrous effect on bread supply for the population.

At the end of February, 1947, Politburo member Andrei A. Andreyev, who was in charge of agricultural matters, reported on the agricultural situation in the country to the plenary session of the All-Union Central Committee and sharply criticized the local authorities for their failure to reach the prewar production and delivery levels. The Ukraine occupied a conspicuous place in Andreyev's report. In the resolution adopted by the plenum, the Ukraine was blamed for "serious lagging behind in production of spring wheat." The resolution deemed it "intolerable that such a valuable food crop as spring wheat had been neglected year after year in the collective and state farms of the Ukrainian S.S.R., while the fertile black-earth soils were sown with less valuable crops, especially barley."[8] The Ukrainian leadership was also criticized for the decrease of production and delivery of sugar beets, tobacco, and other crops.

These were serious charges, and the consequences for Khrushchev were potentially grave. The plenum had hardly finished its work when Khrushchev's former teacher and trainer, Lazar M. Kaganovich, was sent to the Ukraine to take over from Khrushchev the control of the Ukrainian Party. This left only the chairmanship of the Council of Ministers under Khrushchev's jurisdiction.

On March 4, 1947, the Ukrainian papers officially announced that the change had been made because the separation of the top posts in the Party and government was "expedient," and had been done for the purpose of "strengthening Party and Soviet work."[9] The next day, however, an editorial in *Pravda Ukrainy* unequivocally mentioned the "serious and big shortcomings in the management of the Ukrainian agriculture" and extolled the resolution of the February plenum of the All-Union Central Committee as a "historical" achievement, praising it for having exposed the Ukrainian shortcomings with "Stalinist profundity and clarity." The editorial urged its readers "not to whimper, not to chatter, not to show the white feather . . . but to attack the difficulties, to attack in the same manner as genuine Bolsheviks are able to do, as our wise leader, Comrade Stalin, has taught us to do." Finally, the article called Kaganovich an "outstanding personality of the Bolshevik Party and the Soviet state" whose dispatch to the Ukraine was "striking proof" of Stalin's concern for the Ukraine and its people.[10] This standardized phraseology would not have meant much if it had not been for the special mention of the shortcomings in the management of agriculture which had been for years identified with Khrushchev's name. Although his name was not mentioned, even the least informed collective farmer knew how to interpret Kaganovich's arrival in the Ukraine.

Khrushchev tried to save face by blaming his subordinates for the shortcomings which, as such, he fully acknowledged. In his report before a special session of the Ukrainian Central Committee held on March 10-13, 1947, Khrushchev himself raised the question: "How did it happen?" How could it happen that spring wheat had been neglected year in year out? The answer was: "Because there was [sic!] an underestimation of this important food crop. The fault lies primarily with the Ministry of Agriculture."[11]

On March 22 and 24, Khrushchev "asked" to be relieved from the posts of the Kiev Provincial and City Party Committees[12] in view of the separation of the Party and government posts. From May to September, 1947, the Ukrainian press did not mention Khrushchev's whereabouts. He was absent from the Supreme Soviet session and the plenary session of the Ukrainian Central Committee held in June. Reports about him began again to appear in the papers only in September.

Khrushchev's demotion in 1947 had been, of course, a decision taken with Stalin's acquiescence, but it must be doubted that Stalin had been the initiator of this move. If Stalin's confidence in Khrushchev had been shaken, Khrushchev would have been ousted altogether, since the Ukraine was an extremely sensitive spot. Khrushchev managed to disentangle himself from the temporary setbacks with the ease of a skillful politician. Kaganovich's "visit" lasted only ten months and was followed by Khrushchev's reinstatement in his prior position as Party boss.

Whatever the reason for Kaganovich's recall to Moscow might have been, Khrushchev replaced him as First Secretary of the Ukrainian Central Committee, reorganized the Party apparatus, and appointed his henchman, Demyan S. Korotchenko,* as Chairman of the Council of Ministers, thus regaining control over both top positions. For two more years Khrushchev continued to rule over the Ukraine. He offset his blunders and failures by continually demonstrating his unlimited faithfulness to Stalin and by the successes he achieved in squeezing out more goods than one would expect under the circumstances from the undernourished, ill-clothed, and ill-sheltered population in exchange for starvation wages.

Another success scored by Khrushchev was the forced recollectivization of agriculture in the western provinces. In the short period of fifteen months, beginning in September, 1939, when these provinces were first seized, Khrushchev had succeeded in "organizing" 571 collective farms comprising 34,000 households.[13] During the war these collective farms disintegrated again, although the German occupation authorities did not encourage their dissolution. Then, after the war, the resistance to collectivization was greater than in the prewar period of Soviet occupation. This is evident from the fact that during a similar period of fifteen months—from October, 1944, when the western provinces were reoccupied, until January 1, 1946—

---

* Demyan S. Korotchenko was known in Moscow in the 'thirties as Korotchenko and Korotchenkov, the difference between both names being that the first sounds Ukrainian, while the second, ending with a "v," implies Great Russian origin. In 1930, Korotchenko worked under Khrushchev as chief of the Agitation Department in the Bauman District Party Committee. In 1932-33, he had been identified as Chairman of the Bauman District Soviet and in January, 1934, as a member of the bureau of the Moscow City Party Committee, of which Khrushchev was First Secretary. In December, 1934, his name appeared in its new spelling—Korotchenkov —(*Pravda*, December 4, 1934) and remained so until 1938, when he was transferred to the Ukraine. There he became again Korotchenko. He worked closely with Khrushchev as Chairman of the Ukrainian Council of Ministers, Second Secretary of the Ukrainian Central Committee, and then again as Chairman of the Council of Ministers. At present, he occupies the post of Chairman of the Presidium of the Ukrainian Supreme Soviet. In June, 1957, following the purge of Malenkov, Molotov, and Kaganovich, he became alternate member of the All-Union Party Presidium.

only 177 collective farms with 5,293 households could be re-stored.[14] The resistance of the once-free farmers was certainly connected with the presence in these provinces of strong detach-ments of the Ukrainian Insurgent Army (UPA) whose ultimate purpose was an independent Ukrainian state. In his first postwar speech Khrushchev implied that this resistance was substantial and warned that those unwilling to "lay down arms" would face "severe punishment as traitors of the people," as enemies of the Motherland."[15]

The task of liquidating the Ukrainian insurgents was assigned to the Ukrainian NKVD which employed for that purpose not only its regular units but also the Soviet partisan detachments* who, prior to their new duties, had fought the Germans. The "severe punishment" with which Khrushchev threatened the Ukrainian nationalists was death. Most of them, however, dis-regarded Khrushchev's warning and continued to harass the Soviet authorities for a few more years; this was probably the reason for Khrushchev's slow progress in collectivizing the western provinces. In March, 1947, almost two and a half years after the reoccupation of these provinces, the prewar collec-tivization level had not yet been reached (504 collective farms with 33,000 households as compared to 571 collective farms with 34,000 households). After the resistance was crushed by the NKVD, which at the time was headed by Timofey A. Strokach, the former chief of the Ukrainian Partisan Movement, Khrushchev succeeded in forcing through the collectivization of the western provinces at high speed: in less than nine months, from March, 1947 to January, 1948, the number of collective farms increased from 504 to 1,668, and almost trebled in 1948, reaching 5,071 as of January 1, 1949.[16] In his report at the Six-teenth Ukrainian Party Congress in January, 1949, Khrushchev implied that this tremendous success was achieved in spite of the resistance of the peasants, or, as Khrushchev put it, the collectivization was "a crushing blow to the kulaks and the Ukraino-German nationalists."[17]

---

* The famous Kovpak division was taken over by the NKVD on August 18 1944. (David Bakradze, *Kroviu geroyev* [Tbilisi, 1956].) After they had been cleared of "doubtful" elements, this and other guerrilla units continued to operate as NKVD detachments against the Ukrainian nationalists.

On the opening day of the Sixteenth Ukrainian Party Congress, *Pravda* editorially stressed the "remarkable victories the Bolsheviks of the Ukraine [scored] in all branches of the national economy, in the development of culture, science, and art."[18] Then *Pravda* spelled out the "victories": pre-schedule fulfillment of the postwar Five-Year Plan; a 43 per cent increase of industrial production in 1948; pre-schedule grain delivery to the state in 1947 and 1948; surpassing the amount of grain delivered in 1948, compared with that in 1940, by 77 million poods,* and this despite the fact that the prewar sowing area had not yet been reached. The enumeration of these achievements was a clear recognition of Khrushchev's personal successes in fulfilling the Kremlin's assignments. Khrushchev was not mentioned by name, in accordance with the Kremlin's custom of reserving all praise of any kind for the dictator himself. *Pravda*, however, went beyond its usual reserve when it wrote in the same editorial that the Ukrainian people were led "by their militant Bolshevik vanguard," meaning, of course, the Ukrainian Party leadership headed by Khrushchev.

In December, 1949, Khrushchev's Ukrainian mission came to an end. He was called to Moscow to become First Party Secretary of the capital and its province, and one of the five secretaries of the All-Union Central Committee. Two decades earlier he had arrived in Moscow as an unknown Party trainee clinging to the coattails of Lazar M. Kaganovich. Now he re-entered the capital as a full-fledged member of the Politburo, with twelve years of experience in ruling over 40 million people, and as one of the "closest companions-in-arms" of Stalin. When Khrushchev had left Moscow in 1938, Malenkov had been an important wheel in the Party machine, but otherwise an unknown figure; Beria had not yet stepped into Nikolai Yezhov's shoes and was still busy with the fulfillment of the later's bloody orders in his native sunny Georgia; and only Molotov, Kaganovich, Voroshilov, and Andreyev had played important roles in shaping the Kremlin's policies through the dictator's assignments.

An entirely different situation awaited Khrushchev in 1949. Of the eleven Politburo members in 1938, one (Kalinin) had

* One pood is equal to 36.11 pounds.

died a natural death; the death of another (Zhdanov) is still a mystery; two (Kosior and Chubar) had been executed in the Great Purge; and the sadistic secret police chief, Nikolai Yezhov, had disappeared forever. Molotov still appeared to be Stalin's big favorite, while Kaganovich had moved from second place to seventh; two news stars, Malenkov and Beria, had come into the limelight, occupying the second and third places among the dictator's closest collaborators. After Zhdanov's mysterious death in August, 1948, the Zhdanov-Malenkov controversy had found its natural end in Malenkov's complete victory. Many Zhdanovites had been liquidated, among them the First Deputy Chairman of the U.S.S.R. Council of Ministers and Politburo member N. A. Voznesensky, and one of the secretaries of the Party Central Committee, A. A. Kuznetsov—later described by Khrushchev as "talented and eminent leaders"—and other leaders identified with the so-called Leningrad affair, also mentioned by Khrushchev in his 1956 secret speech.[19]

Among the victims who had been purged but not killed was Grigori M. Popov who, prior to Khrushchev's transfer to Moscow, had occupied the very positions to which Khrushchev was now assigned. Popov had been relieved "in connection with his transfer to a responsible job in city construction."[20] In March, 1953, he was appointed to another "responsible" job as Ambassador to Poland, a place where later other former prominent Party men (Mikhailov, Melnikov, and Ponomarenko) sojourned for short periods. The whereabouts of Popov, after he finished serving as Ambassador, have remained unknown.

Despite various opinions expressed on the subject of the Malenkov-Zhdanov controversy, the real issues involved are not known, nor is Khrushchev's position in it. Prior to Stalin's death it was generally assumed that all major post-Zhdanov changes in the composition of the Central Party apparatus reflected the outcome of this controversy. The replacement of Popov by Khrushchev was therefore considered one of the telling signs that Khrushchev had belonged to the Malenkov "faction." This approach can hardly be sustained today, after the curtain behind which the past had been tightly concealed was somewhat raised in Khrushchev's secret speech, and after he has now revealed himself as the most astute aspirant for Stalin's mantle. Rather, because of his own ambitious designs, Khrushchev was not interested in committing himself to either side. It is possible that at various stages of the controversy Khrushchev switched from one side to another, closely watching which side was getting the dictator's support.

Khrushchev's appointment as Secretary of the Central Committee was connected with agricultural matters. Until 1950, Andrei A. Andreyev had been the official Politburo spokesman on agricultural policy. His eclipse had begun in February, 1950, when an unsigned article in *Pravda* had openly criticized him for advocating the small work team, the so-called *zveno*, instead of the large brigade, for work on the collective farms. Since the late 'thirties, the *zveno* had been considered the basic work team. At the Eighteenth Party Congress in March, 1939, Andreyev had emphasized that the "depersonalization of labor in large brigades is the main obstacle to the increase of labor productivity in the collective farms."[21] This opinion was shared by other Soviet leaders. The resolution adopted unanimously by the Congress explicitly stressed the "necessity of a large-scale transition" to small work teams on the collective farms.[22] Thus, in criticizing Politburo member Andreyev, *Pravda* actually repudiated the "unanimous will" of the Eighteenth Party Congress, which is supposed to be the supreme organ of the Communist Party. In other words, in 1939, the Party had endorsed Andreyev's position in favor of the *zveno*, but in 1950, *Pravda* attacked him for it. No doubt Khrushchev was behind the attack. In a series of speeches delivered in March, 1950.* only a few weeks after the appearance of the *Pravda* article against Andreyev, Khrushchev praised the article and urged "every agricultural worker to draw the necessary conclusions from it." This open attack on Andreyev heralded a profound change in agricultural policy in the direction of greater depersonalization of labor on the collective farms and further eradication of whatever was left of intimate ties between the farmer and the soil he had once owned.

* Khrushchev made a speech strongly advocating the switch from small work teams to large brigades on March 7, 1950, which was published in *Pravda* the next day. On April 25, 1950, *Pravda* published two additional speeches delivered by Khrushchev on this subject on March 16 and 31, 1950.

A further step in the same direction was the merger of small collective farms which began immediately after Khrushchev became the Kremlin's spokesman on agricultural matters. Khrushchev opened the merger campaign only a few weeks after the attack on Andreyev. In his speech of March 7, 1950, he made the important announcement that "in many collective farms [of the Moscow province] the collective farmers express the desire to unite and create economically powerful collective farms."[23] In Communist countries it is customary to represent major policy changes as having been initiated by the "wide masses." The collectivization of the privately owned farms in the early 'thirties—a measure which resulted in the loss of millions of peasants' lives and the destruction of large amounts of property—had also been described as "urgently desired by the peasants."* When Khrushchev spoke of the "desire" of the collective farmers to amalgamate, he said in the same breath that "the task of the Party and Soviet organizations is to assist [sic] the collective farmers in carrying out this measure." Another Soviet source, however, leaves no doubt that the measure was imposed upon the collective farmers. According to S. S. Sergeyev, "the Party organizations, executing the instructions of the Party and the Government, organized and directed this movement..."[24]

It is no coincidence that the important changes in agricultural policy took place immediately after Khrushchev's arrival in Moscow. It is possible that he actually initiated the changes while he was still in the Ukraine, and after persuading Stalin of their necessity was called to Moscow to carry them out. Be that as it may, the fact that the amalgamation drive began in Moscow province, of which Khrushchev became First Party Secretary, shows that the Kremlin regarded him as highly qualified for pioneering the tremendous job. Khrushchev fulfilled the assignment with his usual speed and energy. In June, 1950, he announced that in less than six months the number of collec-

---

* In the *History of the CPSU* (Short Course) one reads: "The peasants would come in crowds to the state farms and machine and tractor stations to watch the operation of the tractors and other agricultural machines, express their enthusiasm and then and there resolve: 'Let's join the collective farm'" (*Istoria VKP(b). Kratkii kurs* [Moscow, 1942], p. 284).

tive farms in the Moscow province had decreased from 6,069 to 1,668. This meant that more than 72 per cent of the collective farms had "decided" to terminate their independent existence, or, as Khrushchev put it, "the overwhelming majority of the collective farmers deeply realized the vital necessity of this measure." [25]

Both measures—the promotion of the brigade instead of the small work team, and the amalgamation of the collective farms into larger units—were officially motivated by the alleged economic advantages of larger work teams and larger collective farms. The main purpose of these measures, however, was to tighten Party control over the collective farmers. The collective farm merger enabled the Party to spread its tiny reserves in the countryside more economically and effectively, and thus close some of the gaps where the passive resistance of the Soviet peasantry had been breaking through.

In connection with the amalgamation of the collective farms, Khrushchev had also urged the creation of large "collective-farm settlements" or "agro-cities" which would replace the small villages. This grandiose plan was born in Khrushchev's mind while he was still Party boss in the Ukraine. Already in January, 1949, he tried to convince the delegates to the Sixteenth Ukrainian Party Congress of the possibility of "transforming all our villages in the very near future." [26] At that time his pet project was "complete transformation" of the entire Cherkassy district in the Ukraine. He presented his plan as a "big step on the path of liquidating the contradictions between the city and the village." [27]

In March, 1950, in his double capacity as Secretary of the Party Central Committee and First Secretary of the Moscow Provincial Party Committee, Khrushchev delivered two speeches in which he recommended the "resettlement of the collective farmers from small comfortless villages" to new, centrally located cities where "good everyday living and cultural conditions will be created." Just as he had proclaimed in his 1949 speech in Kiev, Khrushchev promised that the reconstruction of the villages could and must be done "in the very near future."

In two speeches presented in June, 1950, Khrushchev became more impatient and specific as far as the reconstruction of villages in the Moscow province was concerned. He insisted that the mass integration of villages into large settlements was an immediate task, and he urged the collective farms to take the necessary measures in the spring of 1951, to move the homes of the collective farmers from the small villages to new sites where "large, comfortable houses will be gradually constructed later . . ." [28]

"It should be kept in mind," Khrushchev reasoned, "that in one year the collective farms are unable to build homes for all the collective farmers. This cannot be done because of lack of labor and material means. Where then is the solution for collective farmers who live in small villages? After all, it is impossible to wait until the collective farms can construct houses in the new villages for all the collective farmers." In his speeches, Khrushchev asserted that his resettlement idea was motivated by the "desire of the collective farmers to live in good houses" and to enjoy the amenities of city life. If this had been Khrushchev's real motive, he would not have insisted on moving the old comfortless peasants' huts to new sites where the construction of new "good" houses would take place later and depend on many uncertain factors. Rather, there were other considerations behind Khrushchev's plan for amalgamating the small villages. Before the establishment of the larger collective farms the farmers had lived in one or two villages near the land to be taken care of. The merger of several collective farms into larger units caused difficulties in controlling the collective farms' manpower and in transporting the workers to and from work. In addition to these purely geographical and administrative considerations, there was also a political motive: the political "supervision" of geographically concentrated communities would have been far easier than that of dispersed small villages and hamlets. Finally, Khrushchev's resettlement plan was aimed at the separation of the farmers' personal plots from their homes. This would have been a further step in the direction of elimination of the last vestige of private ownership in the Soviet countryside. In his speech of January 18, 1951, Khrushchev proposed to limit the private plots adjacent to the farmer's houses to 0.10-0.15 hectares (one-fourth to one-third of an acre) instead of the previous 0.25-0.50 hectares. "This is quite enough to build a home to live in and the necessary outbuildings, to lay out a small orchard of fifteen or twenty trees, and a small vegetable garden," Khrushchev asserted. As for the remaining portion of land to which the collective farmer is entitled, Khrushchev proposed that it be integrated into a "mass of private plots . . . located outside the settlement."*

In the winter of 1950-51, Khrushchev's plan was put into practice, primarily in the Moscow province. What the resettlement looked like and what it meant for the farmers can be seen from an article published in *Izvestia* on February 13, 1951, by Y. Petrov, chairman of a collective farm in the Kalinin district. In this collective farm, 112 homes were simply moved from four villages to a fifth which had existed before the amalgamation of the collective farms and which had no better "cultural" establishments than the abolished villages. The moving costs were borne by the farmers themselves, and not by the collective farm or by the state. The Khrushchev plan met with considerable resistance from the farmers. Opposition to his plan grew also within the Party hierarchy itself and reached a climax early in March, 1951. On March 4, 1951, three Moscow newspapers—*Pravda,* the central organ of the Party; *Moskovskaya Pravda,* organ of the Moscow Party Committee; and *Sotsialisticheskoye Zemledeliye,* organ of the Ministry of Agriculture—carried Khrushchev's article, "On Construction and Organization of Public Services in the Collective Farms," which was based on his speech delivered on January 18 at a conference convoked to discuss these matters. The next day, all three newspapers carried an identical "note from the editor" explaining that a footnote to the effect that "the article by Comrade N. S. Khrushchev is open for discussion . . . was omitted by an oversight." After March 5, 1951, Khrushchev's project was not given further mention in the press, and the resettlement campaign ceased abruptly.

---

* This was partly realized in 1956, when on many collective farms, in fulfillment of the decree of March 6, 1956, the collective farmers allegedly freely decided to proceed in accordance with Khrushchev's 1950 proposal. For instance, the private plots adjacent to the homes of members of the Molotov collective farm (by now the name has been changed) in the October district, Tadzhik S.S.R., were reduced to 0.06 hectares (0.15 acres); in addition to this amount, the collective farmers were entitled to 0.03 hectares for every able-bodied member of their families, if they fulfilled the prescribed production norm. These additional parcels, however, do not adjoin the farmers' homesteads but are part of a separate "private-plot fund" which can be taken away if the work norms are not fulfilled.

The fact that Khrushchev's pet project was called off after March 4, 1951, was a serious defeat for him and reflected the state of the struggle within the Kremlin for influence over Stalin. The defeat was so serious that even lesser dignitaries, such as the former First Secretary of the Armenian Communist Party, Arutinov, dared to label Khrushchev's resettlement plan "fantastic." It was Malenkov who dealt the final blow; he clearly aimed at Khrushchev when he denounced "some of our leading officials" in his report to the Nineteenth Party Congress in 1952:

> It should be noted that certain of our leading officials have indulged in a wrong approach, a consumer's approach, to problems of collective farm development, particularly in connection with carrying out the amalgamation of small collective farms. They proposed forcing the pace of mass integration of villages into large collective farm settlements, suggesting that all the old collective farm buildings and collective farmers' homes be pulled down and large "collective-farm settlements," "collective-farm towns" or "agrocities" be built on new sites, and viewed this as the most important task in strengthening the farms organizationally and economically. The mistake these comrades made was that they overlooked the collective farms' major tasks—the tasks of production. . . . The Party took timely measures to overcome these mistaken tendencies in the sphere of collective farm development." [29]

Malenkov did not explain the nature of the "timely measures" taken by the Party, but it seems that Khrushchev was relieved of handling agricultural matters and assigned to deal with Party organizational affairs. This assumption is supported by the fact that at the Nineteenth Party Congress in October, 1952, he was the rapporteur on changes in the Party statutes. It is not surprising, however, that Khrushchev retained and, as shown elsewhere, even improved his standing in the Kremlin; Stalin had no doubts about Khrushchev's faithfulness to him, and the only reproach he deserved in Stalin's eyes was for his "gigantomania" and hastiness in trying to solve problems which needed time.

Khrushchev, as in prior cases, did not admit his personal guilt in connection with launching the project. The only reference to his failure was an impersonal remark he made in September, 1952, in his report to the Tenth Moscow Party Conference, that "shortcomings and mistakes were tolerated which consisted of a wrong approach to problems of collective-farm construction, in attempts to speed up the resettlement of villages into large collective-farm settlements." [30]

On March 5, 1953, after thirty-one years of tyrannical rule, Stalin died. "The heart of Lenin's comrade-in-arms and the continuer of genius of his cause, of the wise *vozhd* and teacher of the Communist Party and the Soviet people—Yosif Vissarionovich Stalin—has stopped beating." [31] Khrushchev was given the honor of presiding over the commission to organize the funeral, and Malenkov, Beria, and Molotov were assigned to deliver the farewell speeches.

People in the streets wept, and foreign correspondents could not make up their minds whether the tears they saw were tears from shock, joy, or sorrow. Uncertainty and hope might have been additional reasons for the emotions that swept through the cities and villages of the Soviet empire. But all this did not matter, because it was not for the people to decide who should succeed the dead dictator.

Stalin's body was not yet buried when his top companions-in-arms went into a huddle from which they emerged as a "collective leadership" in the form of a ten-member Party Presidium. The Party and government announcement of March 7, 1953, listed them in the following order: Malenkov, Beria, Molotov, Voroshilov, Khrushchev, Bulganin, Kaganovich, Mikoyan, Saburov, and Pervukhin. Thus, from the seventh place which Khrushchev occupied shortly before Stalin's death, he moved up to the fifth.

The Council of Ministers underwent reorganization, and eight members of the Party Presidium (Malenkov, Beria, Molotov, Bulganin, Kaganovich, Mikoyan, Saburov, and Pervukhin) were represented on it. Malenkov, as Chairman of the Council of Ministers, headed its Presidium, which consisted of himself and four newly appointed first vice-chairmen—Beria, Molotov, Bulganin, and Kaganovich. Only two members of the Party Presidium, Voroshilov and Khrushchev, were not included in the supreme executive organ of the Soviet State. Marshal Voroshilov was made Chairman of the Presidium of the U.S.S.R. Supreme Soviet, a minor position in spite of its high-sounding title, and Khrushchev's position in the apparatus of the Central Committee remained the same as before Stalin's death—that of one of the secretaries. He was, however, released from the post of First Secretary of the Moscow Province Party Committee, since, according to the March 7 communiqué, "it [was] acknowledged as necessary to ask Comrade N. S. Khrushchev to concentrate on work within the Central Committee." This was not a curtailment; it reflected rather a short phase in the struggle for power which broke out immediately after and might have had its beginning before Stalin's death. Not even two weeks passed, when Malenkov, "at his own request," relinquished his duties as senior Secretary of the Central Committee,[32] and Khrushchev thus became in fact its First Secretary, in which position he was officially confirmed in September, 1953. This was the first major setback for Malenkov. The rise of Beria during the first few months after Stalin's death and the sudden purge and subsequent execution of the once powerful chief of the Soviet secret police were other signs of the bitter struggle for power. Whoever might have been the temporary victor, Beria's fall accentuated the rise of Khrushchev. He now occupied a position similar to that of Secretary General held by the late dictator after the death of Lenin—a position which enabled him to fill the Party machine with his faithful followers and turn it into a bastion from which he could attack his main rival, Malenkov.

At the frequently convoked plenary sessions of the Central Committee, Khrushchev was the main rapporteur on many problems which fall under the jurisdiction of the Council of Ministers. On September 3, 1953, he delivered an unexpectedly frank report on the disastrous situation in agriculture and proposed a number of concessions to the collective farmers in the form of material incentives which would increase their interest in raising the production in the collectivized agriculture. These measures improved somewhat the agricultural situation, but did not solve the grain production problem as expected. In his September, 1953, report Khrushchev asserted that "generally speaking we are satisfying the country's need for grain crops, in the sense that our country is well supplied with bread. We have the necessary state reserves and are exporting wheat on a fixed scale." [33] Khrushchev's main worry was at that time the "growing need of the population" for dairy products. But five months later, in his February, 1954, report on putting virgin and idle lands in cultivation, he admitted that the "level of grain production so far has not met all the requirements of the national economy." It is necessary, therefore, Khrushchev said, to "meet fully the growing requirements of the entire population for bread and other grain products," to "supplement the state grain reserves," to "ensure feed grain for all livestock," and to "increase grain exports." [34]

Experienced observers of the development of Soviet "socialized" agriculture were aware of its serious chronic shortcomings long before Khrushchev revealed them in 1953 and 1954. Soviet agriculture did not deteriorate overnight; it was a lengthy process initiated by the collectivization of private landholdings and cattle and continued under further experiments whose purpose was the liquidation of the last vestiges of private ownership in the countryside. The effect of this policy was particularly disastrous in the sphere of livestock production. In fact, the cattle population in 1953 declined by about two million head compared with the number of cattle in 1916, when Czarist Russia entered the third year of World War I. [35] The significance of these figures becomes particularly clear in view of the increase of the population by approximately 36 million during the same period.

It was not until 1956 that Khrushchev, in his de-Stalinization speech before the Twentieth Party Congress stated that "all those who interested themselves even a little in the national situation saw the difficult situation in agriculture." [36] "Our situation on the land was a difficult one and . . . the situation of cattle breeding and meat production was especially bad," [37] Khrushchev continued. In the same speech Khrushchev blamed Stalin alone for the "difficult situation in agriculture." "Our project" to improve the situation "was not accepted, and in February, 1953, it was laid aside entirely," Khrushchev said.[38] In connection with this project, Stalin allegedly proposed to increase the tax load on the collective farms and their members by 40 billion rubles, although the total collective farm revenue in 1952 from produce delivered and sold to the government was less than 27 billion rubles. "In such cases," Khrushchev asserted, "facts and figures did not interest Stalin. If Stalin said anything, it meant it was so—after all he was a 'genius,' and a genius does not need to calculate, he only needs to look and can immediately tell how things should be. When he expresses his opinion, everyone has to repeat it and admire his wisdom."[39]

The project to improve cattle breeding was allegedly rejected by Stalin in February, 1953, just before his death. Five months later, *Pravda* stated officially that "it has now been established that Beria, under various fictitious excuses, hindered in every way the solution of very important, urgent problems in the sphere of agriculture."[40] And in February, 1955, the down-graded Malenkov was forced to declare in his letter of resignation that he saw particularly clearly his own guilt and responsibility for the unsatisfactory state of affairs which had arisen in agriculture, because for several years (before Stalin's death) he, Malenkov, had been entrusted with the duty of controlling and guiding the work of central agricultural organs and the work of local Party and Soviet organizations in the sphere of agriculture.[41]

In his reports on agriculture delivered in September, 1953, and February, 1954, Khrushchev blamed the top government agencies for the shortcomings in agriculture. "Facts show," Khrushchev said in 1953, "that the U.S.S.R. Ministry of Agriculture and Procurements and the U.S.S.R. Ministry of State Farms have lagged impermissibly far behind the demands of life. . . ." In 1954, Khrushchev went further and attacked by name the Minister of State Farms, Kozlov, the Minister of Agriculture, Benediktov, and the Vice-Chairman of the State Planning Committee in charge of agriculture, Dmitriyev, for impeding the grain production.

The fact, however, remains that in the early 'fifties Khrushchev himself was the official spokesman on agricultural matters and promoted measures which were to a great extent responsible for the plight of Soviet agriculture.

Less than a year after Stalin's death, Khrushchev became the indisputable authority on agricultural matters qualified to pass judgment on the work of the top agricultural bureaucracy. This was Khrushchev's first success in establishing the primacy of the Party under his leadership over the managerial group entrenched in the government apparatus.

The problem of relations between Party and the executive branch of government was not acute in the Stalin era, because he was commander of all branches of the totalitarian dictatorship. With the establishment of "collective leadership" after Stalin's death, differences between the Party and government bureaucrats came into the open and were one of the major aspects of the struggle for power. The second blow Khrushchev dealt to the managerial "class" was the decentralization of industry undertaken in December, 1956, and February, 1957.[42] The reorganization had put an end to the rigid, highly centralized economic machine concentrated in Moscow and at the same time had given the Party bosses in the economic regions far greater authority in controlling the newly established Councils of National Economy.

Molotov, Kaganovich and Malenkov obviously failed in their desperate fight against economic decentralization, and this was one of the main reasons for their downfall in June, 1957. For his victory over the "anti-Party group," as they have been officially called, Khrushchev depended upon the support of the military caste headed by Marshal Zhukov. After the ouster from the Party Presidium of the "anti-Party group," Zhukov was "elected" a full-fledged member of the Party Presidium, which was considered at the time an indication of the strengthened position of the military hierarchy within the dictatorship. The subsequent purge of Marshal Zhukov in November of the same year shows how unsubstantiated this assumption was. Khrushchev completed his victory in March, 1958, when he succeeded Bulganin as Chairman of the Council of Ministers without relinquishing his post of First Secretary of the Party's Central Committee.

Thus it took Khrushchev less than five years to "catch up and overtake" his rival, Malenkov; Malenkov's successor, Bulganin; his teacher and protector of the 'thirties, Kaganovich; the hard-boiled Molotov; and the "savior of Russia from the Nazi hordes," Marshal Zhukov. Today, in their solitude, they have plenty of time to analyze their fatal moves on the political chessboard and how it happened that they overestimated their authority in the Party and underestimated the loquacious, low-brow, *enfant terrible* of the Kremlin.

18

The Preacher of "Peace"

Nowhere in the world is foreign policy so intimately connected with problems of domestic policy as in Communist countries, and particularly in the Soviet Union. This is so because the rulers of the Communist bloc are convinced that *they* are the promoters of a new social order that will inevitably conquer the world,* and that the stronger the bloc becomes economically and militarily the sooner this will happen. Lenin said in 1920: "As soon as we are strong enough to defeat capitalism as a whole, we shall immediately take it by the scruff of the neck." [1] Lenin never explained what means he would have used to perform this operation, but this is of less importance today, in the midst of the atomic age. There can hardly be any doubt that if Lenin could rise from the mausoleum on the Red Square he would have chosen other means than war to conquer the world, not because of moral scruples, but because he would have shared Khrushchev's secret belief that a nuclear war would be disastrous both for civilization and for the Com-

* *The History of the CPSU* published in 1959 puts it this way:
"The greatest international significance of the October Revolution consists not only in the fact that it has moved the entire course of world history forward, but also in the fact that it has shown that the basic features of that Revolution must inevitably be repeated in a socialist revolution in any country" (*Istoria Kommunisticheskoi Partii Sovetskogo Soyuza* [Moscow, 1959], p. 241). It is noteworthy that the previous version of the *History of the CPSU (Short Course)* published in the Stalin period claimed only that the October Socialist Revolution "ushered in a new era in the history of mankind—the era of proletarian revolutions" (*Istoria Vsesoyuznoi Kommunisticheskoi Partii [bolshevikov]* (Moscow, 1942), p. 214).

249

munist cause. What is important are not the means, which are to be chosen according to the circumstances, but the essense of the Communist belief that capitalism will be "taken by the scruff of the neck," or, to use Khrushchev's expression "buried." In this respect, nothing has changed. It is in the light of this belief that Khrushchev's foreign policy pronouncements and actions should be analyzed. But before proceeding with the analysis it is necessary to describe under what circumstances Khrushchev emerged as the Preacher of "Peace."

Stalin's death created a vacuum in the sense that none of his heirs (and, as events have shown, not even Malenkov, whom most observers considered his successor) could claim the empty throne and, if necessary, support such a claim by force. In their first post-Stalin communiqué of March 7, 1953, they declared that "in this difficult time for our Party and country . . . the most important task of the Party and the Government [is] to ensure uninterrupted and correct leadership of the whole life of the country, which in turn demands the *greatest unity of leadership and prevention of any kind of disorder and panic . . .*" [2] The fact that Stalin's heirs were apprehensive over the possibility of "disorder and panic" after the death of the "beloved leader" and felt that "greatest unity of leadership is necessary" reflected the state of affairs which Stalin left behind him. The horrible wounds of the war were not yet healed despite the fact that eight years had elapsed since the end of hostilities; nearly 100 million people who derived their living from working the soil were struggling under enormous stress and poverty; the overwhelming majority of workers in plants and factories were rewarded with only a small fraction of the value of the goods they were turning out and were living in overcrowded, unsanitary quarters; and the intellectuals were craving less conformity and more freedom of thought and expression.

If one disregards the strikes in the slave labor camps which were brutally halted by bullets, there were no visible signs of "disorder and panic." But underneath the official tranquillity, the pulse of life, warmed by rays of hope, began to beat faster. The fall of Beria intensified that feeling of longing and expectation.

Two ways were open to the "unified" post-Stalin leadership;

either a continuation of the Stalin era with all its characteristics, or a gradual change in which the needs and the desires of the population would be taken into consideration; either continued stress on heavy industry and production of armaments at the expense of the consumer goods industries, or a drastic increase in the rate of growth of industries producing the necessities of life and a lowering of the rate of growth of industries nonessential from the standpoint of the people's well-being; either continued strict control of all aspects of intellectual life, or a relaxation of that control so that some of the thoughts and feelings so long suppressed could come out into the open.

Continuation of the Stalinist foreign policy of threats to the international peace would exclude the possibility of concessions to the population, and the screws of the totalitarian dictatorship would have to be kept as tight as during the Stalin period. But if his heirs chose a policy of honest negotiations aimed at genuine relaxation of international tensions, then, of course, the road toward a real liberalization of the regime would be open.

Which road did Stalin's heirs choose? The answer to this is that during the Malenkov period (1953-55) Soviet policy, generally speaking, was inconsistent. While Malenkov was mostly concerned with promoting measures which would raise the level of living of the Soviet people, Molotov did his best to continue the hard Stalinist foreign policy line which would logically require a steady increase of investments in heavy industry and armaments, thus undercutting Malenkov's plans. Khrushchev's exact position is of course unknown to outsiders, but, judging from his pronouncements during the Malenkov period and from the events that followed Malenkov's dismissal from the premiership it can be assumed that Khrushchev was not only aware of this discrepancy but that he developed his own plan for restoring the logical connection between Soviet domestic and foreign policy. On the one hand, he believed that no successful Communist foreign policy could be conducted without having the arms to support it, without gaining superiority over the West in the creation and production of intercontinental ballistic missiles and solving, as a by-product, problems of space exploration with huge satellites. On the other hand, he realized the necessity for improving living conditions in the country. Therefore, he went along with Malenkov in promoting and pioneering changes in agricultural policy aimed at a "drastic" increase of production of grain and dairy products, but he definitely disagreed with Malenkov's views as far as a substantial diversion of funds from heavy industry to light industry was concerned. He was not opposed to Molotov's continual harassing of the West along Stalinist lines, but he was definitely against using the old Stalinist style. Khrushchev's plan was to postpone Malenkov's measures until equality with or superiority over the West in producing nuclear weapons and means of delivery was achieved, and to prepare the ground for an offensive by a means unknown as yet in the history of Soviet foreign policy, namely personal diplomacy and attacks on the psychology of the world public with waves of intensive propaganda on "peaceful coexistence" coupled with rocket-rattling threats.

The above assumption is to a large extent confirmed by the following facts:

In March, 1953, Malenkov stated: "In the sphere of domestic policy *our main task* is ceaselessly to strive for further improvement of the material welfare of the workers, the collective farmers, the intelligentsia and all the Soviet people." [3] In his election speech of March, 1954, he devoted far more attention to the "task of achieving a sharp increase in consumer goods production in two or three years" than to heavy industry, which he said "we will continue ceaselessly to develop as the basis for continuous growth and advancement of the entire national economy and as a reliable support of the country's defense." [4] On the other hand, Khrushchev, in his speech delivered on the same occasion,[5] stressed in detail "how the industrial might of the Soviet Union has increased over these years" (from 1950 to 1954) and praised "the wise policy of socialist industrialization of the country" which was carried out under the leadership of the Party "headed by I. V. Stalin, the great continuer of the cause of Lenin." Although he mentioned the possibility of "speeding up the development of light and food industries," he emphasized in the same breath that this should be done "without relaxing attention to the further development of heavy industry which is the very foundation (*osnova osnov*) of Soviet economy." Thus, already at the beginning of 1954, there seemed to be differences on the question of how far the government should go in promoting consumer goods industries.

Nine months later Khrushchev made the following statement: "The industrialization of the Soviet land has been carried out thanks to the fact that our Party has undeviatingly put into practice the instructions of Lenin and Stalin. This has been and will continue to be *our main task*. We must develop heavy industry in the future in every possible way." [6]

A comparison of Malenkov's and Khrushchev's statements makes it clear that while Malenkov considered "our main task" to be a "ceaseless" development of light and food industries, Khrushchev insisted that "our main task" has been and will continue to be the development of heavy industry "in every possible way." The controversy ended with Khrushchev's victory. On January 24, 1955, *Pravda* blasted those who assert that since 1953, "the center of gravity has shifted to developing light industry, to production of consumer goods," which would mean that "the development of our heavy industry, which is the backbone of the socialist economy, would take a descending line." Furthermore, *Pravda* emphasized that while "the forces of imperialist reaction, armed to the teeth and arming even more, are nurturing plans for another world war . . . every possible strengthening of the might of the Soviet country and its defense capacity are the first, sacred, patriotic and international duty of the Soviet people." Two weeks later Malenkov was forced to resign.

Molotov's star was also on the decline. At the Geneva Conference of the four heads of the Great Powers, Khrushchev, in no other official capacity than as a "member of the Presidium of the U.S.S.R. Supreme Soviet," represented the Soviet Union together with Bulganin and Molotov, and his name was listed second after Bulganin's, preceding that of Molotov. A few months later he and Bulganin paid official visits to India, Burma, and Afghanistan. This was Khrushchev's starting point in his "peaceful coexistence" drive.

The slogan of peaceful coexistence of states with different social systems is not new. It had been used in the Stalin era, but it has been worked up into a "principle" of Soviet foreign policy and incorporated into the treasures of Communist ideology (in its Soviet interpretation) only in the Khrushchev era. The cornerstone for this "principle" was laid by him in his 1956 published report delivered at the Twentieth Party Congress. Khrushchev argued that the Marxist-Leninist precept that wars are inevitable as long as imperialism exists should be reappraised because "the situation has changed radically." This precept, Khrushchev conceded, remains valid in the sense that "as long as imperialism exists, the economic base giving rise to wars will also remain," but "war is not only an economic phenomenon," because whether there is to be war or not depends in large measure on the correlation of social and political forces, which, according to Khrushchev, have changed in favor of the forces of "socialism and democracy." Therefore, he concluded, "War is not a fatalistic inevitability."

It seems that the revision of the Leninist theory on imperialism and war did not convince all Communist ideologists, particularly in the Far East, despite Khrushchev's assurances, made in 1956, that the principle of peaceful coexistence "has become one of the cornerstones of the foreign policy of the Chinese People's Republic."[7] * That was the reason it became necessary for Khrushchev to elaborate on his thesis of peaceful coexistence by disassociating himself more emphatically from Lenin's teaching on imperialism and war. In his speech at the Third Congress of the Rumanian Workers' Party (June 21, 1960) Khrushchev said:

* Today there is ample evidence that a bitter ideological controversy has broken out on the subject between Khrushchev and the Chinese ideologists.

In his book *Socialism and War* (August, 1960), the Yugoslav Communist ideologist Edvard Kardelj, pointed out that the "attacks in the Chinese press and in the speeches of Chinese leaders, including the highest, on Yugoslavia's concept of peaceful active coexistence between states with different social systems . . . indicate that something much more important is in question than Chinese displeasure with Yugoslavia's foreign policy, with the policy of a minor European country. . . . Evidently the pressure of the Chinese attacks is aimed against the entire front of international affairs of present-day socialism for the purpose of obtaining certain solutions in the dilemma confronting socialist forces in the world today." (TANYUG, Radioteletype in English to Europe, August 11, 1960.) It is obvious that the Chinese, pressing their attacks on Yugoslavia, had in mind the "big brother" Khrushchev.

The thesis enunciated at the Twentieth and Twenty-first Congresses of our Party to the effect that war is not inevitable in our time is directly related to the policy of peaceful coexistence. The tenets on imperialism that Lenin advanced hold true; they serve as before and will go on serving as a lodestar for us in our theory and practice. But it must not be forgotten that Lenin's tenets on imperialism were put forward and developed by him decades ago, when many phenomena that have now become decisive for the development of the historical process and for the entire international situation did not exist . . .

Therefore, one must not repeat without considering the concrete setting, without considering the change in the correlation of forces in the world, what the great Lenin said in altogether different historical conditions. If Lenin could rise from the grave he would take such people by the ear, as they say, and would teach them how the essence of the matter should be understood.[8]

Thus, Khrushchev based his thesis of peaceful coexistence on a revision of Lenin's tenets on the inevitability of war in the epoch of imperialism. But, at the same time he has, as shown below, persistently asserted that Soviet foreign policy is based on *Leninist* principles of peaceful coexistence.

Speaking at the National Press Club in Washington in 1959, Khrushchev declared that Soviet policy is in full conformity with the principles which "were bequeathed to us by Vladimir Ilyich Lenin, the great founder of the Soviet state."[9] Lenin, he stated, was for peaceful coexistence—and so are the present leaders of the U.S.S.R.

Such assertions are not new to Khrushchev. At the end of 1955, when he and the former Premier Bulganin visited India, Khrushchev addressed the Indian Parliament in the following terms:

"We are guided by the immortal teachings of the great Lenin who held that the people of every country are entitled to live as they wish, without interference by other countries in their affairs. . . . We have never attempted to force our ideas of social reconstruction on anybody."[10]

In 1956, at the Twentieth Party Congress, Khrushchev declared:

"The Leninist principle of peaceful coexistence of states with different social systems has always been and remains the general line of our country's foreign policy." [11]

Similarly in 1958, in reply to a question from the Australian editor of *The Herald*, John Waters, he stated:

". . . Over the span of more than forty years, Soviet foreign policy has been consistent—it has always been, is and will continue to be the Leninist policy of peaceful coexistence." [12]

And in 1959, at a reception in Peking, Khrushchev declared:

"During the first years of Soviet power, the great Lenin defined the general line of foreign policy as a line of peaceful coexistence of states with different social systems. For a long time ruling quarters of the Western Powers rejected these truly humanistic principles." [13]

Yet how truthful is Khrushchev's portrayal of Lenin's view on relations between capitalist and "socialist" states? How truthful is his claim that Lenin had always and consistently been in favor of peaceful coexistence? A cursory glance at the historical record supplies the answer to these questions—and the answer is, in brief, that Khrushchev's claims are hardly in accord with the facts.

An examination of the text of the "Decree on Peace" to which Khrushchev alluded in his article in *Foreign Affairs* (October, 1959) shows conclusively that it does not contain any deviation from the concepts on war and peace which Lenin had formulated at the start of World War I, and to which he steadfastly adhered till his death. A "democratic peace," Lenin wrote in January, 1917, "can be concluded . . . *only by proletarian* governments after they have overthrown the rule of the bourgeoisie and begun to expropriate it." [14] And on the very day Lenin drafted the Decree on Peace, he said in a speech before the Petrograd Soviet:

"One of our urgent tasks is the necessity to end the war immediately. But it is clear to everybody that in order to end the war, which is intimately bound up with the capitalist system, it is necessary to overcome capital itself." [15]

In other words, peace through war—"class war," that is. And indeed, the Decree on Peace itself spells out this principle in no uncertain terms:

". . . class-conscious workers [must] understand the duty that now lies upon them . . . and by comprehensive, determined and supremely energetic action [they must] help us to bring the cause of peace to a successful conclusion and, together with this, the cause of the liberation of the toiling masses from all forms of slavery and all forms of exploitation." [16]

The Decree on Peace was only the first of a series of similar documents. On December 19, 1917, an appeal issued by the People's Commissariat of Foreign Affairs openly admitted that the Soviet Government "does not consider the existing capitalist governments capable of concluding a democratic peace," and went on to say:

> The revolutionary struggle of the working masses against the existing governments alone can bring Europe nearer to such a peace. . . . While entering in negotiations with the existing governments the Soviet Government has set itself a double task: first, to bring an end as quickly as possible to the disgraceful and criminal slaughter which is laying Europe waste; and second, to use all means to overthrow the rule of capital and to seize political power." [17]

On December 30, 1917, the Commissariat of Foreign Affairs again urged the peoples at war to sweep away their governments and promised "full support to the working class in every country who would rise in revolt against their national imperialists, against the chauvinists, against the militarists—under the banner of peace, fraternity of peoples and socialist reconstruction of society." [18]

Evidence that the Soviet Government fully intended to make good on its promise to support revolutionary movements in other countries is contained in an interesting document, quoted verbatim by the American journalist and Communist sympathizer, John Reed, author of *Ten Days that Shook the World* —a book which originally appeared with a preface by Lenin, then was relegated to the "memory hole" by Stalin, and which

was recently "rehabilitated"—along with its author—by Khrushchev himself.[19] This document—a resolution passed by the Soviet
Government on December 23, 1917, and signed by Lenin—
made it plain that the Soviet Government "deems it necessary
to come to the assistance of the Left International wing of the
labor movement in all countries by all possible means, including funds, whether the said countries are at war with Russia,
allied to Russia, or occupying a neutral position." Specifically,
the resolution stated that "the sum of two million rubles shall
be placed for the needs of the revolutionary internationalist
movements." [20]

In the same article, Reed also revealed that early in November
of the same year—that is, immediately following the Bolshevik
coup—a "Bureau of International Revolutionary Propaganda"
was established in the Commissariat of Foreign Affairs. This
bureau had to be abolished shortly thereafter, in accordance
with the provisions of the Brest-Litovsk Peace Treaty, but it
continued to exist unofficially as a "committee," its budget having in the meantime been augmented by 20 million rubles.[21]

The fact that information regarding the "Bureau of International Revolutionary Propaganda" is not to be found in any
official Soviet source does not mean, of course, that the Soviet
Government, under Lenin, was necessarily reticent about its
revolutionary goals. There is, for instance, the official reply
from Adolf A. Yoffe, first Soviet Ambassador in Berlin, to accusations of Soviet interference in internal German affairs.
Charged with fomenting revolutionary outbreaks against the
social-democratic government which was formed after the
overthrow of the Kaiser, Yoffe openly admitted the existence
of a fund of 10 million rubles "placed directly at the disposal
of Dr. Oskar Cohn in the interest of the German revolution." [22]

It is evident that the comparatively forthright statements by
Lenin and his associates in the early years of the Soviet regime
are a source of acute embarrassment to present-day Soviet "theoreticians," who are at pains to square their claims of peaceful
coexistence with Lenin's call for world revolution. Yet if square
they cannot, falsify they can. A good illustration of this is a
recent book on the aforementioned Decree on Peace, written by
S. Y. Vygodsky. Vygodsky writes:

V. I. Lenin pointed out: "People live in states and every state lives in a system of states . . ." This means that the establishment of economic ties between individual states is an objective law that is valid independently of the will and desire of the peoples. It was the idea of indiscriminate cooperation, based on this objective law, that was decidedly pronounced in the Leninist Decree on Peace.[23]

As we have seen, the Decree on Peace "decidedly" did not constitute a pronouncement of "indiscriminate cooperation" (not even in the purely economic sense) with capitalist states, but—in addition to pressing for an end to the hostilities—was aimed at inciting the "toiling masses" against their governments. However, not even Lenin's speech of 1920, from which Vygodsky quoted, has anything to say about "indiscriminate cooperation" between Soviet and capitalist governments. Here are three passages which convey the spirit of that speech:

> As long as we have not conquered the whole world, as long as from the economic and military standpoint we remain weaker than the capitalist world, we must adhere to the rule that we must know how to take advantage of the antagonisms and contradictions existing among the imperialists. Had we not adhered to this rule, every one of us would have long ago been hanged from an aspen tree, to the satisfaction of capitalists.[24]
>
> What would have saved us still more would have been a war between the imperialist powers. If we are obliged to tolerate such scoundrels as the capitalist thieves, each of whom is preparing to plunge a knife into us, it is our direct duty to make them turn their knives against each other. When thieves fall out, honest men come into their own.[25]
>
> As soon as we are strong enough to defeat capitalism as a whole, we shall immediately take it by the scruff of the neck.[26]

Perhaps better than anything else, the essential character of Lenin's "peace" policy was wrapped up in an introduction to a collection of Soviet documents covering the years 1917-27, published in 1929. Here are some relevant passages:

> The entire grandoise peace activity of the Soviet Government, reflected in innumerable documents officially addressed to various governments or leaders of bourgeois countries, is essentially an appeal addressed over their heads to the multimillion masses of working and oppressed peoples of all parts of the world and, in the first place, to their vanguards—the international proletariat—who, by their class struggle and class battles, concretely and efficiently support this unprecedented peace activity of the first proletarian government in the world. In its peace policy, as well as in all its other activity, the Soviet Government, under the leadership of the Communist Party, carries out an offensive against the bourgeois world; struggles for influence on the wide multimillion masses; endeavors to imbue them with ideas which have inspired the workers and the peasants who have accomplished the greatest revolution, and calls upon them to actively check the resistance of the bourgeois world and to defeat it . . .[27]
>
> The working people of the Soviet Union are firmly aware of the fact that the final triumph of their peace aspirations is possible only when imperialists will be disarmed and defeated by the international proletariat.[28]

These, then, are the facts concerning the "Leninist policy of peaceful coexistence." They show that Lenin's approach to the problem of "coexistence" with capitalist states had been subordinated to the concept of world revolution which he expected to break out immediately after the October upheaval. When he realized that revolutions in the West were not forthcoming, he adopted a policy of tolerating "bourgeois" governments, in the hope that they would then be willing to render assistance to Soviet Russia, both in terms of credits and technological know-how. By taking advantage of the "antagonisms and contradictions existing among the imperialists," he expected to bring them into conflict with each other. Such a conflict, Lenin thought, would change the relations of forces in favor of the Soviet Union, making it strong enough to "defeat capitalism as a whole" by taking it—in his picturesque phrase—"by the scruff of the neck."

Lenin's view on foreign relations was a perfectly understandable one. Moreover, it was presented to the world in a startlingly forthright fashion. This forthrightness was completely abandoned by Stalin, who preached "world revolution" on the one hand and "peaceful coexistence" on the other, while at the same time engaging in cautious piecemeal imperialist aggrandizement (Lithuania, Latvia, Esthonia, West Ukraine, Bessarabia, the East European satellites, etc.). Khrushchev now claims that Soviet foreign policy has no aggressive plans. Whether this is so remains to be seen.

What is perfectly clear, however, is that Khrushchev's version of Leninism is, on the face of it, a radical departure from the original version. Whereas Lenin based his hopes on world revolution—in the pristine and actual sense of the term—Khrushchev says no word about it. Whereas Lenin explicitly recognized Communist parties throughout the world as allies in the struggle for universal socialism, Khrushchev—in his pronouncements on peaceful coexistence—is almost oblivious of their existence. Whereas Lenin made no secret of his loathing for the "capitalist thieves," and called upon the "workers of the world" to overthrow them, Khrushchev—though of course voicing criticism of "capitalism"—nevertheless maintains that he has not the slightest intention of interfering with its course of development: history, he blithely and good-naturedly predicts, will "prove" which system is better. Yet at the same time he calmly ascribes *his* views to Lenin—and thus engages in gross distortion.

The problem remains *why* he and his "theoreticians" so blatantly and crudely distort Lenin's views on peaceful coexistence (a term, incidentally, which Lenin *never* employed). Without going into detail, suffice it to say that if Khrushchev persists in distorting Leninism and in identifying himself with it (the two processes are intimately interrelated), it is because his position as chief of a totalitarian state dictates ideological continuity—in this case, continuity between the present theoretical formulations of Soviet foreign policy and the "holy tenets" of Marxism - Leninism. Ideological continuity, in turn, of necessity involves distortion: the price which Khrushchev and his propagandists are ready to pay for maintaining an ideological bridge with the past is a deliberate misrepresentation of Lenin's views and practices.

Whatever the reason for Khrushchev's persistence in identifying his foreign policy with Leninist principles might be, it would be a mistake to assume that he does so for practical purposes alone— to build up his authority in the Communist world as the recognized "great continuer of Lenin's cause," or that he pays only lip service to ideological matters and, as a noted pragmatist and unpredictable politician, might some day show willingness to dismiss the basic tenets of Leninism. In numerous statements made not only before Communist audiences but also before neutralist and anti-Communist gatherings Khrushchev warned his enemies not to take his desire to compete peacefully with capitalist states for a sign that the Bolsheviks had abandoned "their political plans." In 1955, at a reception in Bombay, Khrushchev said:

"We have never abandoned, and never will abandon, our political line which Lenin mapped for us; we have never abandoned, and never will abandon, our political program. . . . And so we say to the gentry who are expecting the Soviet Union to change its political program: 'Wait until the crab whistles!' And you know when the crab whistles." [29]

In 1956, at the Twentieth Party Congress, Khrushchev denounced "some people" who "attempt to transfer into the sphere of ideology the absolutely correct thesis of the possibility of peaceful coexistence of countries with different socio-political systems." Khrushchev declared this to be a "harmful error":

"The fact that we are for peaceful coexistence and economic competition does not at all lead to the conclusion that the struggle against bourgeois ideology, against the remnants of capitalism in people's minds, can be relaxed. Our task is to expose bourgeois ideology tirelessly, to show its hostility toward the people, and disclose its reactionary nature." [30]

The purpose and aim of this struggle are clear. They are the same as Lenin envisioned them—establishment of Communist rule throughout the world. Khrushchev differs from Lenin only insofar as the means are concerned. The only weapon Lenin possessed was the Communist International which he created in 1919, but he lacked such means as military might, economic strength, and the political prestige of a leader of a Great Power. All these weapons are at Khrushchev's disposal. Applying different means and forms of struggle, Khrushchev is faithful to Lenin who wrote in 1920, after his hopes for a world-wide social revolution had vanished, the following:

"The Communists must exert every effort to direct the working-class movement and social development in general along the straightest and quickest road to the victory of world-wide Soviet power and the dictatorship of the proletariat. That is an incontestable truth. But it is enough to take one little step further —a step that might seem to be in the same direction—and truth becomes an error! We have only to say, as the German and British Left Communists say, that we recognize only one road, that we do not agree with tacking, maneuvering, compromising— and it will already be a mistake which may cause, and partly has already caused, and is causing, very serious harm to Communism. . . . It is our duty as Communists to master all forms, to learn how, with maximum rapidity, to supplement one form with another, to substitute one for another, and to adapt our tactics to every such change not called forth by our class, or by our efforts." [31]

Khrushchev's peace offensive is only another form of the struggle for Communist world domination. In a recent article in *Pravda*, the Soviet ideologist of the international Communist movement, B. Ponomarev, made it perfectly clear that Khrushchev's principle of "peaceful coexistence" is, among others, based on the alleged fact that ". . . under the conditions of peaceful coexistence the class struggle in capitalist countries has not died down but has strengthened, sharpened, making it possible for the working class to carry on an offensive, up to the most decisive actions, against the capitalist monopolists and their domination; that the possibilities for the national liberation movement, for revolutions aimed at the overthrow of the colonial and imperialist yoke, are not only preserved but increased to an enormous extent." [32]

As Stalin would have said: "Clear, one would think."

19

The Unfinished Act

The story of Khrushchev's spectacular rise after Stalin's death to the most powerful position in the Kremlin is so rich in events that their detailed analysis would demand a special study. This book is a retrospective analysis of Khrushchev's political past in the light of his present position rather than an analysis of his post-Stalin transmutations. It aims at tracing the most important phases of Khrushchev's past and conveying Khrushchev's characteristics as a political leader.

The Khrushchev of today is, of course, a product of the Stalin era, but he differs from Stalin's other heirs in one respect: he is not a standardized product of this era. Even during the Stalin era Khrushchev displayed initiative in promoting his audacious and in some cases unrealistic projects. Given some freedom for experimentation, he sometimes failed and was reprimanded. Now that he has succeeded in consolidating the Party's control over the government machine and the army, and has established his leadership of the Party and the government, Khrushchev has almost unlimited freedom to promote and carry out reforms of far-reaching significance. Some of them are on the brink of failure, others may succeed, Khrushchev is, therefore, unpredictable. His mind is preoccupied with finding short cuts. A man with no inclination for ideological matters, he may even pull some of the secondary stones out from under the Communist ideological edifice, provided that such an operation would speed the achievement of the final goal.

Khrushchev has reached the zenith of his political career. Will he re-establish a one-man rule of the Stalinist type or will he tolerate some sort of "intra-Party democracy"? Some observers believe that one day Khrushchev may return to the bloody practices of the Stalin era. They believe that history can repeat itself. Their reasoning is like this: When Lenin died, Stalin held the same position in the Party as Khrushchev did after Stalin's death. Stalin eliminated Trotsky with the assistance of the other two members of an earlier triumvirate, Kamenev and Zinoviev; similarly, Khrushchev liquidated Beria with the support of Malenkov and Molotov. Then Stalin eliminated Kamenev and Zinoviev with the assistance of Rykov and Bukharin, who were also purged subsequently; similarly Khrushchev, supported by Zhukov, ousted Malenkov, Molotov, and Kaganovich, and then got rid of Zhukov. Later Stalin liquidated all his rivals and their supporters and, with the assistance of those who survived him, became the charismatic leader, the *vozhd*, the charisma being maintained by an all-embracing propaganda and a powerful terror machine. It took Stalin a decade to lay the cornerstone of his personal dictatorship. Does it not seem that Khrushchev has gained enormous ground in this short post-Stalin period and might repeat Stalin's old game? To put it differently: Is a totalitarian system a stagnant socio-political phenomenon which can be destroyed only by force from without, or is it subject to change into another "higher," still totalitarian form? If such development is possible, can a totalitarian system, having remained for a certain period in that "higher" form, return to its original stage? Speaking in chemical terms the question might be: Is such a change a reversible or irreversible reaction?

Any attempt to analyze this question inevitably leads to speculations based on small bits of information from Soviet sources, on large chunks of hearsay, and, finally, on the widespread theory that a one-man rule of the Stalinist type is inherent in the totalitarian system. But speculation is a trap. The theory of totalitarian monocracy is based on a comparatively short period of experience. The Soviet totalitarian system, established in the 'thirties, has existed less than a quarter of a century; the fascist system in Italy survived for only two decades, and that in Germany for a little over one decade. These short historical periods do not seem to be a sufficient basis for far-reaching theoretical generalizations. Relying on facts alone, one would have to examine three major events pertinent to the question raised above: the liquidation of Beria, Khrushchev's secret speech of February, 1956 on Stalin's cult, and the 1957 purges.

After Stalin's death none of his heirs possessed the qualities and power to become a charismatic leader. In the first days after the demise of the *vozhd*, Malenkov's followers made initial steps to create a new leader-image of him, but his abdication from the secretaryship of the Party proved that their efforts had met with decisive resistance on the part of his colleagues in the post-Stalin Presidium. Whether Beria, who occupied the second place after Malenkov in the post-Stalin hierarchy, actually attempted to reach for Stalin's mantle is not known. The real significance of the Beria case lies, however, in the subsequent downgrading of the power of the secret police, the fearful weapon developed by Stalin for the very purpose of establishing and maintaining his personal rule. It seems that the liquidation of Beria was not so much a dramatic event in the struggle for power as the second act of the Stalin tragedy, an epilogue to an era.

Khrushchev's de-Stalinization speech started a chain of reactions and created conditions under which a return to the Stalin era would, to say the least, produce political convulsions which might threaten the very existence of the dictatorship. It was because of these reactions that the Kremlin labeled revisionism, i.e., the gradual relaxation of theories and practices, the major danger to Stalinist dogmatism. This partial reversal has the same significance as Khrushchev's statement that he and his colleagues were Stalinists as far as "the cause of socialism" and "fighting the imperialists and the enemies of Marxism-Leninism" were concerned. There can be no doubt that, except for the lessening of the police terror, no signs of a genuine change in what is generally known as Stalinism are noticeable. Nevertheless, the preservation of the basic principles of Stalinism in no way weakens the tremendous effect Khrushchev's de-Stalinization speech has had on the Communist movement everywhere. The "genius of mankind," the man who had "lit the sun," has been desecrated, and the ugly face of the tyrant has been exposed. Khrushchev dared to perform this operation despite the fact that he himself had contributed to the idolization of the late dictator. Khrushchev must have had valid reasons for so doing; but by doing so he blocked the path to the empty throne with the debris of the idol he had smashed.

Only the third event—the ouster of Malenkov, Molotov, Kaganovich, Bulganin, and Zhukov—points in the same direction as the gradual elimination of a score of old Leninists undertaken by Stalin on his path toward personal rule. The parallel loses its validity, however, when one recalls that after Lenin's death the economic, political, and social conditions were fundamentally different from those which Stalin's heirs inherited from him in 1953. When Stalin took over the reins of power, the Soviet Union was at a crossroads and the struggle for power was connected with the question of which road should be followed—the road of the liberal economic policy announced by Lenin in 1921, or that of collectivization of agriculture and concentration on the development of heavy industry at the expense of consumer goods production. Prior to the purge and the liquidation of the dissenters, Stalin was forced to allow various opinions on this basic question to be debated openly; only gradually could he silence the voices of criticism and establish complete "unanimity." To achieve this the Party machine was rejuvenated with people willing to follow blindly all the zigs and zags of the Party line, which was the line of its Secretary General, Stalin.

On the other hand, Stalin's heirs inherited from him a ready-made totalitarian machine and a general Party line from which no major deviations could be made without destroying the foundations of the totalitarian regime. Moreover, his heirs were free from the necessity of bringing their differing opinions into the open: they could thrash out their different opinions behind closed doors and announce dramatic decisions without giving the defeated members of the ruling circle a chance to present their case to the people. And finally, the late dictator's heirs inherited a highly industrialized country with an economy extremely lopsided in favor of heavy industry. The industrialization of the country was accompanied by the creation of a new privileged class of managers, scientists, engineers, technicians, and a large group of "cultural" workers—writers, artists, composers, and the like—whose duty it was to reshape the minds of the people in accordance with the aims of the totalitarian regime.

Unlike the pre-revolutionary intelligentsia which was almost entirely extinguished by natural or violent death, this new class has felt entitled to, and been given, material and social privileges as pioneers and participants in this economic upheaval. This Soviet aristocracy, faithful to the Party, has gradually become conscious of the important role it plays in the structure of the regime. After Stalin's death, it took advantage of the lessening of the terror and displayed its desire to limit the Party's tutelage in non-political activities. This "anti-Party" tendency might become a chronic phenomenon, and Khrushchev may have to use all means short of terror to bring the "revisionists" and "dogmatists" back under full Party control. For the time being persuasion and economic pressure may be sufficient to smother these trends. On the other hand, Khrushchev's popularity has risen. Through the introduction of incentives he has succeeded in improving the living conditions, particularly in the countryside. Like Stalin, Khrushchev has maintained and even intensified the control of the Party machine over all aspects of Soviet life. But, unlike Stalin, he has established a *modus vivendi* with the population and thus created a new political pillar to support his leadership in the Party and government and to intensify his control over the aristocracy. Like Stalin in the period of his ascendancy, Khrushchev is striving to rejuvenate the Party and the leading cadres, but unlike Stalin he is using far less crude methods to get rid of the stale and inflexible remnants of the Stalinist bureaucracy.

Under these conditions, it is unlikely that Khrushchev will take the tremendous risk of re-establishing Stalin's practices, not because of moral scruples, but because they are not needed at present or in the foreseeable future. This is only logical. Yet logic is not always a favorite consultant to heads of totalitarian regimes. The history of all totalitarian states contains many examples of irrational actions, and it is not impossible that the unpredictable Khrushchev may become a victim of illogical thinking, much like his predecessors. If that happens, the world might witness outbursts of atrocities that would top Stalin's crimes. Khrushchev's experience in this field would then burst into full bloom. For the time being, however, no signs of such a development are in sight.

In the sphere of foreign policy, Soviet interests have not changed. Communist aspirations for world conquest have become even more emphatic than in the Stalin era. Khrushchev has departed from Stalin's policy of "self-isolation" and of employing the bayonette for probing the enemy. Instead, he has resumed Lenin's methods of an active foreign policy and the simultaneous spreading of world-revolutionary ideas by means of unprecedented propaganda devices. Khrushchev has established a new approach based on his experience as a domestic Party agitator and propagandist. He exploits and creates opportunities to express his views on any subject in simple, catchy words, always keeping in mind their impact on world public opinion. No statesman in history has flooded the world with so many speeches and interviews as Khrushchev has done in so short a period. It is debatable whether Khrushchev's public appearances, such as his spectacular and noisy visits to uncommitted Asian countries, or his shoe-banging performance at the United Nations have left a lasting impression on public opinion. It is, however, certain that they have succeeded in laying the groundwork for a general impression that Khrushchev's policy might be basically different from that of Stalin and Molotov. Those who have only a limited knowledge of Khrushchev's political past might lend a credulous ear to his persistent peace declarations and to his indignant denials that the Soviet Union has ever had any imperialistic designs anywhere in the world. The more the credulous and the uncertain are impressed by Khrushchev's simplicity and "likableness," the greater would be their surprise to learn that in March, 1944, for instance, he publicly insisted that indisputably Polish territory be annexed to the Soviet Union, a demand which even Stalin rejected.

In broad terms, Khrushchev's policy is a policy of adaptation to reality without making compromises about the final goal. To carry out this policy Khrushchev is the best man the Kremlin has at its disposal: a "man from the people," with such features as simplicity, inventiveness, and concentrated innate energy, combined with shrewdness and cynicism. The main problem the free world faces today is how to resist Communism in its new attire, a smooth-faced and smooth-tongued enemy whose weapon is not open assault, but organized hypocrisy, planned deception, and concealed infiltration.

Epilogue: *Quo Vadis?*

In January, 1959, when the Soviet Communist Party convened for the twenty-first time, Nikita Khrushchev, an offspring of a poor Kursk peasant, a former shepherd and locksmith, stood on the rostrum of the Great Kremlin Palace that for centuries witnessed Russian history in the making and delivered perhaps the longest speech ever made by a Party and government official. For the first time in the Party's history, foreign correspondents had been invited to witness the performance. "The speech will be long," he warned them on the eve of the big event, "you'd better bring your lunch with you." He wanted to be heard all over the world. And he was. The communication wires and air waves were crowded, the printing presses rushed the news to the public, commentators strained their brains, and analysts in foreign ministries looked for clues to his next moves.

He spoke with the air of a man whose wisdom is the deepest, whose knowledge the widest, and whose foresight the most accurate. He painted the future of the peoples he rules in minute detail, a future so happy and bright that all the other peoples on earth who have not yet embraced the teaching he preaches would follow its path. The speech was colorful. Now he brandished rockets and sputniks, and now he promised peace and togetherness if his demands were met; now he pledged not to interfere in other countries' affairs, and now he pledged support for his fifth columns in these countries; now he mocked his enemies, and now he invited them to take part in peaceful talks. No corner inside or outside his empire was forgotten in that speech. It was universal, conclusive, comprehensive. On that cold January day he appeared to have reached the summit of power and the apex of self-confidence. But was he really so self-confident?

In June, 1957, Khrushchev fought desperately for survival against his highbrow comrades, the "theoreticians" and the "bookworms" who knew by heart all the quotations from Marx, Lenin, and Stalin. He achieved a victory, but it was not a complete victory. He failed to eliminate them entirely, not for reasons of principle, but because the smell of the Stalin era was still emanating from the Pandora box which he himself had opened in 1956. None of the remaining old Party Presidium members would have supported such a dangerous turn of events. Almost three years have passed, and most of the high-ranking oppositionists—Malenkov, Kaganovich, Molotov, Bulganin, Pervukhin, Saburov, and Shepilov—are still alive. Molotov was even given a "promotion" and moved from the Soviet Embassy in half-civilized Outer Mongolia to lovely Vienna. But the attack against the opposition has never stopped. In December, 1958, Khrushchev said that his "tongue can hardly turn to call such men comrades, even though they have remained Party members." One month later, at the Twenty-first Congress, he called them "the despicable group of factionists and dissenters" who used "the basest methods of factional, dissenting struggle." Some delegates, certainly not against Khrushchev's desire, went even further, and the head of the secret police, Shelepin, accused them of "conspiracy against the Party." And yet, they still remain Party members, and some of them members of the Central Committee.

There are no obvious signs of a new power struggle behind the Kremlin walls, but there are evidences of a constant shuffle within the top Party leadership. The resonance of the 1957 purge has not yet died down, and three other top Party figures —Belyaev, Kirichenko, and Aristov—have been ousted from the Party machine and demoted. Neither Lenin nor even Stalin had ever dared to humiliate publicly Politburo members while they still occupied prominent positions, as Khrushchev does at plenary sessions of the Central Committee. While these lines are being written, Khrushchev is preparing the Party machine for the forthcoming Twenty-Second Party Congress, to be held in October, 1961. Considerable changes can be expected in the direction of a rejuvenation of the Central Committee membership. Will the old guard give up its positions without a fight?

Furthermore, Khrushchev is constantly subjected to an ever-growing demand for more consumer goods. The 1960 setback in Soviet agriculture has shown that this demand can be met only after a basic change in Soviet economic policy. But such a change involves a radical departure from Communist ideology. Marx and Engels created a philosophy which was based on economic conditions prevailing in advanced European countries a century ago. Lenin tried to apply this philosophy in a backward country by means of terror. He scored a political "victory" but was unable to overcome the economic resistance of the people. In 1921, he was forced to admit defeat and proclaim a policy of peaceful coexistence with the farmers and with small business. Seven years later Stalin repeated Lenin's early attempt, employing even more terror. He scored a "victory" in creating an economic monster, a wasteful system producing complicated machinery and weapons of death and destruction, while unable to satisfy the people's daily needs.

Chronic economic disease is one of the reasons for the ideological and political crises Communism is undergoing at the present time. The Communist system, allegedly created by the workers for the workers, has been faced with unrest in which workers play a leading role. "Proletarians have nothing to lose but their chains!" This dictum from the Manifesto of the Communist Party pronounced more than a century ago by Marx and Engels was used to encourage workers to fight for political and economic freedom. Today this dictum, paraphrased into "Peoples have nothing to lose but their chains!" was on the lips of the Berlin, Poznań, Warsaw, and Budapest workers in their fight against Communist oppression. Analyzing the history of Communism, the future historian will have to draw a descending line showing the gradual withering away of the spirit and philosophy of Marxism and Leninism, and of the enthusiasm it once inspired in a large part of the working people throughout the world.

Will Khrushchev be able to solve the chronic economic disease caused by the failure of Communist ideology and, at the same time, preserve the tenets of Marxism-Leninism?

Another source of pressure is inherent in the new gigantic Communist power that emerged at the end of the Stalin era and now endangers Soviet supremacy in, and control of, the Communist world. Ideological differences, dissension over problems of practical domestic and foreign policy, and the looming geopolitical strifes have deeply marred the unity of China and the Soviet Union. Although one cannot foresee or even imagine a break between them in the near future, the ideological rift limits Khrushchev's mobility in his "peaceful coexistence" drive. Will Khrushchev overcome Mao Tse-tung's opposition?

To solve the problems he faces is Khrushchev's urgent task. Time is running out. The Grand Tactician has evaded many pitfalls during his political career. But never before has he been overburdened with such tremendous responsibilities. He is at a crossroad. A step in the wrong direction may be fatal.

Notes

1. THE BELATED BOLSHEVIK

(pp. 3-14)

1. V. Poliakov, *Kalinovka idet vpered* (Moscow, 1957).

2. Clarence A. Manning, *The Story of the Ukraine* (New York, 1947), p. 295.

3. F. A. Brokgauz and I. A. Yefron, *Entsiklopedicheskii slovar'* (St. Petersburg, 1903), XXXVIIA, 753.

4. *Pravda*, February 16, 1958.

5. *U.S.S.R.* (Washington, D.C.: Soviet Embassy), No. 10 (37), p. 2.

6. Press release of Soviet Embassy in the U.S.A., April 16, 1959.

7. *Nikita Sergeyevich Khrushchev* (New York: International Arts and Sciences Press, 1959), p. 1.

8. Press release . . . , p. 1; Khrushchev stated in one of his speeches that he had spent his "childhood and youth" at a mine among the children of miners (speech in Reims, France, March 29, 1960). On another occasion he remarked that he worked in his "childhood" at a factory (tape-recorded speech in New York, September 17, 1959). However, in the official Soviet version of that speech, "childhood" was changed to "youth" (*Let Us Live in Peace and Friendship, The Soviet Visit to the U.S.A.* [Moscow, 1959], p. 108).

9. *Pravda Ukrainy*, February 27, 1945.

10. Speech in Reims . . . ; *Pravda*, March 30, 1960.

11. *Let Us Live* . . . , p. 192. This Soviet-English version differs from the original tape-recorded Russian version, which is as follows: "I began working as soon as I learned to walk. I worked till the age of fifteen, I tended calves . . . calves . . . do you know what they are like? A calf is a small cow, as foreigners call it. I tended calves of the landlord, I tended cows of the capitalist. All that before I was fifteen."

12. *U.S.S.R., loc. cit.*, p. 2.

13. Brokgauz and Yefron, *op. cit.*, XXA, 765.

14. *Ibid.* (1904), LXXXI, 327; *Bolshaya Sovetskaya Entsiklopedia* (1st ed.; Moscow, 1947), pp. 652-653.

15. N. A. Bulganin and N. S. Khrushchev, *Rechi vo vremia prebyvania v Indii, Birme i Afganistane* (Moscow, 1955), p. 173.

16. *Britain's Guests, Nikolai Bulganin and Nikita Khrushchev, Their*

Lives and Work, Soviet News Booklet (London, April, 1956), No. 13, p. 20.

17. *Ibid.*

18. *Nikita Sergeyevich Khrushchev,* p. 1; press release. . . .

19. *Pravda,* March 27, 1958.

20. Press release . . . ; *Britain's Guests* . . . , p. 20.

21. *Nikita Sergeyevich Khrushchev,* p. 2.

22. *Pravda,* April 2, 1960.

23. V. Modestov, *Rabocheye i professionalnoye dvizhenie v Donbasse do Velikoi Oktyabrskoi Sotsialisticheskoi Revolutsii* (Moscow: Profizdat, 1957), p. 65.

24. *Istoria Ukrainskoi SSR* (Kiev, 1956), I, 738.

25. *Ibid.,* I, 739.

26. Modestov, *op. cit.,* p. 81.

27. *Istoria Ukrainskoi SSR,* p. 762.

28. Modestov, *op. cit.,* p. 87.

29. *Ibid.,* p. 95.

30. Akademia Nauk URSR, Institut Ekonomiki, *Narysi ekonomychnoi geografii URSR* (Kiev, 1952), II, 195.

31. Modestov, *op. cit.,* pp. 89-90, 96.

32. *Pravda,* April 2, 1960.

33. *Z istorii borot'bi za vstanovlennya radyanskoi vladi na Ukraini* (Kiev, 1957), p. 89.

34. *Ibid.; see also* Modestov, *op. cit.,* pp. 100, 114.

35. *Pravda,* January 14, 1948.

36. *U.S.S.R., loc. cit.,* p. 2.

37. Press release . . . , p. 1; *Britain's Guests* . . . , p. 20.

38. *Polityka,* No. 28, July 11, 1959, p. 3. It is noteworthy that the author of the article enclosed the phrase "in the name of the revolution" in quotation marks, as if he offers a slight apology for using it.

39. *Ibid.*

40. *Istoriko-revolutsionnyi kalendar* (Moscow, 1939), p. 183.

41. *Istoriko-revolutsionnyi kalendar* (for 1941 [Moscow: released for printing October 31, 1940]), p. 221.

42. *Visti VTsVK,* January 28, 1938.

43. *See* notes 40 and 41.

44. *Sovetskaya Ukraina,* April 11, 1941.

45. A. V. Likholat, *Razgrom nationalisticheskoi kontrrevolutsii na Ukraine, 1917-1922 gg* (Moscow, 1954), p. 91.

46. *Istoria grazhdanskoi voiny v SSSR (History of the Civil War in the U.S.S.R.)* (Moscow, 1957), p. 136.

47. *Bolshaya Sovetskaya Entsiklopedia* (1st ed.; Moscow, 1947), LII, 654; *ibid.* (2nd ed., 1952), XV, 102. *See also* S. F. Markov, *Otechestvennaya voina ukrainskogo naroda protiv germanskikh interventov v 1918 g* (Moscow, 1941), pp. 12-14.

48. *Visti VTsVK,* March 22, 1929.

49. *Istoria Kommunisticheskoi Partii Sovetskogo Soyuza* (Moscow, 1959), p. 314.

50. S. F. Nayda, *O nekotorykh voprosakh istorii grazhdanskoi voiny v SSSR* (Moscow, 1958), p. 21.

2. THE RISE OF A POLITICAL STAR
(pp. 15-26)

1. Press release . . . , p. 1; *Nikita Sergeyevich Khrushchev,* p. 3.
2. *Britain's Guests* . . . , p. 21.
3. Bulganin and Khrushchev, *op. cit.,* p. 173.
4. *Pravda Ukrainy,* June 15, 1946.
5. *Ibid.*
6. *Pravda,* January 15, 1924, p. 5.
7. *Ekonomicheskaya Zhizn,* November 22, 1923, quoted from *Sotsialisticheskii Vestnik,* No. 1 (71), 1924, p. 11.
8. *IX-yi Vseukrainskyi z'izd rad robotnychykh, selesnskykh ta chervonoarmyiskykh deputativ, 3-10 travnia 1925 roku* (Stenographic report; Kharkov, 1925), p. 286.
9. *Sotsialisticheskii Vestnik, loc. cit.,* pp. 7-8.
10. *Pravda,* October 25, 1959.
11. Press release . . . , p. 1.
12. *Nikita Sergeyevich Khrushchev,* p. 4.
13. *Bilshovik Ukrainy,* No. 3, 1940, p. 38.
14. *Kommunist* (Moscow, 1956), No. 9, p. 18.
15. "Secret Speech of Khrushchev Concerning the Cult of the Individual," delivered at the Twentieth Congress of the CPSU, February 25, 1956, quoted from *The Anti-Stalin Campaign and International Communism* (New York: Columbia University Press, 1956), p. 6.
16. "Secret Speech . . . ," p. 7.
17. *XIV s'ezd Vsesoiuznoi Kommunisticheskoi Partii (B)* (Stenographic report; Moscow-Leningrad, 1926) p. 713.
18. *Ukrains'kii istorichnii zhurnal,* No. 4, 1959, p. 141.
19. Press release . . . , p. 1.
20. *U.S.S.R., loc. cit.,* p. 3.

3. IMPATIENT GRAVEDIGGER OF DEMOCRACY
(pp. 27-38)

1. *Pravda,* October 7, 1926.
2. *Visti VTsVK,* October 20-21, 1926.
3. *Ibid.,* October 21, 1926.
4. *Ibid.,* October 22, 1926.
5. *Ibid.*
6. *Pravda,* October 17, 1926.
7. *Visti VTsVK,* November 29, 1927.
8. "Secret Speech . . . ," p. 21.

4. THE SOVIET COUNTRYSIDE BECOMES A COLONY
(*pp. 39-48*)

1. *Visti VTsVK*, April 12, 1929. Italics added.
2. I. V. Stalin, *Sochineniya* (Moscow, 1949), XI, 212.
3. *Pravda,* February 3, 1955.
4. Stalin, *op. cit.*, XI, 159.
5. *Ibid.*, XI, 188-189.
6. *Ibid.*, XII, 51.
7. "Secret Speech . . . ," pp. 10-11. Italics added.
8. *Sotsialisticheskii Vestnik*, No. 22-23, 1928, p. 21.
9. Stalin, *op. cit.*, XI, 231.
10. *Ibid.*, XI, 236.
11. *Sotsialisticheskii Vestnik*, No. 6, 1929, p. 10.
12. Stalin, *op. cit.*, XII, 100.

5. THE FORMATION OF A STALINIST
(*pp. 51-68*)

1. *Bolshaya Sovetskaya Entsiklopedia* (1st ed.; 1937), XXX, 514.
2. *Sotsialisticheskii Vestnik*, No. 6-7, 1930, p. 18.
3. *Ibid.*, No. 1-2, 1937, p. 20.
4. *Bolshaya Sovetskaya Entsiklopedia* (1st ed.; 1946), LV, 204.
5. A. Kamensky, "Pervyi vypusk Promyshlennoi Akademii," *Pravda,* April 26, 1930.
6. Stalin, *op. cit.*, XII, 230.
7. Institut po povysheniu kvalifikatsii administrativnogo i inzhener-notekhnicheskogo personala VSNKh SSSR, *Plan seti kursov na 1929-30 g.* (Moscow, July, 1929), p. 6.
8. *Visti VTsVK*, January 11, 1928.
9. *Ibid.*, January 28, 1938.
10. *Ibid.*, May 24, 1938.
11. *Istoriko-revolutsionnyi kalendar* (for 1941), p. 221.
12. *Sotsialisticheskii Vestnik*, No. 5, 1930, p. 14.
13. *Bolshaya Sovetskaya Entsiklopedia* (1st ed.; 1937), XXX, 517.
14. Stalin, *op. cit.*, XII, 167.
15. *Sotsialisticheskii Vestnik*, No. 8, 1930, p. 16.
16. *Izvestia*, November 26, 1929.
17. *Ogoniok*, No. 32, November 20, 1932, p. 5.
18. From a condolence by Politburo members and their wives, *Pravda,* November 10, 1932.
19. A. S. Alliluyeva, *Vospominania* (Moscow, 1946), p. 153.
20. Victor Kravchenko, *I Chose Freedom* (New York: Charles Scribner's Sons, 1946), p. 238.

21. *Pravda,* November 10, 1932.
22. *Ibid.,* May 26, 1930.
23. *Ibid.,* June 3, 1930.
24. *Ibid.,* June 1, 1930.
25. *Ibid.,* May 29, 1930.
26. *Ibid.,* May 31, 1930.
27. *Britain's Guests . . . ,* pp. 22-23.
28. *Visti VTsVK,* May 24, 1938.
29. Kamensky, *loc. cit.*

6. THE SETTING OF THE MOSCOW ACT
(*pp. 69-73*)

1. *Izvestia,* August 24, 1931. Italics added.
2. Solomon M. Schwarz, *Labor in the Soviet Union* (New York: Frederick A. Praeger, 1952), pp. 138-139.
3. *Ibid.,* p. 149.
4. Schwarz, article in *Sotsialisticheskii Vestnik,* No. 10, 1931.
5. *Bolshaya Sovetskaya Entsiklopedia* (1st ed.; 1944), L, 531.

7. IMPROVING THE STALINIST STYLE OF WORK
(*pp. 74-85*)

1. *Pravda,* January 9, 1931.
2. *Rabochaya Moskva,* January 29, 1931.
3. *Pravda,* February 26, 1931.
4. *Rabochaya Moskva,* February 25, 1931.
5. *Pravda,* July 26, 1931.
6. *Ibid.,* July 16, 1931
7. *Rabochaya Moskva,* January 6, 1932.
8. *Ibid.,* January 8, 1932.
9. *Pravda,* January 5, 1932.
10. *Ibid.*
11. Stalin, *op cit.,* XIII, 101.
12. *Pravda,* December 15, 1931.
13. *Rabochaya Moskva,* January 8, 1932.
14. "Secret Speech . . . ," p. 10.
15. *Istoria Kommunisticheskoi Partii . . . ,* p. 441.
16. *Istoricheskie zapiski (Historical Notes)* (Moscow: U.S.S.R. Academy of Sciences, 1956), No. 58, p. 310.
17. *Pravda,* July 5, 1933.
18. *Ibid.,* September 6, 1933.
19. *Ibid.*
20. *Ibid.,* April 11, 1934.

8. THE PARTY BUILDS A SUBWAY

(*pp. 86-100*)

1. *Istoria metro Moskvy; Rasskazy stroitelei metro* (Moscow, 1935), I, 38-39.

2. *Ibid.*, p. 11.

3. *Ibid.* (longer version), p. 44.

4. *Pravda*, February 7, 1935.

5. *Istoria metro im. L. M. Kaganovicha; Kak my stroili metro* (Moscow, 1935), p. 276.

6. *Ibid.*, p. 592.

7. *Ibid.*, p. 531.

8. *Pravda*, March 16, 1935.

9. *Istoria metro Moskvy* . . . (shorter version), p. 433; (longer version), p. 487.

10. *Ibid.* (shorter version), p. 223; (longer version), p. 263.

11. *Ibid.* (shorter version), p. 372; (longer version), p. 427.

12. *Moskovskii Komsomol na metro* (Moscow-Leningrad, 1934), p. 29.

13. *Istoria metro im. L. M. Kaganovicha* . . . , p. 109.

14. *Ibid.*, p. 41.

15. *Ibid.*, p. 226.

16. *Ibid.*, p. 231.

17. *Piat' let metro* (Moscow, 1940), p. 34.

18. *Ibid.*

19. Valentin Gonzalez and Julian Gorkin, *Life and Death in Soviet Russia* (New York: G. M. Putnam's Sons, 1952), p. 80.

20. *Istoria metro Moskvy* . . . (shorter version), p. 230; (longer version, p. 270.

21. *Ibid.*

22. *Pravda*, April 6, 1935.

23. *Istoria metro Moskvy* . . . (both versions), p. 42.

24. *Moskovskii Komsomol na metro*, p. 47.

25. *Istoria metro Moskvy* . . . (shorter version), p. 427; (longer version), p. 481.

26. *Ibid.* (shorter version), p. 428; (longer version), p. 482.

27. *Ibid.* (shorter version), p. 431; (longer version), p. 485.

28. *Istoria metro im. L. M. Kaganovicha* . . . , p. 24.

29. *Ibid.*, p. 235.

30. Z. Troitskaya, *The L. M. Kaganovich Metropolitan Railway of Moscow: Moscow's Metro*, (Moscow, 1955).

31. *Moskovskii Komsomol na metro*, p. 17.

32. *XVII s'ezd Vsesoyuznoi Kommunisticheskoi Partii (B)* (Moscow, 1934), p. 454.

33. *Narodnoye khozyaistvo SSSR. Statisticheskii sbornik* (Moscow, 1956), p. 87.

34. *XVII s'ezd Vsesoyuznoi Kommunisticheskoi Partii (B)*, p. 504.

35. *Istoria metro im. L. M. Kaganovicha* . . . , p. 181.

36. *Pravda*, November 10, 1955.

9. THE EVASIVE WITNESS
(pp. 101-125)

1. "Secret Speech . . . ," pp. 25-26.
2. *Ibid.*, p. 14.
3. *Ibid.*
4. *Ibid.*, p. 15. Italics added.
5. *Pravda*, December 2, 1934.
6. "Secret Speech . . . ," p. 25.
7. *Izvestia*, December 6, 1934.
8. *Ibid.*, December 12, 1934.
9. *Ibid.*, December 18, 1934.
10. *Ibid.*, December 30. 1934.
11. "Secret Speech . . . ," p. 25.
12. *Ibid.*
13. *Ibid.*, pp. 6, 9.
14. *Ibid.*, p. 14.
15. *Ibid.*, p. 12.
16. *Ibid.*, p. 29.
17. *Ibid.*, p. 41.
18. *Ibid.*, p. 39.
19. *Pravda*, February 1, 1934.
20. *Ibid.*, June 10, 1936.
21. *Ibid.*, March 17, 1937.
22. *Ibid.*, May 24, 1937.
23. *Ibid.*, May 30, 1937.
24. *Ibid.*, June 6, 1937.
25. *Visti VTsVK*, May 27, 1938.
26. "Secret Speech . . . ," p. 28.
27. *Ibid.*, p. 12.
28. *Ibid.*, p. 13.
29. *Pravda*, December 4, 1934.
30. "Secret Speech . . . ," p. 14.
31. *Pravda*, July 6, 1937.
32. *Ibid.*
33. *Ibid.*, August 24, 1937.
34. "Secret Speech . . . ," pp. 11-12.
35. *Ibid.*, p. 27.
36. *Ibid.*, p. 37.
37. *Pravda*, June 10, 1936.
38. *Izvestia*, August 23, 1936.
39. *Pravda*, November 24, 1936.
40. *Ibid.*, January 31, 1937.
41. "Secret Speech . . . ," pp. 15-16.
42. *Ibid.*, p. 22.
43. *Ibid.*, pp. 16-17.
44. N. M. Shvernik's speech in *Pravda*, July 7, 1957.

10. FACELESS SYCOPHANTS AND MEN WITH A SPARK OF HONESTY
(*pp. 126-135*)

1. *Pravda,* February 19, 1937.
2. "Secret Speech . . . ," p. 69.
3. *Pravda,* October 28, 1936.
4. *Ibid.,* February 22, 1937.
5. "Secret Speech . . . ," p. 28.
6. *Ibid.*
7. *Ibid.,* p. 29.
8. *Ibid.,* p. 82.
9. *Ibid.,* pp. 22-23.
10. *Ibid.,* p. 81.
11. *Ibid.*
12. *Ibid.,* p. 82.
13. *Ibid.,* p. 65.
14. *Ibid.,* p. 40.
15. *Ibid.,* p. 82.
16. *Ibid.*

11. CLIMBING OVER CORPSES
(*pp. 139-155*)

1. *Bilshovik Ukrainy,* No. 1, 1938, p. 53.
2. *Visti VTsVK,* May 23, 1938.
3. *Ibid.,* June 17, 1938.
4. *Ibid.,* February 14, 1938.
5. *Pravda,* December 21, 1937.
6. *Ibid.,* December 20, 1937.
7. "Secret Speech . . . ," p. 65.
8. *Visti VTsVK,* June 1, 1937.
9. *Ibid.,* January 18, 1937.
10. *Ibid.,* February 1, 1937.
11. *Ibid.,* March 18, 1937.
12. "Secret Speech . . . ," p. 42.
13. *Bilshovik Ukrainy,* No. 6, 1938, p. 10.
14. *Visti VTsVK,* April 2; September 16 and 27; November 22, 1936.
15. *Ibid.,* June 2, 1937.
16. *Ibid.,* May 30, 1937.
17. *Ibid.,* June 18, 1938.
18. *Ibid.,* May 22, 1938.
19. *Ibid.,* June 21, 1938.
20. *Ibid.,* May 23, 1938.
21. *Ibid.,* June 18, 1938.
22. *Ibid.,* June 9, 1939.

23. *Ibid.*, November 24, 1940.
24. *Ibid.*, January 8, 1940.
25. *Ibid.*, June 21, 1938.
26. *Ibid.*, May 23, 1938.
27. *Bilshovik Ukrainy,* No. 7, 1938, p. 25.
28. *Visti VTsVK,* June 17, 1938.
29. *Ibid.*, June 24, 1938.
30. *Ibid.*, June 4, 1937.
31. *Ibid.*, January 24, 1954.
32. *Ibid.*, June 20, 1938.
33. *Ibid.*, May 18, 1940.
34. "Secret Speech . . . ," pp. 22-23.
35. *XVII s'ezd Vsesoyuznoi Kommunisticheskoi Partii (B)* (Stenographic report; Moscow, 1934) pp. 680-681; *XVIII s'ezd Vsesoyuznoi Kommunisticheskoi Partii (B)* (Stenographic report; Moscow, 1939), p. 688.
36. "Secret Speech . . . ," p. 23.
37. *Ibid.*
38. *Ibid.*, p. 24.
39. *Visti VTsVK,* May 27, 1938.
40. *Bilshovik Ukrainy,* No. 6, 1938, p. 7. Italics added.
41. *Ibid.*
42. *Pravda,* May 31, 1937.
43. *Bilshovik Ukrainy,* No. 7, 1938, p. 11.
44. "Secret Speech . . . ," p. 49.
45. *Ibid.*
46. *Visti VTsVK,* June 21, 1938.

12. THE HISTORY OF A CULT
(*pp. 156-168*)

1. *Inostrannaya Literatura,* No. 6, 1957, p. 205.
2. "Secret Speech . . . ," p. 69.
3. *Ibid.*, p. 24.
4. *XIV s'ezd Vsesoiusznoi Kommunisticheskoi Partii (B)*, p. 181.
5. *Ibid.*, p. 335.
6. *Ibid.*, p. 336.
7. *Ibid.*, p. 274.
8. *Ibid.*, p. 275.
9. *XV s'ezd Vsesoiuznoi Kommunisticheskoi Partii (B)* (Moscow, 1927), p. 324.
10. *Izvestia,* December 21, 1929.
11. *Pravda,* December 21, 1929.
12. "Secret Speech . . . ," p. 69.
13. *Rabochaya Moskva,* January 26, 1932.
14. *Pravda,* January 19, 1933.
15. *Ibid.*, June 2, 1933.

16. *Ibid.*, December 5, 1933.

17. *Ibid.*, January 26, 1934.

18. *XVII s'ezd Vsesoiuznoi Kommunisticheskoi Partii (B)*, p. 145.

19. *Ibid.*, p. 126.

20. *Ibid.*, p. 253.

21. Leon Trotsky, *Stalin* (3rd ed.; New York: Harper & Bros., 1941), p. 389.

22. *Pravda*, November 1, 1936.

23. *Ibid.*, November 22, 1936.

24. *Ibid.*, November 25, 1936.

25. *Ibid.*, November 30, 1936.

26. *Ibid.* Italics added.

27. *Kommunist Ukrainy*, No. 7, July, 1957, p. 30.

28. *Pravda*, August 23, 1936.

29. *Ibid.*, January 31, 1937.

30. "Secret Speech . . . ," p. 40.

31. *Pravda*, December 12, 1937.

32. *Rechi na sobraniakh izbiratelei v Verkhovnyi Soviet SSSR* (Moscow, 1938), p. 34.

33. *Pravda*, December 2, 1937.

34. *Ibid.*, November 26, 1937.

35. *Ibid.*, February 22, 1937.

36. "Secret Speech . . . ," p. 69.

37. *Bilshovik Ukrainy*, No. 7, 1938, p. 11; *Visti VTsVK*, September 11, 1938, and November 20, 1939.

38. *Visti VTsVK*, March 3, 1939.

39. *XVIII s'ezd Vsesoiuznoi Kommunisticheskoi Partii (B)*, p. 174.

40. *Pravda*, December 21, 1939; *Visti VTsVK*, November 20, 1939.

41. *Pravda Ukrainy*, October 21, 1944; *XVI z'izd Kommunistychnoi partii (B)* (Kiev, 1949), p. 14.

42. *Pravda Ukrainy*, May 13, 1945.

43. "Secret Speech . . . ," pp. 43, 52, 53, 54.

44. *Ibid.*, p. 51.

45. *Ibid.*, p. 50.

46. *Pravda*, June 10, 1936.

47. *Ibid.*, June 29, 1936.

48. *Visti VTsVK*, April 6, 1939.

49. *Pravda*, December 14, 1944.

50. *Velikomu Stalinu. Narodni pisni ta dumy* (Kiev, 1949), p. 325.

51. *Sovetskaya kultura*, April 16, 1960.

52. *Pravda*, April 17, 1960.

13. RUSSIFIER IN DISGUISE
(*pp. 169-180*)

1. Calculated on the basis of a table on page 18 of *Narodnoye Khozyaistvo SSR, Statisticheskii sbornik* (Moscow, 1956).

2. *KPSS v resolutsiakh i resheniakh s'ezdov, konferentsiy i plenumov TsK* (7th ed.; Moscow, 1954), Part I, p. 345.

3. For a more comprehensive description of Khvylovism and other "deviations," *see* Basil Dmytryshyn, *Moscow and the Ukraine, 1918-1953* (New York: Twayne Publishers, 1956), pp. 91-121.

4. Stalin, *op cit.*, VIII, 149.

5. *Pravda*, July 8, 1933.

6. *Bilshovik Ukrainy*, No. 7, 1938, p. 51.

7. *KPSS v resolutsiakh . . .*, Part III, p. 198.

8. *Ibid.*, Part I, p. 713.

9. *Bilshovik Ukrainy*, No. 7, 1938, p. 51.

10. *Ibid.*, No. 6, 1938, p. 13.

11. *Ibid.*, No. 7, 1938, pp. 6-7.

12. *Visti VTsVK*, July 29, 1938.

13. *Ibid.*, August 6, 1938.

14. *Ibid.*

15. Frederick C. Barghoorn, *Soviet Russian Nationalism* (New York: Oxford University Press, 1956), p. 98.

16. *Visti VTsVK*, July 29, 1938.

17. *Ibid.*, August 21, 1938.

18. *Ibid.*, July 15, 1938.

19. *Ibid.*

20. *Stalinskoye plemya*, May 22, 1940.

21. *Visti VTsVK*, October 11, 1938.

22. *Ibid.*, March 16, 1939.

23. *Sovetskaya Ukraina*, January 14, 1941.

24. *Pravda Ukrainy*, July 15, 1945.

14. THE POSTWAR JUGGLING WITH NATIONALITY POLICY
(*pp. 181-190*)

1. *Bolshevik*, No. 6, March, 1944, pp. 33, 34.

2. *Pravda*, May 25, 1945.

3. *Ibid.*, January 23, 1947.

4. *Pravda Ukrainy*, June 30, 1946.

5. *Ibid.*, August 24, 1946.

6. *Ibid.*, September 1, 1946.

7. *Ibid.*, September 5, 1946.

8. Ukrainian broadcast from Kiev, March 19, 1960.

9. *Kommunist*, No. 12, August, 1957, p. 26.

10. *Pravda Ukrainy*, December 11, 1948.

11. *Ibid.*, January 12, 1946.

12. Maksym Rylskyi, *Poezii* (Kiev, 1950), p. 105.

13. Rylskyi, *Izbrannoye* (Moscow, 1954), p. 27.

14. Rylskyi, *Poezii*, p. 140.

15. Rylskyi, *Izbrannoye*, p. 27.

16. *Pravda*, June 13, 1953.

17. *Ibid.*, July 27, 1953.
18. "Secret Speech . . . ," p. 64.
19. *Ibid.*
20. *Moskovskaya Pravda,* January 13, 1953.
21. *Pravda,* April 6, 1953
22. *Ibid.*, April 7, 1953.
23. *Jewish Life* (now *Jewish Current*), February ,1957, p. 40.
24. *Bolshaya Sovetskaya Entsiklopedia* (1st ed.), XXX, 747; *ibid.*, XXX, 75; *ibid.*, SSSR, 1947, 60; *Malaya Sovetskaya Entsiklopedia* (1st ed.), III, 609; *ibid.*, III, 838, 841; *ibid.*, VII, 507; *ibid.*, VIII, 645, 647; *ibid.*, IX, 31, 34; *ibid.*, IX, 811; *ibid.* (2nd ed.), V, 137; *ibid.* (3rd ed.), IV, 33; *Narodnoye Khozyaistvo, statisticheski sbornik, 1959* (Moscow, 1960), p. 14.
25. Léon Leneman, *La tragédie des Juifs en U.R.S.S.* (Paris: Desclée, de Brouwer, 1959).

15. "LIBERATOR OF THE OPPRESSED BROTHERS"
(*pp. 191-207*)

1. *Krasnaya Zvezda,* September 23, 1939.
2. *Ibid.*, September 20, 1939.
3. *Ibid.*
4. *Ibid.*, September 27, 1939.
5. *Ibid.*, October 2, 1939.
6. *Stalinskoye plemya,* May 22, 1940.
7. *Ibid.*
8. *Visti VTsVK,* September 21, 24, and 29, 1939.
9. *Ibid.*, September 30, 1939.
10. *Ibid.*, September 22, 1939.
11. *Trybuna Ludu,* May 1 and October 14, 1955.
12. *Ibid.*, February 19, 1956.
13. *Bilshovik Ukrainy,* No. 10, 1939, p. 15.
14. *Stalinskoye plemya,* October 22, 1939.
15. *Ibid.*, November 15, 1939.
16. *Ibid.*, November 14, 1939.
17. *Ibid.*
18. *Ibid.*, October 26, 1939.
19. *Ibid.*, January 4, 1940.
20. *Ibid.*
21. *Visti VTsVK,* October 10, 1939.
22. *Stalinskoye plemya,* October 10, 1939.
23. *Ibid.*, October 12, 1939.
24. *Visti VTsVK,* October 20, 1939.
25. *Stalinskoye plemya,* October 23, 1939.
26. *Pravda,* March 26, 1940.
27. *Stalinskoye plemya,* May 18, 1940.
28. *Pravda,* December 17, 1940.

Notes 287

29. *Ibid.*
30. *Bilshovik Ukrainy,* No. 3, 1940, p. 62; *Izvestia,* January 29 and October 18, 1940.
31. Khrushchev, *Itogi plenuma TsK VKP(b) i zadachi Moskovskoi partiinoi organizatsii* (Moscow, 1935), p. 32.
32. *Ibid.,* pp. 34-35.
33. *See* John L. Snell (ed.), Forrest C. Pogue, Charles F. Delzell, and George A. Lensen, *The Meaning of Yalta* (Baton Rouge: Louisiana State University Press, 1956), p. 82.
34. "Declaration of the Soviet Government on Soviet-Polish Relations," *Pravda,* January 12, 1944.
35. *Pravda,* January 12, 1944.
36. *Ibid.,* March 16, 1944.
37. *New York Herald Tribune,* April 11, 1944.
38. *Bolshaya Sovetskaya Entsiklopedia* (2nd ed.; 1955), XXXIV, 49.
39. *Pravda,* April 17, 1944.

16. THE MILITARY ADVENTURES OF A CIVILIAN GENERAL
(pp. 208-225)

1. *Malaya Sovetskaya Entsiklopedia* (Moscow, 1947), XI, 494; *Kratkaya Sovetskaya Entsiklopedia* (Moscow, 1948), pp. 297-298; *Entsiklopedicheskii slovar'* (Moscow, 1955), III, 567; *Bolshaya Sovetskaya Entsiklopedia* (2nd ed.; 1956); XLV, 390-391.
2. *Bolshaya Sovestkaya Entsiklopedia* (2nd ed.; 1951), VII, 163.
3. *Istoria Kommunisticheskoi Partii Sovetskogo Soyuza,* p. 520.
4. *Bolshaya Sovetskaya Entsiklopedia* (2nd ed.; 1951), VII, 194.
5. *Ibid.* (1953), XXII, 234.
6. *Ibid.* (1957), L, 239.
7. *Istoria Kommunisticheskoi Partii Sovetskogo Soyuza,* p. 526.
8. *Bolshaya Sovetskaya Entsiklopedia* (2nd ed.; 1951), VI, 172.
9. B. S. Telpukhovsky, *Velikaya pobeda Sovetskoi Armii pod Stalingradom* (Moscow, 1953), p. 40.
10. *Ibid.*
11. Akademia Nauk SSSR, *Ocherki istorii Velikoi Otechestvennoi voiny (1941-1945)* (Moscow, 1955), p. 162.
12. *Vazhneyshie operatsii Velikoi Otechestvennoi voiny* (Moscow, 1956), p. 112.
13. *Bolshaya Sovetskaya Entsiklopedia* (2nd ed.; 1957), XL, 430.
14. *Ibid.* (1957), L, 236.
15. N. I. Suprunenko, *Ukraina v Velikoi Otechestvennoi voine Sovetskogo Soyuza* (Kiev, 1956), p. 124.
16. K. I. Kovalevsky, *Velikaya Otechestvennaya voina Sovetskogo Soyuza (1941-1945)* (Moscow, 1959), p. 91.
17. *Ministerstvo vysshego obrazovania SSSR: Kommunisticheskaya Partia-vdokhnovitel i organizator pobedy Sovestkogo naroda v Velikoi Otechestvennoi voine (iyun 1941g.-1945)* (Moscow, 1959), p. 54.

18. *Pravda Ukrainy,* February 1, 1946. *See also* issues of November 11, 1943, and February 6, 1947.

19. *Ibid.,* January 12, 1946.

20. *Ibid.*

21. *Britain's Guests . . . ,* p. 26; press release . . . , p. 2.

22. "Secret Speech . . . ," p. 49.

23. *Ibid.*

24. *Ibid.,* pp. 51-52.

25. M. Kuznetsov, "Pravda o generale Podlase," *Svoboda,* No. 53-54, pp. 36-38.

26. *Vazsneyshie operatsii . . . ,* p. 112.

27. *Ibid.*

28. *Pravda Ukrainy,* February 6, 1947.

29. *Pravda,* February 13, 1943.

30. *Ibid.,* April 11, 1943.

31. *Ibid.,* August 28, 1943.

32. *Ibid.,* May 23, 1945.

33. *Bolshaya Sovetskaya Entsiklopedia* (2nd ed.; 1951), VII, 178.

34. *Ibid.* (1955), XXXII, 163.

35. Akademia Nauk SSSR, *op. cit.,* p. 144.

36. *Bolshaya Sovetskaya Entsiklopedia* (2nd ed.; 1956), XLIV, 97.

37. S. A. Kovpak, *Stalinskii reid* (Moscow, 1947); P. P. Vershigora, *Ludi s chistoi sovestiu* (Moscow, 1948, 1952, 1953, and 1959); A. F. Fedorov, *Podpolnyi obkom deistvuyet* (Moscow, 1951 and 1954); David Bakradze, *Kroviu geroyev* (Tbilisi, 1956).

38. Fedorov, *op. cit.,* p. 10.

39. Vershigora, *op. cit.* (1952), p. 670.

40. Cf. Vershigora, *op. cit.* (1952), p. 671; and (1959), p. 63.

41. *Bolshaya Sovetskaya Entsiklopedia* (2nd ed.; 1956), XLIV, 97.

42. *Ibid.,* p. 102.

43. K. V. Basilevich, S. V. Bakhrushin, A. M. Pankratova, and A. V. Fokht, *Istoria SSSR* (Moscow, 1956, 1957, and 1959), p. 242.

44. Suprunenko, *op. cit.,* p. 41

45. *Ibid.,* p. 107.

46. *Bolshaya Sovetskaya Entsiklopedia* (2nd ed.; 1955), XXXII, p. 163.

47. Basilevich *et al., op. cit.,* p. 242.

48. *Ukrainskyi istorichnyi zhurnal,* No. 1, 1960, p. 139.

49. *Ibid.,* p. 142.

50. *Ibid.*

17. THE POSTWAR UPS AND DOWNS
(*pp. 226-248*)

1. Marshall MacDuffie, *The Red Carpet* (New York: W. W. Norton & Company, 1955), p. 200.

2. *Ibid.*, p. 197; *see also Ukraina*, No. 10-11, 1945, p. 1; and *Pravda Ukrainy*, January 24, 1948.

3. *Pravda Ukrainy*, August 25, 1946.

4. *Pravda*, August 23, 1946; *see also* editorial in *Pravda Ukrainy*, August 25, 1946.

5. *Pravda Ukrainy*, June 8, 1946.

6. *Visti VTsVK*, August 3, 8, and 18, 1938.

7. *Ibid.*, November 29, 1940.

8. *Pravda*, February 28 and March 7, 1947.

9. *Pravda Ukrainy*, March 4, 1947.

10. *Ibid.*, March 5, 1947.

11. *Ibid.*, March 23, 1947.

12. *Ibid.*, March 25 and 26, 1947.

13. *Pravda*, February 6, 1941.

14. From Khrushchev's speech, *Pravda Ukrainy*, January 30, 1946.

15. *Bolshevik*, No. 6, March, 1944, p. 16.

16. *Pravda Ukrainy*, January 19, 1949.

17. *Ibid.*, January 27, 1949.

18. *Pravda*, January 25, 1949.

19. "Secret Speech . . . ," p. 83.

20. *Pravda Ukrainy*, December 18, 1949.

21. *XVIII s'ezd Vsesoiuznoi Kommunisticheskoi Partii (B)*, p. 117.

22. *KPSS v resolutsiakh . . .* Part III, p. 364.

23. *Pravda*, March 8, 1950.

24. S. S. Sergeyev, *Organizatsionno-khozayaistvennoye ukreplenie melkikh s. -kh. artelei* (Moscow, 1950), pp. 119-120.

25. *Moskovskaya Pravda*, June 28, 1950.

26. *Pravda Ukrainy*, January 27, 1949.

27. *Ibid.*

28. *Moskovskaya Pravda*, June 28, 1950.

29. *Pravda*, October 6, 1952.

30. *Moskovskaya Pravda*, September 28, 1952.

31. *Pravda*, March 6, 1953.

32. *Ibid.*, March 21, 1953. It is interesting to note that the decision of the Plenary Session of the Central Committee to relieve Malenkov from his Party post was adopted on March 14 and made known only on March 21, in contrast to the usual procedure of publishing Party decisions on organizational matters a day or two after they are taken.

33. *Ibid.*, September 15, 1953.

34. *Ibid.*, March 21, 1954.

35. *Narodnoye khozyaistvo SSSR. Statisticheskii sbornik*, p. 118.

36. "Secret Speech . . . ," p. 77.

37. *Ibid.*

38. *Ibid.*, p. 78.

39. *Ibid.*

40. *Pravda*, July 10, 1953.

41. *Ibid.*, February 9, 1955.

42. *Ibid.*, December 25, 1956, and February 16, 1957.

18. THE PREACHER OF "PEACE"
(*pp. 249-263*)

1. V. I. Lenin, *Sochineniya* (4th ed.; 1950), XXXI, 413.
2. *Pravda,* March 7, 1953.
3. *Ibid.,* March 19, 1953. Italics added.
4. *Ibid.,* March 13, 1954.
5. *Ibid.,* March 7, 1954.
6. *Ibid.,* December 28, 1954. Italics added.
7. *Ibid.,* February 15, 1956.
8. *Ibid.,* June 22, 1960.
9. *New York Times,* September 17, 1959.
10. Bulganin and Khrushchev, *op. cit.,* p. 39.
11. *Pravda,* February 15, 1956.
12. *Ibid.,* June 25, 1958.
13. *Ibid.,* October 1, 1959.
14. Lenin, *op. cit.,* XXIII, 202.
15. *Ibid.,* XXVI, 208.
16. *Sovetskii Soyuz v borbe za mir. Documenty i vstupitelnaya statia* (Moscow, 1929), p. 29.
17. *Ibid.,* p. 33.
18. *Ibid.,* p. 40
19. Khrushchev pictured Reed as "a remarkable representative of the American press" who "in 1917 paved the way to an objective understanding and description of our life for the West" (*Pravda,* February 16, 1958).
20. John Reed, "How Soviet Russia Conquered Germany," *The Liberator, Journal of Revolutionary Progress,* January 19, 1919.
21. *Ibid.,* pp. 19, 24.
22. *Izvestia,* December 17, 1918.
23. S. Yu Vygodsky, *Lenininski Dekret o Mire* (Leningrad, 1958).
24. Lenin, *op. cit.,* XXXI, 410-411.
25. *Ibid.,* p. 419.
26. *Ibid.,* p. 413.
27. *Sovetskii Soyuz v borbe za mir . . . ,* p. 8.
28. *Ibid.,* p. 23.
29. *Pravda,* November 26, 1955.
30. *Ibid.,* February 15, 1956.
31. Lenin, *op, cit.,* XXXI, 83.
32. *Pravda,* August 12, 1960.

Index

(The subject of this biography, Nikita S. Khrushchev, is not indexed. However, most of the entries in this index relate either directly or indirectly to Khrushchev's political career.)

291